To: Ryan

♡: Heather

Christmas 2010

I ♡ U!

xo

AS TOLD TO AL STRACHAN

DOUBLEDAY CANADA

Special thanks to Martha Leonard of Doubleday Canada for putting up with me. —DC

Library and Archives of Canada Cataloguing in Publication has been applied for.

ISBN: 978-0-385-67003-6

For photo credit and permissions details, please see page 263.

Printed and bound in the USA

Published in Canada by Doubleday Canada,
a division of Random House of Canada Limited

Visit Random House of Canada Limited's website:
www.randomhouse.ca

10 9 8 7 6 5 4 3 2 1

Strathcona Tank Corps
A squadron at a forward operating base a few miles from Kandahar, Afghanistan.
This picture was taken right before they began a major mission where there were
heavy casualties and a trooper was killed.

*To all the Canadian wounded and fallen in all of our wars,
and especially to the men and women in active duty in
Afghanistan: You're the best.*

On the *Hockey Night in Canada* set with Ron, my grandson Del, Bobby Orr, and my daughter, Cindy.

FOREWORD

DURING THE 2006 STANLEY CUP FINAL between the Carolina Hurricanes and the Edmonton Oilers, a member of the Oilers staff brought some guests into our television studio to meet Don. The men worked for Edmonton public utilities and EPCOR, a company hired by the city to look after draining and sanitary sewer services. One of the men said, "Don, I have a confidential tidbit for your next contract negotiation with the CBC: our records reveal that toilet usage goes up 500 per cent right after 'Coach's Corner.'"

I thanked the man for leaking the information.

I remember a lot of moments from that one final. Prior to game one in Carolina, Doug Weight of the Hurricanes reported that his stomach was in knots, but then, as he skated out onto the ice, he noticed Don wearing one of his wild, flowered jackets, a blue wig and shades. Doug let out a laugh and instantly overcame his nerves.

I also recall having a heated interview, during game four, with NHL senior vice-president Colin Campbell about the rising numbers of penalties called and of players diving to draw penalties. I was pilloried in the media for having an old-school attitude.

During game five, we showed an infraction on "Coach's Corner," and I said, "Definitely a good call—that's a penalty." Grapes immediately replied, "Oh, I get it. They're after ya in the papers, so now you're trying to bail. Quit sucking around. You said it 'cause you mean it. Don't apologize. Be a man!"

After the camera went off, I was seething . . . at myself. It did sound like I was a little too eager to hand out a bouquet in the wake of the write-ups. Don, of course, sniffed out my weakness.

"Geez, ya look upset, what's the problem? Are you mad at me?"

"No," I muttered.

"Well, are you mad at the guys in the truck?"

"No, no," I replied.

He kept at it. "Well, is it David Sealy [the studio director]? Is it Bob [Cole] and Harry [Neale, the announcers]? Someone must have set ya off. What's wrong?"

Finally, I exploded: "I'm mad at myself!" Grapes killed himself laughing. Got me again!

Twenty-five years, and I always fall for it. But the truth is, I do get a kick out of it, and it's because I know what a good heart Don has.

Two last examples. In game seven, with less than two minutes to play in a one-goal game, Don saw Aaron Ward of Carolina flip the puck behind his net, directly out of play. That would call for a delay-of-game penalty. It was a tricky angle, a bang-bang play. No one saw it. At game's end, Grapes said, "I'm not showing it. It's not fair to anybody, and it will only incite Edmonton. Too tough to tell for sure, and too loaded to make an issue of."

Grapes always, always puts himself in the shoes of others.

Over the years, when we'd sit down for a beer, I'd trot out some philosophies and Don would often say, "Ron, you're living in the land of Billiken."

Now, Billiken was a charm doll invented by Florence Pretz of St. Louis in 1908. The elf-like Billiken was the god of how things ought to be. At the turn of the twentieth century it was as popular as pet rocks, mood rings or Cabbage Patch dolls would be later on. It was thought to bring luck, especially if received as a gift.

A few years ago, Don gave me his. With this note: "To Ron MacLean—Found at Belle Island, Kingston, Ontario, in 1952 by Don Cherry while working for P.U.C. [the Public Utilities Commission] Travelled to Rochester, Boston, Denver, Sudbury,

Three Rivers, Spokane, Kitchener, Springfield and Hershey."
With that, I'll take the odd bit of torture.

All those places . . . all these stories. He really is flush. If this were
"Coach's Corner," I'd say, "It's the pee, you see!" (That's P.U.C.,
Grapes.) Enjoy.

Ron MacLean
July 20, 2010

Me, a twenty-year-old rookie with the Hershey Bears of the AHL.

IT'S JUNE 2010—THE STANLEY CUP FINALS between the Chicago Blackhawks and Philadelphia Flyers. Ron MacLean and I have been goin' since April 8, every other night for two months.

It's not bad. The first two series we do out of the CBC studio in Toronto. For the semifinals and finals, we are on the road.

Our first night on the road, we're in Philadelphia. Ron and I have a few too many pops, kind of deliberately. The playoffs remind me of when I played: you come to camp in good shape, but you all get together the first night and have a session. You'd be good all summer, and then just before camp, you ruin it.

So about ten the next morning, Ron and I are in this cab and we're bakin', it's so hot. We're in our shirts and ties because we always travel that way in the States. (People at airports think we're detectives, as there's usually an older cop and a young cop.) I always think my shirts look good, but they're murder in the summer. The cab, as usual, is so small my legs are jammed up against the front seat. Why is every American cab dirty and small, with no air-conditioning and windows that don't roll down? And, of course, I'm on the side where the sun shines through.

And the extra pops don't help. When will we ever learn?

Folks, this is not the glamorous life everybody thinks it is. There are ticket lines at the airport. And security lines. The customs guys always seem to be ticked off about something. You get to the hotel and the rooms aren't ready. Eventually, you unpack (I've got tons to unpack and Ron seems to have nothing).

So here I am, sittin' in this hot cab, thinkin' all these things and feelin' sorry for myself. I look at Ron and he says, "Never mind. Just think of the twelve cold ones we'll have on ice for after the game tonight."

I do. Everything is right with the world.

* * *

Still in the finals. Now we're into Chicago, and we land. We're walking through the tunnel between O'Hare Airport and the airport hotel. As we walk along the tunnel—and we're the only ones in it—we come to a guy with a little organ, and he's singin'. He really sounds great.

Ron says, "Isn't that guy a wonderful singer?" and before I can say anything, he has dropped a fiver into the guy's hat.

I say, "You jerk. That guy's not singing. It's a record. That's Sam Cooke singing. The guy is only lip-synching."

Ron says, "You know, you're too cynical. You should wake up to the world. There aren't people like that. You couldn't be more wrong."

So about four days later, we're on our way back. Same tunnel. Same guy. Now the guy is letting on he's playing a violin. He sounds like Stratovarigus, or whatever his name is. I drop a fiver into his hat as a reward for being such a good con artist.

Ron gets taken every time. He never passes a guy who needs a handout, no matter what. But he definitely does get taken a lot.

For instance, we're in Anaheim one night, and after a few pops in the bar, we're walkin' back to the hotel. This guy comes up to us and gives us this song and dance.

"Can you guys help me out? I've spent all my money on the bar, and now don't have any money for a taxi to get home. I was wondering if you guys could help me because now I'm over the limit, and I don't want to drive my car."

Believe it or not, Ron bites on this one and gives the guy twenty-five bucks to get home.

I say, "Are you nuts?"

He answers, "Yes, I know. He could be lying. But what if it was true? I would never forgive myself, and I'd feel so guilty if he drove and hurt somebody."

Hoo boy.

* * *

It's in Philly, right between the fifth and sixth games. We go out to a bar.

Now, usually, we stay in Ron's room at night and have a twelve-pack on ice and watch TV and have a few munchies and cheese and we have a grand time. But we figured this series is going to wind up pretty soon, so the night before the sixth game, we go out to a bar for a little celebration. Believe it or not, the bartender knows all about my Bruins back when I was coachin' them against Philly's Broad Street Bullies. He knows everything.

I know he's not a phony because he remembers the one game — the second game of the semifinals — that we were up 3–0 and we blew a three-goal lead, with Bobby Clarke tyin' it up with two minutes to go. He has it all down, and he remembers how Terry O'Reilly got the winner for us in the second overtime.

Ron, who not only gives money to guys who drink too much, tips bartenders — and waitresses — like he's paying off the national debt. This time, he tips the guy fifty bucks.

I say, "Hey, fifty bucks? What are you doing?"

He says, "Everybody's gotta live."

So on the way back to our hotel, we're strollin' along, feelin' no pain, and we see a young guy who is really down on his luck, and he has a little dog on a piece of rope with him.

Ron says to me as we cross an intersection, "Doesn't it break your heart to see a young fellow like that? And isn't it wonderful how that dog loves him and sticks with him?"

So we're halfway across the intersection by now, and I say, "Well, if you feel that way, why don't you go back and help him out?"

I was just kiddin'. It was just a joke. He says, "I'll do that," and he goes back and says to the young fella. "Don't take this the wrong way. I just want to help you out a little. I want to give you a little something to help you out, you and your dog." And he slips him a fifty as well. What a guy! He falls for everything.

* * *

Sometimes you tell stories that were funny at the time, but they come across later as mean-spirited. For instance, Ron MacLean and I were travelling to Philly for the 2010 Stanley Cup semifinal between the Flyers and the Canadiens. We were walking from the plane towards the customs area, and Ron, who was a little behind, hollers, "Hey Grapes. There's a young hockey player here who wants to say hello to you. You're his hero."

So I walk back, and the kid is about five or six. I say, "Hello, kid. How are you doin'?"

He says, "I see you on TV all the time. You're Don Cherry." Then he turns to Ron and says, "I don't know you," and all the people laughed. They really thought it was funny.

Later on, I tell this story to a bunch of people, and when I end it, there's silence. I couldn't figure it out. But then I thought the people must have felt sorry for Ron, and must have figured I was a jerk for laughing at him. Here he had been so kind to the kid and me, and I make fun of him.

It was no use explaining to the people that the person who laughed the loudest when the kid said "I don't know you" was Ron.

* * *

So we're in Philly between games. Ron and I and some of the crew from *Hockey Night in Canada* go over to the old Spectrum, where we're filming a bit for the *Rock'em Sock'em* video about old times between the Big Bad Boston Bruins and the Broad Street Bullies.

We finish, we come back, we go into the hotel, we order lunch. Halfway through the lunch, the waitress comes in, screaming, "There's a man drowning in the river!"

Ron jumps up, runs and grabs one of those ropes that they use in restaurants to get you to stand in line, runs outside, scales two walls and runs down to the dock.

Now, the guy is in the water, but it's fifteen feet down. It's one of those docks for big boats. Ron climbs halfway down and gives the guy the rope, and with the help of another guy who had seen it and jumped in the water, Ron pulls the guy out of the river.

They try to say afterwards that the guy Ron saved was trying to commit suicide, but listen to this: he had duct tape wrapped around his neck a few times, and his arms and legs were tied with rope. Later on, I tell a police officer I know about it—and about the tape and rope. He laughs and says, "That's no suicide. He was taken for a one-way swim."

So Ron becomes a hero on TV and in the papers and the Red Cross wants to give him an award.

But when he comes back to the table, I just say, "Nice guy. You ruined the whole lunch."

* * *

I just read back these stories that I've told about Ron. And I don't know how this happened, but I look like a jerk, and he looks like a good guy.

How did that happen? That's not the way it's supposed to be!

* * *

On one of my "Coach's Corners" in the Stanley Cup finals, I was talkin' about meeting our soldiers in the airports. When I say to them that they must be glad to be back in Canada, they say, "Yeah. For sure." But then they always say that they can hardly wait to get back to their buddies—or "teammates," as they call them, because they feel they're all a part of a team.

But the one complaint they have is that opposition politicians, for their own good, try to make points against the government by voicing their concerns about the detainees that our soldiers hand over to the Afghan authorities. These politicians are very concerned about the way these Taliban terrorists are treated.

The soldiers say, "Hey, be more worried about us, the guys who do it for you, than the guys who are trying to blow us up."

I knew it would be tough for the media to find a way to argue against that, but they found a way to ridicule me and the soldiers, and here's how they did it.

A couple of days after I said that, Laurie Hawn, the parliamentary secretary to the minister of national defence, commented in Parliament about the soldiers' feelings. He had just come back from a week in Afghanistan with the troops, and he said, "Grapes gets it. Our government gets it. The Canadian people get it. And in the words of Don Cherry, I say, 'Amen to that.'"

This is how *Maclean's* magazine responded to that: "For four years now, the government has publicly worried that various members of the House hold some sympathy for the enemy. Perhaps now it is time for the government to summon the courage of its convictions and formally pursue these charges. For sure Mr. Cherry would seem to be a fine choice to head up such an official inquiry.

"From the House yesterday, Laurie Hawn, the parliamentary secretary to the minister of national defence, cites the human rights and international law authority of Don Cherry on one of the more complicated moral questions of modern global conflict."

You can always count on the left-wing media to put a spin on things, to ridicule anything they see as right wing. I'm fair game, and I expect it; but it's too much to make light of our troops' feelings.

It is just too much.

* * *

In June 2010, the Toronto Maple Leafs made Dion Phaneuf their captain. He was the obvious choice. He was the type of guy GM Brian Burke says he wants on his team.

It makes me laugh, though, that the one big thing Burke has always mentioned that Phaneuf did last year to set the standard was to change the music in the dressing room, then crank it up, when he first walked in.

Being captain of a team does not have the same ring now that it had a few years ago, when the guys voted for their captain.

The Leafs' captains have always been the obvious choices—Darryl Sittler, Doug Gilmour, Wendel Clark, Rob Ramage. But it's still not the same unless it is voted by the players.

For instance, Gary Roberts should have been the captain on every team he played for. And believe me, the players would have voted for Roberts every time. Why was he not picked as captain by management on any team? That's easy. Because he was a guy who would have walked in and demanded things for the players. No fooling around. Full speed ahead. You couldn't snow him, and he had no fear for his job. He would have gone to the wall for his players.

Management wanted no part of Gary or any player like that.

Let me ask you a question: If you had a company, and you wanted to make a foreman, would you make a guy like Gary your foreman? I guess not.

That's why all the players loved Gary. He was a players' captain. You could even say he was a captains' captain. But unfortunately, too much of a captain for management. And so he was never a captain.

That's the way it is now. Management picks a guy they can work with—and they usually pick the right guy.

But to me and to the players, it's not the same as when you sit down and you say, "Okay, vote for your leader and captain."

You put in your vote, and when it comes out, this is your captain. That's the way it was when I played. That's the way it should be.

But the day of the players picking their own leader is long gone.

Mats Sundin didn't do a bad job as captain of the Maple Leafs, but I'm sure Mats would have rather just played the game and not had to deal with the media.

He was a good player for the Leafs, but did you notice that he always got around the same number of goals each year? Hey, he always had a good year, but it was always around the same number of points. If you keep your points the same, they can never say that you had a bad year. I always thought that if he wanted to, he could have scored fifty goals, but he only played when he felt like playin'.

I had a canary once that was a great singer, but it only sang when it wanted to. I named it Mats.

* * *

The 2010 final between Philly and Chicago again. Ron and I are in a taxi, driving to the game.

Ron says, "Look at the old Hilton Hotel."

I say, "I thought they tore it down."

He says, "No. Take a look."

I take a look, and it's beautiful. I'm kinda happy because, when I coached, that's where all the teams stayed when we were in Philly, because you could walk to the Spectrum from there. But it was shut down a long time ago and was deserted for years. Someone took it over and turned it into a gem.

There were a lot of great memories there from when we walked into Philly and won the first two games to put them down 2–0 in the semifinals. But it also had bad memories too. When I was with Colorado, we weren't beating too many teams in those days. We went into Philly, stayed at that hotel, walked over to the Spectrum and got beat. It was a nice hotel, but it was a long way from downtown, and I knew that the guys wanted to have a few beers. I also knew that if the guys took a cab into town and back, it was going to cost them a hundred bucks for the taxi. If they did that, they were going to stay out a long time. I mean, you're not going to spend a hundred bucks to go there and back and not stay out for a while. I knew there would be trouble.

So I did something that you really shouldn't do, but I did it for the players—and to keep trouble down. I said, "You guys can drink in the hotel bar tonight."

Usually, the hotel bar is off-limits to the players, but this time it seemed smarter to break the rule. So they went into the bar of the hotel and they were acting good. I was there too. I never had anything against drinking with the players. I had done it for most of my coaching career—but not in the hotel bar. This time, I was with them, and we all had a few beers and I see one of our scouts walking by. I invite him in. I say, "Sit down. Have a drink."

So he sat down and had a few drinks. Unbeknownst to me, afterwards, he got up and phoned Ray Miron, the Rockies' general manager, to give him more ammunition against me. He said, "Do you know that Cherry is letting the players drink in the hotel bar?"

Boy, you meet a lot of great characters in hockey.

We'd had no real problem at all, but there was just one little thing that caused trouble.

There was no food in the hotel by that time, so two guys went out to a convenience store and got some chocolate cakes. Well, you know what kids are like with chocolate cake—and they were kids. They started to throw chocolate cake around, and some of it got on the floor.

That's the only thing that happened. I know, because I went around and checked all the rooms before we left.

I should have been smart enough to go—and I blame myself for this one—to the housekeeping lady and give her a couple of hundred bucks to clean the rug. Well, I didn't, and she complained to the Colorado Rockies about the chocolate. More ammunition for Ray Miron to go to the owner and say I didn't have control of the club.

So sometimes you run into things, and sometimes you have great memories about places. I had great memories about that hotel, but

I'll never, ever forget about the scout coming in and having a beer with me then gettin' up and goin' out and phonin' Ray Miron. That was a toughie.

* * *

That's why Doug Harvey quit the New York Rangers—'cause he couldn't go and drink with the guys. He was the player-coach of the Rangers and he put 'em in the playoffs. They hadn't made the playoffs in three years. Remember when they traded him from the Canadiens? He put the Rangers in the playoffs, then he quit. They asked him why he quit. He said, "When the players turned left and I had to turn right, I knew I couldn't do it."

With me, it started in Rochester because I got made coach halfway through the season. I was the same age as the players, and it just followed that the players never took advantage of me. They knew they could go only so far with me. I don't recommend for a coach to do it. I was treading on thin ice doing it in Boston, but we were young. So I got away with it. I didn't get away with it in Colorado.

* * *

I'm often asked how it feels to get ripped in the papers day after day.

It's funny how it works with the press. The first year or two, it's like a honeymoon. They leave you alone. But if you get too popular, look out.

When Ron MacLean first started with *Hockey Night in Canada*, I told him, "Hey, you'd better watch it. You're getting too popular. You'd better be ready. You're going to get it!"

He just laughed at me. He didn't believe me. He thought it was funny. Finally, after a year and a half or so, he hosted the National Hockey League awards show. It was in Calgary, in his home province of Alberta, and he did a good job. But he picked up the paper the next day, and he had got it—both barrels. He couldn't believe how he got it. Even though he was good, it was his time. It was his time to get it.

I gotta tell you, he was really hurt. He just couldn't understand it. I said, "It was just your time."

* * *

Just before we went on the road for the 2010 playoffs, I went downtown on a Sunday afternoon to tape *Grapeline*. That's the syndicated radio show I do with Brian Williams, and we usually tape the five shows for the week on a Sunday.

I go into the Rogers building, and there's nobody there except this young radio reporter from 680 News in Toronto. He comes up to me and says, "I want you to give your opinion of Dr. Charles Tator, the concussion guy who says you're the cause of concussions and head injuries."

I said, "No. I'm not giving it to you," and kept on walkin'.

He kept following me and goin' on, and I said, "I'm not giving it to you."

He kept going on, so I said, "Look, why would I give it to you? I have my own show."

So he made like he was putting his microphone away, and he says, "Are you sure you won't?"

And I says, "Look. Would you f*** off? If I was gonna do it, I'd do it on my own radio show, now f*** off."

Well, the guy was pretty sharp. He had the mike still goin', and they're so powerful these days that even though it looks like they've been put away, they still pick everything up. So what he did was, he took it back and put it up on his own Internet site, and boy, everybody in the world heard it. It was all over the place. Everybody was all upset. I didn't mind it. I was ripped in the paper. It went on and on. Column after column after column about how bad a guy I was. At 680 News, they weren't upset that he did it to me; they

were upset that he took it home and put it on his home Tweeter—
or whatever you call those things, I don't know.

They were gonna fire him, I guess. But I said, "Aw, don't worry
about it. It doesn't matter to me at all." They just give him a
week's suspension.

On the other stations, they had talk shows about it. One of them
went over two hours. A lot of people were ripping me, but one guy
said, "I'm kinda glad that he did that. If he hadn't a did that, I woulda
been disappointed in him."

* * *

When I left Boston to coach the Colorado Rockies in 1979, I gotta
admit, it was a tough go. I went from a team that rarely lost a
game to a team that rarely won a game. I knew it was not gonna
be a piece of cake when I went there, so I shouldn't have been
upset. But upset I was. It was so bad on my nerves that I couldn't
sleep at night, and when I did sleep, I ground my teeth so bad that
the dentist said I had to wear a mouth guard so I wouldn't break
my teeth.

But we were slowly gettin' better. We had a great bunch of guys,
and one day the general manager, Ray Miron, comes to me and
says, "Would you like to have Lanny McDonald?"

I says, "Are you kiddin'? I'd trade Blue for him."

I was just kiddin' about that, of course.

I said, "How come he's comin' here? I thought he was a hero
in Toronto?"

Miron says that Punch Imlach, the general manager of the
Maple Leafs, is having a fight with Darryl Sittler, but he can't trade
Sittler because he has a no-trade contract. So he's gonna get rid of
his buddy Lanny instead, just to show Sittler who's boss. I find out
that to get Lanny, we've got to give up Wilf Paiement, who is
playin' great for us. Okay. I'm sorry, Wilf, but if I've got a chance
to get Lanny, you've got to go.

I felt bad, because I really liked Wilf. In fact, the week before, his dad, who used to hunt moose, gave me a great big set of moose antlers, and here I am a week later, tradin' his kid. I also felt bad because Wilf said he was afraid. He said he didn't want to go to Toronto because he was French-Canadian, and he'd get picked on there.

I says, "Are you kiddin'? They'll love you there."

They did. Up until a couple of years ago, he was the highest-scoring right winger in the Leafs' history, so he had great success there.

So it was all set, but then I found out that Lanny didn't want to come. Now, I really didn't blame him. His wife, Ardell, was gonna have a baby shortly. He's heartbroken leavin' Toronto and his buddy Darryl, and he's goin' to a losing club. I figure, "Boy, I gotta get a hold of Lanny and do a sell job fast." My plan is just to let him play the games and stay with Ardell in Toronto the rest of the time.

Let's let Lanny tell what happened. This is from his book, *Lanny*, written with Steve Simmons. He says that when he heard he was traded to the Colorado Rockies, he said to himself that he couldn't go.

Then the phone rang and on the other end of the line was Don Cherry, the coach of the Rockies, and when I hung up, I knew I was on my way to Denver.

If there was a bright spot in being traded to one of the worst teams in hockey, it was playing for the man they called Grapes. No doubt he was the man I most enjoyed playing for, and from the moment I was traded to Denver, he did everything he could for me and my family. He told me I would be allowed to commute to Toronto between games to be with Ardell, who was two weeks away from giving birth.

I'll just give my thoughts on Lanny playin' great. In fact, he was playin' unbelievable, even though one player said, "Lanny, the stick boy spends more time in the room than you do." He was just kiddin', though.

Believe it or not, Lanny scored 25 goals in 45 games for a last-place club. It doesn't get any better than that.

Back to what Lanny said in his book:

The players accepted it, and I've always been grateful to Grapes for what he did for me. Hockey may be great, but it's not number one. Family is.

Playing for the Colorado Rockies could have been a horrible experience except for Don Cherry. After leaving Punch Imlach and the Toronto turmoil, Grapes made hockey fun again. All he asked was to give your best. Grapes may not have been the best technical coach in the world, but he was a tremendous motivator.

He would say little things about pride and love for the game that would give you a little boost and keep you going. He'd throw little things in all the time that would make the game much more enjoyable. Grapes knew how to keep our enthusiasm in the game.

* * *

It's 1979, and things are not going well in Colorado. I'm coaching the Colorado Rockies, where I was hired with much hullabaloo and fanfare. It was the whole deal, but things are not going good.

The very first day I met Arthur Imperatore, the owner, I could tell he was one of the toughest guys you're ever going to meet. He was an independent trucker in New Jersey, in the heartland of the Teamsters empire, so you can imagine how tough he is.

In mid-season, I was summoned to New Jersey. Ray Miron was the team's general manager. When they hired me, I was the highest-paid coach in the National Hockey League, and they asked me if I could coexist with Ray Miron. And, like a fool, I said I could.

His nickname was "The Carp." I won't go into the reasons, but it was pretty obvious. You figure it out. He didn't like the name much, and I was told that he went down to visit the farm team in Fort Worth, and a rookie was sitting beside a veteran. The rookie saw Miron come in, and he said, "Who's that?"

The veteran said, "That's Carp."

Later, Miron comes around, shaking hands, and when he gets to the rookie, the kid says, "Hello, Mr. Carp."

Another time, some kids at the game hung a banner in the stands saying "Fire the Carp." When Miron saw it, he called the security guys and had them go over and tell the kids to take it down. They did. They moved over and sat in front of Miron's box and hung it up there. So there's Miron, sitting in his box, watching the game over a sign that says "Fire the Carp."

The guys were all laughing on the bench. They loved that one.

* * *

Miron did a number on me from day one. The first game of the exhibition season, we played the Winnipeg Jets and we lost. Unbeknownst to me, Frank Millen, the agent, had a few pops with Miron after the game and Miron said, "Well, Cherry didn't look so hot."

It was the very first exhibition game!

When I first arrived there, Miron showed me, as a joke, a book called *All I Know About Hockey* by Ray Miron. When you opened it up, all the pages were blank. Little did I know it was more truth than humour!

I was looking at the team we had in Colorado compared to the one I had in Boston, where we had five psycho guys and the rest of the team were all tough too. Compared to the Bruins, the Rockies looked like little boys.

I knew I was in trouble right from the start. We had a first-round draft choice, Mike Gillis, who is now the general manager of the Vancouver Canucks. He was making around $125,000, which was a lot of money back then. One of the problems we had on the club was that Barry Beck, who was a legitimate great player—this guy was dynamite—was making only $85,000. He was ticked off, and so he should have been.

In training camp, we had one of my type of guys—Ronnie Delorme. The funny thing is, he's now the chief scout for Vancouver. I'm surprised Gillis, Vancouver's GM, kept him.

Anyways, back then it came down to those two for the final spot. Ronnie Delorme had done everything. He had busted his tail. He had worked. He had done everything. There was no way I could send him down. So I sent down Mike Gillis.

I knew even then that my days were numbered, because Miron went to Imperatore and Armand Pohan, Imperatore's stepson, who did a lot of the day-to-day management for his father. I'm sure he said something like, "There you are. Cherry is sending down our most expensive player—a first-round draft choice—to Fort Worth and he's keeping a guy making $18,000. Look at the money he's cost you. He won't work with the first-round draft choice," etc., etc., etc.

* * *

Eventually, we had a pretty good team, but on top of all the other problems, we had Hardy Astrom, the Swedish Sieve. He was a good guy and a good person. His only problem was with pucks.

The first day, we ran a breakout play in practice. The coach flips the puck in to the goalie, who catches it, puts it down, over to the defence, up to the winger. I flipped it in to Hardy, and I scored!

I went home that night and I said, "Rose, get ready to pack. At the end of this year, we're gone."

The sad thing about it, too, was that Dougie Favell, a great little goaltender, was there in Colorado not playing, and he could have been one of our players. But he had a big fight with Ray Miron, so we didn't use him.

That's when I get the call to go to New Jersey and meet Mr. Imperatore. They sent a limo to pick me up at the airport. The driver never said a word. He just put me in the car and we drove off.

It's funny how your mind works. There's all kinds of swamps in that part of New Jersey, and we're driving along by the swamps, and I'm thinking, "I wonder if he's going to drop me off in these swamps, and I'll never be heard of again?"

I get to Arthur Imperatore's office, and I go inside, and his secretary says, "Mr. Imperatore will be with you in a moment."

I sat for fifteen minutes. He let me cool my heels outside.

Then, when she said, "Mr. Imperatore will see you now," I went up to the bulletin board and let on I was reading something and made *him* wait two minutes.

A death wish, I guess.

I go in and open up the door, and you can't believe it. The room looked like something out of *The Godfather,* I swear. There's a table at least forty feet long with a marble top—dark green marble—with wingback chairs all along the side. There's a fireplace at the end. Curtains with gold brocade all over the place. A flowing fountain. It was incredible. I mean, talk about intimidating!

His stepson, Armand Pohan, who looked like Al Pacino, was in the room, sort of hanging in the background, and sitting at the end of the table was Arthur Imperatore, and he was an impressive-looking guy.

I had met him before, and the first time I met him, I knew there was going to be trouble. He had flown me down with a bunch of other employees before training camp, and we were on a big yacht. I was sitting beside him, and he really put on a show. When the wine came, he made them take all the bottles back because they were too chilled.

I remember sitting awake at about three in the morning, thinking, "Donny boy, you've made a big mistake." And how right I was.

Arthur really loved Rose because she was Italian, like him, and my son, Tim, looked Italian. The first thing he said was, "I don't want to hurt Rose and Tim."

I says, "Arthur, don't you worry about Rose and Tim. I'll take care of Rose and Tim."

So he went on to tell me what Miron had to say about me, and he said, "What do you have to say about Mr. Miron?"

I'm not trying to be a hero, but I said, "I'm not talking about Mr. Miron because he's not here."

That's the way it went, so I was dead there. We went back and forth, back and forth. Then he says, "I want to show you something, Don. I've been told you don't work hard enough."

Imagine that! The one thing I *did* do was work hard.

He takes me over to the window, and he looks down. His trucks are all lined up, and his truckers are all lined up watching the guys unload the trucks.

He says, "Look there, Don. You have to work as hard as my truckers."

I says, "Aw, come on, Arthur, who are you kidding? Take a look at your truckers. They're just standing there. The guys that really are working are the guys that are unloading the trucks."

There's that death wish again.

So we sat back down again, and he says to his stepson, "Armand, what did the players think about Don?"

He says, "Well, I have to tell you, I hate to say this, but the players would crawl through fire for him."

I knew I was dead. He just wanted to confirm it when I went there.

* * *

Back in the fifties and sixties, George Chuvalo was the biggest thing around Toronto. He was the hero of heroes. I never missed his fights when he fought in Toronto. Usually, he fought in the summer, and he always seemed to fight on a Friday night. I would take the afternoon off work—I couldn't take the whole day; I couldn't afford it—and Rose and I would travel to Toronto in my '55 Custom Ford.

It was baby blue with a baby-blue interior. Gee, I loved that car. Why did I ever get rid of it?

Rose didn't really like the fights, but she went along for the trip. When we arrived in Toronto, I would park across from Maple Leaf Gardens because we got there early. Then we would go across to a restaurant on Yonge Street called Charles Under the Clock. We'd have Chinese food and finish just in time for the preliminary bouts. I never missed a prelim, much to Rose's regret.

In 1961, George fought a guy called Alex Mittef, who at the time was a top-ten boxer. He was from Argentina but he lived in New York. For a while, Alex gave George a boxing lesson. I think George had too much respect for Alex because he was such a high-ranked boxer. Then, after a while, I think George must have thought he had nothing to lose. He came out like a hockey player coming out for the third period when his team is behind.

Boy, he had fire in his eyes. You never saw such a round in your life. He knocked Alex from pillar to post. It was the worst beating I ever saw. He actually knocked him right out of the ring. The sportswriters pushed him back in, like they did with Jack Dempsey when he fought Luis Firpo.

I've seen crowds go nuts, but in all my years, I never saw anything like this crowd. Guys were jumping out of the balcony to get down near the ring. I was so excited, I grabbed Rose by the bum and I had her in the air, dancin' around and around and around. She must have thought I was nuts.

Somehow, George didn't knock him out, but he won a split decision. Everybody left so happy. As we were outside and making our way to the car, everybody was so happy. Except one guy. He's waiting by my car, and I can tell he's ticked off about somethin'. I can't figure it out. What's his problem? I get there and he says, "This your car?"

I says, "Yep."

He says, "Do you know you've had me blocked in for the last three hours?"

I said, "I'm sorry, but when I parked the car, I told the guy I was going to the fight and I was going to be a long time, but he said that was the place to park."

The guy won't let it go and starts giving me a hard time. Now, folks, I'm never the best guy to give a hard time to at the best of times, but certainly not after I've just watched a fight like that and I'm all excited.

So I grabbed the guy and I said, "Okay, I blocked you in. What are you goin' to do about it?"

He backed down, and I'm glad he did, or I would probably have been in court, but Rose was really ticked. She never liked violence of any kind, and she never talked to me all the way back to Kingston. Not a word. And she never again drove with me to see George fight.

* * *

I'm often asked if the coaches and players ever pay those fines that the NHL levies against them. Yes, they do. But if it wasn't a goofball incident that the player got fined for, the team usually finds a way to get around the fine and get the money back to the player.

You can't just give the player or coach the money back, because if the league checks your books and finds out you repaid them for their fines, there's big trouble. A big fine. So the team would schedule an appearance in the summer—maybe a banquet or a golf tournament—and compensate the player or coach for coming.

Harry Sinden, GM of the Bruins, got me pretty good on something like this. The last year I was in Boston, I got fined by the league for something—I know it's hard to believe, but I probably said something I shouldn't have said—and Harry never helped me pay it.

When the league sent a notice out the next year and said this fine hadn't been paid, Harry sent the letter to me. I knew right away that he had the laugh on me.

I was coaching the Rockies at the time, so I knew Colorado wasn't going to pay a fine I got with the Bruins. And Harry sent me the letter, so the Bruins weren't going to pay it.

So guess who had to pay it? Harry must have been laughin' all the way.

* * *

Don't you wonder where all the money goes from all these tournaments that they have in hockey? The Olympics, the junior world championships, the Spengler Cup, the World Cup. The list goes on.

Millions upon millions of dollars are spent by the fans on memorabilia.

Let's face it. At the Winter Olympics, the driving force is hockey. It's jammed game after game. Millions upon millions for sweaters, jackets, shirts, hats and all kinds of memorabilia. For instance, Sidney Crosby sweaters go for six hundred bucks. Who gets the money? Does anybody in Cole Harbour, Nova Scotia, where he comes from, get any money?

How does any of this money help the parents of young players meet their hockey expenses? Expenses just keep going up and up. I know a family of three young hockey players. They take no vacations. Their car is just about to collapse from taking the kids to tournaments, practices and games. It costs them thousands of dollars just to register their kids in hockey, and believe it or not, they have to pay six dollars apiece to get in to see their own kid play! One day, they went to see all three kids play and it cost them thirty-six dollars—just to see their kids play the game they're paying for.

They get no help from anybody, yet they see millions upon millions of dollars coming in from those tournaments; but it doesn't go to the players who risk their careers. They don't get a dime. Does it go to help parents? No!

I'm afraid there are a lot of guys at the trough, collecting big salaries. Tell me where I'm wrong.

* * *

I always protected our goalies, as a coach and as a player.

My last words as a coach, when the players were going out for the warmup, were "Keep the shots low. Keep the shots low. Just let him feel it."

I also never made the goaltenders skate at the start of practice. They know how to get themselves ready.

As a player, I always felt they were our bread and butter. They should be treated with respect. If you don't have a good goalie, you have nothin'. And as the old saying goes, "Show me a good coach, and I'll show you a good goalie." Or, "Show me a good goalie, and I'll show you a good coach."

One time, Gerry Cheevers, when he was playin' for the Rochester Americans before goalies started using masks, caught a puck in the mouth. We lost the game, and because we didn't play good, our coach, Joe Crozier, was steaming, firing on all cylinders. He said, "Everybody on the ice at 9 A.M."

Now, I'm not the captain or anything—I'm the fourth defenceman, actually—but I go in the back, and I say to Cro, "Are you nuts? Cheevers just lost four teeth and has thirty stitches in his mouth and you want him on the ice at 9 A.M.?"

Joe said, "What are we running here? A country club?"

So I just turned and walked out.

As I get back into the room, I saw Cheevers and he's looking at me. "Do I have to go?"

I said, "Stay home. I'll take care of it."

So everybody is on the ice at 9 A.M. except Cheevers. Joe had cooled down by then. He knew he had made a mistake. He didn't even mention that Cheevers wasn't there or ask where he was or anything. You have to protect those goaltenders.

If you don't protect goaltenders, you're done, and like I say: No goalie, no team.

* * *

I remember this like it was yesterday. We were in the Calder Cup and we were playing the Quebec Aces. Joe Crozier had taken us up into the mountains near Quebec. We were sitting there watching the horse races on TV. I think it was the Kentucky Derby.

The place was like a dining-room bar. The whole team was sitting there. We had one guy—a big guy who played in the National Hockey League—and for some reason, he was bugging Cheevers. The guy wasn't drunk or anything. I guess he was feeling a little good. We all were. He starts saying things like, "I'm going to shoot the puck at your head tomorrow morning in practice." I guess he had a beef with Gerry about somethin'. Well, there was one thing about Cheevers. He couldn't stand guys shootin' high in practice. In fact, if you shot high, he'd walk right out of the practice.

We're goin' to the Calder Cup finals, and here's this guy buggin' our goalie and saying he's gonna shoot at his head. So I get up and I walk over to him, and I say, "Look, cut it out. What are you, nuts? This is our goalie. This is the guy that's gonna win it for us."

He kept it up, kept it up.

So I went over to him one more time, and I said, "Listen, I want you to stop this, and I want you to stop it now. I'm gonna go to the washroom, and when I come back, I don't want to hear any more of it."

I come back, and he's still doin' it, so I picked up a knife from one of the tables, come up behind him, grabbed him around the throat, put the knife at his throat, and I said, "Are you gonna keep that up?"

I kept pushing the knife harder and harder against his throat. Everybody's looking, but they're afraid to move. He shook his head.

I said, "Good," and threw the knife on the table. After the race was over, one of the guys come up to me and he says, "Grapes, would you have really stuck the knife in his throat?"

I said, "Nah!"

But he didn't know if I would or not.

* * *

Gerry Cheevers was one of the greatest money goalies ever. He still holds the record of thirty-two consecutive games undefeated. I started playing with him in Rochester. He was great even back then. He was owned by Toronto, but they had Johnny Bower and everybody, so he got drafted by Boston. He went on to Boston from Rochester, while I just stayed in Rochester. I saw a lot of guys on the way up and a lot of guys on the way down. I just stayed in the middle. But when I got to Boston as coach, Cheevers was my goalie, and when we played, nothin' ever bothered him.

I remember one time when I was coachin' the Bruins, we got beat 7–2 and Harry—this is Harry Sinden, the general manager—come in, screamin', "What's this? We got beat 7–2! Gerry, what's goin' on?"

I can still see Gerry sittin' there in his little underwear, smokin' on a cigarette, and he says, "It's very simple, Harry. Roses are red. Violets are blue. They got seven. We got two."

* * *

Cheevers was a terrific, terrific goaltender. We were playin' Pittsburgh in the playoffs and he won the first two games, so I told him, "Gilbert's playin' the first game in Pittsburgh." I'm thinkin', "If we're gonna get beat, it's gonna be that first game. Poor Gillie."

The trainer, Dan Canney, comes up to me and says, "Gillie can't go."

I says, "What do you mean he can't go?"

He says, "He's got the hives."

I said, "What are ya? Nuts?"

He says, "Come and see."

Gillie was so nervous, his whole body was all covered in little spots—all over. So Gerry, in the meantime, thought he wasn't playin' and had a couple of Cokes and a hot dog, unbeknownst to me.

So here he is, sitting there as the backup, half-asleep with a towel around his head, and I says, "Gerry, you're goin' today."

He says, "You're kidding!"

I says, "Yeah, Gillie's got the hives." You shoulda seen the look on his face. But I gotta tell you one thing: believe it or not, he was absolutely tremendous in that game. In fact, I think it was the best game he ever played. We won 2–1.

He was some goaltender, and they changed rules because of him because he could skate so well. When we were in Rochester, we used to do end-to-ends and he could beat me, even wearing goalie pads. I can hear him as he reads this, saying, "That's not a great feat." He's a wise guy, too. He could handle the puck with the best of them, and he was courageous. The only problem with him was when you were winning 5–1, he'd fall asleep a little, but when it got to be 5–3, then he'd buckle down. He gave a lot of coaches heart attacks because he'd lose interest when he had a big lead, but when it came down to the nitty-gritty, he was always there.

* * *

We went on a winning streak, and we hadn't lost in eighteen straight games, but we were pickin' up bad habits — somethin' like Ottawa did at the beginning of the 2007–08 season, when they went 15–2. We got bad habits, but we couldn't lose. They were bouncin' in off our behinds, off our heads. It was one of those deals where we just couldn't lose, but we were gettin' worse and worse.

I'd tell the guys, "Listen, you guys are goin' to have to smarten up or we're in for a big fall. You can't keep playin' this way." But what are you going to do? We hadn't lost in eighteen. So I went up to Gerry after my big meetin', telling them this stuff and lecturin' them, and I said, "You know, Gerry, nobody listens to ya when you haven't lost a game in eighteen."

He says, "What?"

That was typical of Cheevers. He was one of those goaltenders who you knew nothing was gonna bother him, but if you didn't know him, you might think that he didn't care when he really did. As I said earlier, when you'd get up by a few goals, Gerry would fall asleep on you. It was really maddening. It cost us a couple of games, but I've never seen a better clutch goaltender in my life.

He was a lot of fun, but he hated, hated practice. He would ruin all the scrimmages because he would get out of the way of the puck. That cost him the number-one job for Team Canada in the 1976 Canada Cup, because he would just not scrimmage. He just wouldn't work.

He was like Terry Sawchuk. He did not see any sense at all in working hard in practice when he worked hard in the games.

* * *

I really believe that Gerry Cheevers could have been a stand-up comedian. Jerry Seinfeld always reminded me of the way Gerry had that amused expression on his face.

One time when we were in Rochester, we had just checked into the hotel, and he picked up the phone and said, "Room service?"

They said, "Yes."

"Well, send me up a room."

One time after practice, Gerry didn't go home; he stayed out all night with the group. He went straight to the Garden without going home. Naturally, Betty, his wife, got all upset and she called me. I went and found Gerry. He was sittin' in the trainer's room. I said, "Gerry, phone home. Betty is all upset."

He says, "Well, I don't know."

I said, "Phone home right now."

So he phoned home. His wife answered. He said, "Betty! Betty! Don't pay the ransom. I've escaped."

One time, I thought I was being very clever. We had played a lot of games in a short time and we had to play in Buffalo on Sunday night.

We were playin' in Toronto on Saturday, so I thought I'd bring up a backup goalie for Saturday night, and I thought it would be great to send Gerry ahead to Buffalo so he could rest and be ready for Sunday.

I forgot that he comes from St. Catharines, which is right in between, and he went out and had a few with his buddies over there. I also found out later that Gerry couldn't stand rooming alone.

We got bombed.

* * *

I really don't know what the Vancouver Canucks were thinkin' when they made Roberto Luongo their captain.

To make a goalie the captain of the team has to be one of the goofiest moves in sports. Just think of the pressure on a goalie before the game, during the game and after the game. If he has a bad game, he has to go to the press and explain it. As the captain, he's supposed to be the guy who acts for the team when they talk things over with the referee. Can he skate out and talk things over at the penalty box like the other captains do and wait for an explanation on the penalties? Nope.

A goalie has enough problems focusing on the game without worryin' about dealing with the officials. Does he also have to take on the other players' problems? Does he have to organize meetings?

My point is that Roberto Luongo really hasn't played as well as he did before he was named captain of the Vancouver Canucks. Is it just a coincidence? I don't think so. Roberto got pounded 8–1 in one game, and his coach, Alain Vigneault, said, "I left him in there to toughen him up for the playoffs." And in the playoffs, the same coach called Luongo "the second-best goalie on the ice."

Is this any way to treat your captain? The captain is supposed to be the leader of your club.

The goalie should never have to worry about anything except being a goalie. He should never be a captain. His job is to stop pucks. Period.

* * *

It always amazes me when the TV camera goes to the coach after a goal has been scored against his team and he expresses his frustration with the famous F-word.

It has been said if the F-word was taken out of hockey and sports, it would cease to be. I know some guys say it and don't even know they're saying it, and it amazes me how they can turn it off when they get away from the dressing room and the team.

Also, TV causes a problem when the players are miked. There was the classic case back in the seventies when Bobby Clarke was given a penalty, and there was a microphone beside the penalty box. He called referee Andy van Hellemond a name that I don't want to repeat in this book.

When I think of the time when I coached in Rochester, and we didn't have glass around the rink, and some of the language that I used, I'm sort of ashamed of myself now.

It was the same thing in Montreal and Toronto in the NHL. In those two places, we were right in the crowd. They didn't have security guards all over the place like they do now, and people would be walking behind the bench carrying hot dogs and Cokes. It was ridiculous.

One day, one old lady, after I must have said something pretty bad, shouted, "Cherry, you got a filthy mouth." I looked up, and it was a woman sitting on the aisle up about ten rows, and she looked just like my mother. So during the game—honest, this is during the game, while play is going on—I go up, and I sit down on the stairs beside her and I put my arm around her. The game is still going on, and I said, "Yes, ma'am, I'm sorry I said those words. But you've heard those words before, haven't ya?"

She says, "Yes I've heard them, but I've never before had to pay sixty bucks to hear them."

She had me there.

* * *

I knew of a Roman Catholic college that had a dynamite Junior B club. The language that they used did not sit well with the priest who ran the college. He called a special meeting with the coaches and players and said he was very upset at their language, especially with them using the F-word so much.

He said to the players, "After all, this is a religious college, and we can't put up with this. And boys, does it really help your playing to always, always be saying that F-word?"

And from the back of the room, a voice says, "F***-ing right, father. It really does."

The boy was suspended two games.

* * *

I know you are not going to believe this. In this world of profanity, sometimes the air is blue in the dressing rooms, but you will not hear the Lord's name taken in vain.

I played with guys in the minors who were one step away from barbarians, and their language would make your hair curl, but I tell you the truth: never will you hear a curse in the dressing room from a hockey player with the Lord's name involved.

* * *

There is an email that has been attributed to me that went all over the world about eighteen months ago, and now, in the summer of 2010, it is all over the world again. I've been told that the soldiers have it up on their bulletin boards, even the American soldiers.

The headline on it is YA GOTTA LOVE THIS GUY and this is what the statement is:

God bless Don Cherry. Don Cherry was asked on a local live radio show just what he thought about the allegations of torture on suspected terrorists. His reply was prompt, and he was ejected from the studio but to a thunderous applause from the audience.

His statement: "If hooking up one raghead terrorist prisoner's testicles to a car battery to get the truth out of the lying little camel-shagger will save just one Canadian soldier's life, then I only have three things to say. Red is positive; black is negative and make sure the balls are wet."

I did not say this. It is attributed to me. The soldiers think it is great. They have it up on their bulletin boards and in their tanks and in their trucks, but I did not say it.

But come to think of it . . .

* * *

This goes under the heading of "You can't win them all."

Here are some quotes from a writer called Catherine Ford, who now writes for Troy Media after spending years as a left-wing columnist for the *Calgary Herald*. I quote:

The unintended consequences of wars are the young we send off to fight too often return physically and psychologically damaged. The fault is not theirs, the fault is ours. We continue to perpetuate the lies. It is us who lie to each other, who eagerly listen to Don Cherry on *Hockey Night in Canada* eulogize young soldiers who lose their lives in Afghanistan as if soldiers and hockey players belong together as the epitome of maleness and bravery. We are encouraged to shed a tear, to elevate death in Afghanistan as a sort of Stanley Cup sacrifice of battle.

Afghanistan is not a game and it is outrageous to link the death of our soldiers with a sport, regardless of good intentions.

Soldiers die by accident, by misadventure or sheer bad luck. They die pointless and unnecessary deaths.

I honor their sacrifice, but I cannot glorify it.

I should say to Ms. Ford that they do die by accident. They do die by misadventure and they do die by sheer bad luck. I'd add that they die at the hands of the Taliban too.

Ms. Ford was answered by Brigadier-General D. C. Kettle, the chaplain general of the Canadian Forces. He says:

> I disagree with your analysis entirely. I know Don Cherry well enough to know that when he eulogizes the deaths or serious injuries of our soldiers, sailors, and air personnel in Afghanistan, he does so because he is moved by their devotion to duty. The comparison to a Stanley Cup sacrifice of battle is an image of your own making. Don Cherry does not see operations in Afghanistan as a game nor would he see a comparison between hockey players and Canadian Forces personnel as having much more association beyond their professionalism, devotion to something beyond self, role modeling, audaciousness, and physical courage. There is nothing wrong with such comparisons. Yes some soldiers, sailors, and air personnel die by accident, misadventure, and sheer bad luck, but almost without exception they die doing their duty knowing that it could cost them their lives. They put their lives on the line for what they believe in. I can't speak for you, but I find something extremely noble about that. No one is asking you to glorify it—just to respect what we do and why most of us do it.

I know what you're thinking: "Why put something like this in the book? No one has ever heard of Ms. Ford. Why give her the ink?"

I put it in the book to show that when you are a so-called celebrity, shots come from where you least expect it. Who would ever think that you would be criticized for honouring our dead troops? What kind of a mind would link the winning of a Stanley Cup with the war in Afghanistan and our dead troops? And who would *you* believe? A brigadier-general chaplain in the armed forces, or someone like Ms. Ford?

But Ms. Ford is not the only reporter who disagrees with me honouring the fallen soldiers. One reporter called it maudlin. One reporter said I have a "habit" of honouring the soldiers—a habit sort of like smoking, I guess.

But words from Reverend Kettle and letters from the dead soldiers' mothers and fathers and sisters and brothers encourage me to go on. The words from someone like Ms. Ford and her ilk, who live in ivory towers and have no idea what is going on in the real world, do not discourage me.

In fact, people like Ms. Ford spur me on, and it's ironic that it's because of our brave men and women in the Canadian Forces that people like Ms. Ford can criticize people who honour them.

* * *

Ralph Mellanby, the former executive producer of *Hockey Night in Canada*, was the person who got me started on the show. He was always in my corner. He used to say—and he said it in his book— "Canada is a country with two official languages and Cherry speaks neither." He also said, and he was kidding—I think—that he was the person who inflicted Don Cherry on Canada.

When I got fired by Colorado, Ralph and a fellow by the name of Al Stewart decided to have me on for the Stanley Cup playoffs. I mentioned how I got started on TV in my other book, but I'll tell you again in case you didn't read that one.

I had already been on once while I was coaching the Bruins— with the greatest guy, the late Dan Kelly. Dan was the guy who called Bobby Orr's Stanley Cup–winning goal, the one against the St. Louis Blues where he was flying through the air. Dan helped me a lot. During a game one night, he asked me what I thought of the game, and I said, "I'd tell you, Dan, but this guy keeps talking in my ear."

It was the director. Dan explained to me that that's the director's job.

Even with that, Ralph saw that I wasn't afraid of the camera and had me do some shows for the Stanley Cup playoffs. Originally, I said I wouldn't do it, but it was pointed out that they'd pay my way from

Denver to Toronto, and I could visit my mom in Kingston. It was not much pay, but what the heck, I could visit Mom.

So I sat in the studio, wearing a tan jacket—ultra suede if I remember right—describing breakouts. I did eight of these, and I thought they were awful. They were dead. They came up with a name for these bits: "Coach's Corner." I thought they were awful, but they seemed to like them and they asked me to come back to do some more.

That was the start of my career on *Hockey Night in Canada*.

I was on for about a month, and I thought I was doing pretty good, but the CBC people had a meeting and went to Ralph and said, "Ralph, we've got to get this guy off the air." So I started doing colour, but I got in too much trouble doing colour, so they put me on "Coach's Corner." Ralph thought, "How much trouble can Don get in if he's only on for five minutes?"

But there was one thing Ralph did that I never forgave him for. Well, I guess I shouldn't say I never forgave him for it, but he made me very, very unhappy with him.

We went to a seminar in Quebec at a place called La Sapinière, and he said, "I want you to get up and speak. All the *Hockey Night in Canada* people will be there, and there will be bigwigs from the CBC." I had just started public speaking, and as everybody knows, the greatest fear in the world not death, it's speaking in front of people. And I wasn't very good.

I said, "Ralph, I don't wanna do it. I'm not that good."

He said, "I want you to do it."

Well, I got up to speak, and I did my best. It was terrible. People were talking out in the audience. I looked over at the CBC people to the right of me, and they weren't paying attention, and you must realize that when you're speaking, with hockey people in the crowd or with television people in the crowd, they hope you fail. All you have to do is watch Ron MacLean when he does his awards show. He'll come out, and he'll have some funny lines, and the reaction is nothing.

I was failing. I'll tell you how bad I was failing: while I was speaking, a waiter come up and stood in front of me and asked me if I wanted something to drink. That's how bad it was.

I muddled through, but I'll tell you one thing, I was terrible. I never got any help from anybody except Ralph, and it took me a year before I ever did public speaking again because it sure shook my confidence.

I gave Ralph heck for that one, but if it hadn't been for Ralph giving me help and guiding me through and telling me what to do, I don't know if I would have made it.

* * *

It might have been my very first show, and we were talkin' about some team, and I said, "I think they'll make the playoffs."

Ralph come in and smacked the table as hard as he could and he said, "You don't think. You know! You're the coach."

I said, "Well, Ralph, I *don't* know. How am I supposed to know they're going to make it?"

He said, "I don't care. If you're wrong, people get a kick out of you. You *know*; you don't think."

That's the way it has been. You never hear me say "I think" on "Coach's Corner."

When Ralph left to do other things, he only gave me one bit of advice as he left. He said, "Don't turn professional." I gave him my word that I wouldn't. And if you've watched me on television, you can see that I've kept my word.

* * *

I have to admit the movie about my life, *Keep Your Head Up, Kid*, was pretty good, but it never really captured how low I was when I was unemployed.

I was working as a car salesman, and I'm not putting car salesmen down, but I was not carrying my weight. I couldn't approach people.

I was the worst salesman in the world, and after I did that number on one of the customers where I put him against the wall for saying "All you car salesmen are alike," I knew my days were numbered.

The other salesmen were good guys, and they were so smooth. They tried to help me, but it was no use. I just could not approach people cold.

"How did I get into this state?" I thought. "I'm not qualified for anything. Mum was right when she said I would live to regret it when I quit high school." No trade. No education. What was I thinking? I guess I thought I was going to play hockey forever. I struggled on as a car salesman, but I was being paid next to nothing, which is what I was worth.

I often wondered what Rose thought, with all our dreams of the NHL, and she ends up with a broken-down old hockey player who can't keep a job. We were really hurtin' and countin' our pennies, but somehow she kept faith in me, and she kept me on an even keel and never wavered.

"Don't worry," I remember her saying all the time. "You'll work it out."

I'd say, "Rose, don't you get it? I'm at the end of my tether."

Of course, I kept up a brave front; not even Rose knew how I felt and how dark my mind was.

I'm ashamed to admit this, but I'll tell you how my mind was working. I was driving home from the car lot. In my mind, I was going over my situation. The fix I was in was of my own making. I had no one to blame but myself, and for a fleeting moment as I sped along the highway, going faster and faster, I thought, "I'm better off dead."

It only flashed through my mind for a moment, but it happened. I despised myself for thinking this way, for being such a weakling, not to fight on, to take the easy way out. I despised myself for not being able to keep a job, and most of all, I despised myself for feeling sorry for myself. Other guys had been unemployed and didn't quit. Look at me. I was ready to throw in the towel. I stumbled and struggled on but things just seemed to get darker.

* * *

I consider Punch Imlach to be the smartest guy I ever played for. He never failed to come up with things to keep you on edge or keep you thinking.

For instance, one time, it was the night before a playoff game and he got a card game going. He got some beer in and some sandwiches and we played poker. We thought, "What a great guy." We had two or three beers, and he won all the money, and we went to bed. We got thinking after: "That son of a gun conned us into it. He made sure we all got to bed by eleven-thirty."

One Sunday night, we were playing in Buffalo. I was playing for Springfield and Punch was coaching the team. After the game, all the players always used to go a bar called Pat Slater's. Every hockey team went there. It was just a little wee bar, and the owner was an Irish guy that the players loved. He served the best kummelweck buns with beef. They were unbelievable—roast beef with the juice on a salted bun—and after you'd had a couple of beers at one o'clock in the morning, they were the tastiest thing in the world. But most important, he had the coldest beer. And peanuts and popcorn. It was a hockey player's heaven.

We were there on this Sunday night. The guys stayed until closing time and headed back to the hotel. For some reason, Floyd Smith and I stayed a little longer. As we were ready to get up and leave, who comes walkin' in at 2:30 A.M. but Punch!

I said, "Oh boy, we're in trouble now." We tried to sneak out the back door, but he saw us and he yells, "Come back here and siddown!"

So he pulls up a chair and orders a round. I'm sitting there, and I'm sitting between Punch and Smitty, and the strangest thing happened: Punch started to go through situations in a hockey game and was asking what we would do in those situations.

One of the questions was, if you had your goalie out, would you put out five forwards and a defenceman? Another one was when should you pull your goalie? Questions like that, and it went on and on.

I could see that Punch wasn't interested in my answers, so I let him and Smitty go at it. I was in the middle. Punch would ask a question, then whisper his answer in my ear. Then Smitty would whisper his answer in my ear, and then they'd talk about it. Darned if they didn't agree on everything! This went on for about three-quarters of an hour. It was amazing how they always thought the same thing.

Finally, we called it a morning. Naturally, we couldn't get a cab that late on a Sunday night in Buffalo, and it was a deadly cold walk back to the hotel. Punch says, "Wait a minute. I'm short of breath. I'm struggling a little," and leaned against the wall.

We thought he was kiddin' and kept on goin'. Next morning, we find out he had a slight heart attack and he landed in the hospital. I guess what with the late hours, the beer and the cold, it got to him.

When he saw us the next morning, he said, "Nice guys you are, leaving me when I'm in trouble."

We laughed and said, "That'll teach you to drink with us big boys."

The upshot was that Punch never forgot how he and Smitty were on the same wavelength on situations concerning hockey that night. When he was made the Buffalo Sabres' GM, he hired Smitty as coach. Punch and Smitty went on to long careers in the NHL. I had the next sixteen years to go in the minors.

* * *

Well, as I'm writing this it's June 2010, and the playoffs are finally over. Ron MacLean and I were going from April 8 to June 6, every other night for two months. I have to tell you, it takes me three days to get over it after two months of riding in cabs and going through customs and security. Customs is no fun to go through anymore. It used to be a breeze most of the time, but now it's lineup after lineup. The same for airport security and stuff.

It was a tough go this year, but it was a good go. I was a little disappointed. I knew the Blackhawks were going to win, but I wish they would have won in Chicago. Could you imagine the celebrations and the whole deal? I knew if they won in Philly what would happen afterwards, and sure enough, it did.

Gary Bettman goes out and gets booed—but he expects to get booed all the time. That was okay. But it was the first time—and I've been at the finals for thirty-two years now—that I ever heard a city boo the team that won it and boo the MVP when he got the Conn Smythe Trophy.

In Philadelphia, that's what they're like. They boo Santa Claus, I guess, so I guess they can boo Jonathan Toews. It's a tough city.

* * *

One thing that happened in the 2009–10 season was my "battle" with Dan Carcillo of the Flyers. I didn't like the way he played, and I had given it to him all winter and I'd given it to him all play-offs. Now he was benched this one game in the finals. Before the game, to get to the *Hockey Night in Canada* studio, you have to go by the Philly dressing room, and there was Carcillo, out in the hall on a stationary bike. That's what they do when they're not playing: they do the stationary bike to stay in shape.

Now, I've got to go right by there, and I look up and I see him. I'm thinking, "All right! Get ready! You want a fight? I'm ready for the fight." So we march down the corridor and we're going along, and I come up to him and I look him right in the eye, and he looks at me with those big Bambi eyes of his and he says, "Hi, Don."

Oh boy, I could have cried, so I said, "Hi, Dan," and I kept on going.

The next game, I see him again and I say, "Dan, I'll do my best to get you in there." So I did. I went on TV and I said, "You need

Carcillo in the game. Get him in the game; he'll get you some spark." By golly, he did. The Flyers put him in for that game, but I'll tell you he sure knew how to get me just saying, "Hi, Don," after all the stuff I'd given him.

You can get to me easy. Just be kind to me. You'll own me, too, just like Danny did.

* * *

The next game, if you remember, the Philly goalie, Michael Leighton, got pulled in Chicago, and from the Hawks' bench, Patrick Sharp gave him a hard time. He was yelling at him from the bench. I'd never seen that before. I'd never seen it when a guy — who feels bad enough as it is because he's being yanked — is going off, and here he is getting heck from a guy on the bench of the opposing team.

I didn't like to see that, so I gave it to Patrick Sharp pretty good. Next game in Philly, I come walking down the hall, getting ready to go into the studio, and Kathy Broderick, who seems to run pretty well everything at the CBC, comes up to me and says, "Patrick Sharp wants to talk to you. He's been waiting for you for an hour now."

I figure, "Oh boy, here's another one I'll be getting into an argument with." So I go up and I say, "Hi, Patrick," as he comes towards me. He says, "Don, you know I didn't mean to do that. I don't know why I did that to Leighton. I'm sorry I did that. I'm a good Thunder Bay boy. That's not me at all." He says, "I won't do it again, Grapes. I'll make it up to you."

So I said, "Okay, Patrick, I'll have you iso'd." That means we'd have a camera that watched him all night long. He'd be isolated. So we had him iso'd that night, and if you remember, he got an assist on the winning goal and we had a good shot of it.

I'm glad I made the call, because Patrick Sharp is a good guy and he is a good Thunder Bay boy.

* * *

So it's a never-ending battle the whole time. There's always something happening. It was good playoffs.

I knew Chicago was going to win, but like I said, it would have been a lot better back in Chicago. Could you imagine the parades and the celebrations? It was sort of a little downer that they got booed when they won the trophy.

I have to say that the first time the Canadiens beat us when I was coaching Boston, it was right in Boston. In overtime, too. It was disheartening, but when they got the Stanley Cup and they held the Cup up, the Boston crowd gave them a standing ovation. That's the difference between the Boston fans and the Philly fans.

* * *

I remember my very first game of my comeback like it was yesterday. I worked so hard to get in shape and I was raring to go. Nothing was going to hold me back.

So we make the trip to Cincinnati for the first game of the season, and the morning of the game, I'm standing in the lobby of the hotel and I see coach Doug Adams coming up to me. It doesn't look good, the way he's walking towards me. And yeah, he tells me I'm not playing. It was like a knife in the heart. I have to say that I was so disappointed I had to turn away. I think I had tears in my eyes.

So that night, I'm a "healthy scratch," as they say, and I'm sitting in the stands, watching them get bombed by Cincinnati, happy as a pig in mud. You're shocked? I'm not a team guy? Listen, I was desperate. My family had to eat. Let me tell you something: if players are not playing and they're sitting in the stands and they're honest, they'll confess they're so happy if their team loses because they might get a shot.

Sure enough, I dress the next game. Adams dresses me because he has to dress me after an 8–1 loss. We go and we play in Cleveland,

and the feel is still there. I feel good. I'm in great shape. Believe it or not, I score a goal and get an assist. We win. In Cleveland, they only give one star for the game, and I'm it. Two points in Cleveland and I'm plus-2. Next game, we tie. I get an assist and I'm plus-1.

We come home and we're losing with two minutes to go in Rochester. I let a slap shot go. Jimmy Wiste tips it in. He's our left winger, and he tips it into the top corner. We've got a win and two ties—four points in three games. I'm plus-5. It couldn't be better.

A few days later, the club is making a southern trip. I get a call from Doug. I can still remember where I was standing when I got the call. I was told I'm not making the southern trip.

Boy, it was like I was poleaxed! I've played three games. One star. Leading scorer on the club, and I'm scratched. Imagine that!

I shouldn't blame Doug Adams. He was acting under orders. We were a development club, and that's what the American Hockey League was in those days. They wanted their young players to play. They didn't care about Rochester at all. The rule they had in the AHL was that you could only have six guys over 26 on the roster. I was 36.

It was all downhill from then on. Because I didn't play and my conditioning fell off, the feeling left. When I did play, the feeling just wasn't there. Except one time. We were playing the Boston Braves in the Boston Garden. The Braves were the farm team of the Boston Bruins. They didn't get many people there to watch the games.

I was sitting on the bench, as usual. We were getting beat 6–2, and Adams was really getting ticked off at the power play. It was terrible. So to tell the rest of the team how desperate and how lousy we were, he said, "Cherry, you play the point," as if to say, "You guys are so bad, I'm putting this stiff out."

My legs were cold. They were like lead from sitting, but I'm thinking, "I'm not the stiff he thinks I am." I'm all pumped because I can't believe he is sending me out on the power play. It was the first time he'd done that. I'd never played on the power play; I'm just not a power-play guy. He sends me out there, and I'm cold and I say, "Lord, just don't let me make a fool of myself."

As God is my judge, this is what happened: The faceoff is in the right-hand corner, left-hand draw. The centreman pulls it directly back to me on the left point, I fake a shot and the guy goes for it.

I walk around him, fake another shot. I go to his right and walk around him. Now I'm in on the goalie, and I snap a shot into the top corner. I couldn't believe it.

I'm really ticked. I don't wait for congratulations. I skate right to the bench as fast as I can, spray some snow up, and I sit down. There was nobody at the game, and a guy called Garry Peters on the Braves yells out, "Hey, watch out for that Number 2. He's really dangerous." Everybody on the bench laughed. Maybe it was that the other guys were winning 6–2 and there was only about three or four minutes left. Maybe they didn't try so hard. But I tell you one thing: it felt so good to score that goal. I can't remember feelin' better about a goal.

It was a lousy game, and there was nobody watching, but my heart was just going. I skated to the bench and sat down just as if to say, "I'm not the jerk you think I am!"

That was my last shift playing professional hockey. If you're going to go out, that's the way to go out. Nobody saw it. Nobody even remembers or cares about the goal. Except me.

* * *

I loved playing in Rochester. In fact, it was my favourite city. I played in some pretty good spots—Denver and Boston. Spokane, Washington, was really good, too. Rose's favourite was Kitchener, Ontario. She said it was so clean, it reminded her of Hershey, Pennsylvania, her hometown, with all the "Dutchmen" around. After the games in Kitchener, the fan club would put on a dinner or something, a little smorgasbord or a buffet, and they had roasted pigs' tails, a favourite around Hershey—and around Kitchener, I guess.

I passed on them.

Rochester was my favourite, maybe because my friend Whitey Smith lived there. Whitey rose from a private to captain in combat. We had some dynamite clubs in Rochester. I guess that's what it was that made the town my favourite. We were better than some NHL clubs that we used to beat all the time in exhibition games.

The reason that we had such dynamite clubs was because we were a farm team of the Toronto Maple Leafs, and in those days, the Leafs were absolutely loaded. That's when they were winning all the Stanley Cups. Punch Imlach was the coach and GM in Toronto. Joe Crozier was the GM and coach in Rochester. They were two winners.

Joe and Punch were a combo, sharp as a pair of tacks. They had a piece of the action in Rochester, and they ended up selling it to Vancouver and making some nice coin. But before they did that, they loaded up Rochester and made it a championship club to make it attractive for the sale. They never missed an opportunity.

My first year there was 1964, and I played there for four years. In that time, we won three championships and went to the final the other time.

We won our last championship in Quebec, and I almost didn't play. My lungs were so bad with bronchitis I was going to quit, but Joe said, "You gotta see my doctor, Dr. McVeigh. He'll fix you up."

I said, "Joe, there's no use. I've seen all the doctors and taken all the medicine. I just can't breathe. It's like a vise around my lungs. I can't breathe."

But he insisted, so I went to see Dr. Sam McVeigh. He put me on prednisone—very, very high-potency prednisone—and it did the trick. We won the championship that year. I was captain of the club, and it just happened that when the whistle blew to end the championship game, I had the puck. I saved it, and I was going to give it to Dr. McVeigh for saving my career. I told Cro, "I'm going to give this to Dr. McVeigh."

Cro said, "Give it to me. I'll give it to him." I did, and I don't know why.

I wonder if Dr. McVeigh ever saw it?

* * *

In 1989, the Winnipeg Jets hired Alpo Suhonen, who was gonna be the assistant coach to Bob Murdoch. They didn't hire a kid called Ron Smith, a Canadian coach in the minors. As we were getting to the end of "Coach's Corner," I said, "Why didn't they hire Ron Smith instead of this guy?"

Ron MacLean said, "Well, that's neither here nor there. We wish Alpo good luck."

I said, "I don't wish him good luck. He sounds like dog food to me."

Well, Winnipeg almost went nuts. I was in trouble again. So the CBC hired a lawyer and I had to go to meetings and that, because I was being sued by the Winnipeg Jets.

Barry Shenkarow was the president of the Winnipeg Jets, and he said, "The only way Cherry will ever get out of this is if he goes on 'Coach's Corner' Saturday night and apologizes. That's the only way we're gonna stop this lawsuit." So I went on "Coach's Corner" and I told MacLean, I said, "At the end, turn to me and say, 'That's it?'"

So he did. Near the end of "Coach's Corner," he turned to me and he said, "Is that it?"

Now everybody's waitin' to see if I'm gonna apologize. I said, "That's it."

So the lawsuit was goin' ahead, and I was told by the CBC lawyers, "Don't talk to reporters" and "Keep your mouth shut" and stuff like that. But one of the bigwigs with the Winnipeg Jets called me a racist and a bigot. I said, "That's it!" I had been told you couldn't prove I was a racist and a bigot. You could only prove I was discriminatory. I like that one. So I phoned a reporter out there and I said, "I just heard he called me a racist and a bigot. I'm gonna sue them.

I'm gonna countersue them. I'll own the Winnipeg Jets, believe me. I'm gonna sue them for every penny they got."

Needless to say, their lawsuits were dropped.

Alpo Suhonen? He wasn't a bad guy and he wasn't a bad coach. But I still thought we should have had Ronnie Smith, a Canadian.

* * *

I'm often asked how I enjoyed my venture into junior hockey.

It sounded like a good idea at the time. Mississauga had 600,000 people. It has five hundred companies.

I remember my first meeting about it with my buddy Trevor Whiffen. Trevor was the lawyer I first met when I got into trouble with Alpo Suhonen. He was the lawyer for the CBC, and when Barry Shenkarow was suing me, Trevor and I became friends.

Another guy at the meeting about the Mississauga junior team was a financier, as they call him, Joel Albin. They were all gung-ho. Usually, when I'm gung-ho, I'm successful, but this time, I wasn't that gung-ho. I had a few doubts. I pointed out that Mississauga only has a weekly paper, no radio and no TV. It's not like London, Windsor, Ottawa, Kitchener or those other places where junior hockey is successful. How are we gonna let the people know when the game is on?

I went along and contacted Mayor Hazel McCallion about a new arena. She agreed, and once Hurricane Hazel gets something in her mind, it's done. Although she always said she did it for the Mississauga IceDogs, to tell you the truth, I think she did it for women's hockey. Hazel had the women's world championship tournament there in that arena, and Canada won.

Hazel always gets her way. She has been mayor there since the seventies. She never campaigns, but she gets about 96 per cent of the vote.

She's 89 and she's tough as nails. She got hit by a truck last year, but the truck's okay.

I won't bore you with the schmozzle we went through getting the franchise. Suffice to say we got our money in late, and over in Brampton, their junior club got in just before us, so they got all the first picks, and we got seconds—an indication of things to come.

The arena was late getting built, so we played our first nine games on the road and got murdered. We didn't have a chance. Our first game in Ottawa, we got smoked 10–0. I saw a picture of me on TV on the late news, and my face was red. It went like that all year long. That was the year. Agony.

The next year was no better. If you can believe it, we had a coach who won three games. We could have had the trainer stand back there and do that. But we were getting first-overall draft picks, and we had two guys—Patrick O'Sullivan and Robbie Schremp— who were named rookies of the year, so we were getting stronger.

That was the second year, but in the last year that I was there, when my son, Tim, and I did a lot of the scouting, six of our guys were drafted by the NHL, more than any other team in the Canadian Hockey League.

So back in year two, we were a couple of years away, but we were coming. I just can't let the guy who won three games coach again, but we can't afford to replace him because I am going to honour his contract, which is $80,000. That's a lot of money in junior hockey, but your word is your bond, so I paid him.

Now *I've* gotta coach. The reason I gotta coach is that I'm the only guy who would do it for nothing. Tim says, "Dad, you're going to kill yourself. You've got *Hockey Night in Canada.* You have to travel there. You've got five radio shows a week. You got commercials, and you're going out scouting, too."

He was right, of course, and I have to admit, I did a lousy job of coaching.

Trips to Sudbury, North Bay, Sault Ste. Marie, I'm right back where I started from in the American Hockey League.

One time, we played in the Soo and travelled all night back to

Mississauga in a brutal snowstorm. No sleep. I went home, took a shower and then went downtown to the radio studio and taped five shows.

Long trips on the buses, getting in at six in the morning. It was the same thing as the American Hockey League, only with no beer.

* * *

The years in junior hockey were tough. I remember one game in Ottawa. We were up 3–1 in the third period and blew it. After the game, I had to go to Montreal for *Hockey Night in Canada*, and the other guys had to go back to Mississauga.

One of the players, a wise guy, made a smart crack to me. I get to the hotel in Montreal, and I try to phone both coaches on the team. They're on the way to Mississauga, and there's no answer. I'm ticked at the kid, and I want to send him home. The more often I phone with no answer, the more ticked I get. In the hotel room, there happens to be a glass coffee table with sharp corners. I hit my leg on it, and it starts bleeding. As I'm on the phone again, I look in the full-length mirror and see this red-faced jerk, standing in his shorts with blood running down his leg, trying to get somebody on the phone.

It was not a pretty sight, not a sight I was proud of.

But I toughed it out somehow, even though I think it shortened my life. The one thing that I found strange was that I thought the fans on the road would give me a hard time. But even though we had a lousy team, the fans, for some reason, were good.

I wasn't. I have to admit, I didn't act good. I was sullen. I was ticked off all the time. But I'd sign autographs on the road between periods. At least I could do that for the fans. After the last game of the season, I had the players sit in a row at a long table on the ice and sign autographs for the fans.

It was not a good year. The crowds weren't good, and it was exactly like I said it would be. People didn't know when the games were, and we couldn't advertise with no TV, no paper, no radio. The team was not good. I was getting a rip job every day in the paper, but I'm hanging tough with the autograph-signing at the end of the season.

As we come to the end, a man and his wife take their tickets, rip them up and throw them in my face, screaming at me that the only reason they bought those tickets was that I promised them the playoffs.

As I sat there with bits of their ripped-up tickets all over me, I didn't know whether to laugh or cry.

* * *

Little things I remember about the IceDogs. Just a few things.

I had spread myself too thin, and proof I had spread myself too thin is that I wasn't sharp with the press. Usually, this is my bag, and I can dance with the best. You could never catch me. I know all the tricks, such as this one: The reporter has got his story and that's in the bag. So at the end, he'll try for the killer question, and if you're not smart, you'll get caught. They figure, "Hey, I've got the story in the can. Now I'll try something hard."

I know all the routines, and I can honestly say I never got caught until one day I met a guy—and he was just starting out for the *Toronto Sun*. He was covering junior hockey, and my radar was not very sharp, I gotta admit. I guess I was worn down, but maybe that's nothing more than an excuse.

This guy still writes for the *Toronto Sun*. He seemed like a great young kid, so I thought I'd help him out, and we have a good, long interview. It was good. It wasn't a bad one. The questions weren't bad, but I wasn't on my guard. Nothing serious, and after it was over, I thought, "What a nice young kid. He's going to go a long way."

I'm sorry to say I was duped, as they say. Boy, did he do a number on me the next day. And he followed it up time after time. He was relentless. In fact, it helped his career. He was giving it to the big

TV star Cherry. I have to say, in my forty years of dealing with the press, this guy was the only one I ran into and didn't pick up on his motives. I know I have been ripped many times, and I often expected it; but I can honestly say he was the only guy who fooled me completely.

I have done interviews, and I've said to myself afterwards, "Boy, am I going to get murdered in this one." Hey, you live with it. One guy even attacked my family, but that's the life I live. It's the old story. As Harry Truman said, "If you can't take the heat, get out of the kitchen."

I've got to say this kid did a great job. He murdered me. It taught me a little humility—just a little—and taught me that I'm not as smart as I thought I was.

* * *

My assistant coach when I coached the IceDogs was my nephew, Steve Cherry, who I love. We don't spend much time together, because he's in Kingston and I'm in Mississauga, but he's a great kid. He coaches underprivileged kids twice a week in Kingston. He gets the equipment for them. He got the city of Kingston to donate the ice time for them.

He went to Queen's University, played for the team there, and is a teacher. He decided when I was coaching the IceDogs that he'd like to be my assistant coach, so he took a year off teaching and did a great job coaching and was thinking about getting into coaching as a career.

I didn't have the heart to say to him, "Are you nuts? You want to get into the minefield of coaching, where we're all hired to be fired? We all get it in the end. You could be a teacher with security, pension and all that stuff, and you want to give it up to be a coach?"

Now, I know a lot of people don't know that the difference between a head coach and assistant coach is night and day. The assistant coach is the good guy with the players. They love him.

He's the good cop. They're friendly with him. They talk to him on the ice. They tell him their problems. If you're the assistant coach, you don't have to make any decisions. It's kinda fun.

That's not like being the head coach. He's the bad cop. He's the one who benches guys, doesn't dress guys, chews the players out. If there's too many men on the ice, he gets blamed. He's gotta talk to the reporters all the time. The buck stops with him.

But not the assistant. He just has a good time, and it seems like fun.

You have to learn to be a head coach. That's why last year (2009–10), New Jersey's GM and president, Lou Lamoriello, sent John MacLean down to the American Hockey League to learn how to be a head coach. MacLean had been an assistant for three or four years with the Devils. Lou sent him down for one year, and now he's the head coach of the New Jersey Devils.

Lou knows the pitfalls of life as a head coach, but Steve had visions of the glamour of being a head coach, and I must admit, it's a rush to be the guy in charge of twenty players. But I couldn't let Steve blow his career as a teacher after all that education, so I did a cruel thing.

As we only had two or three games left and were goin' nowhere — and Steve is reading this for the first time — one day I said to Steve, "Would you like to be the head coach tonight?"

The game was in Toronto, at Maple Leaf Gardens, and we were going to play St. Mike's, a first-place club. I showed no mercy.

Well, Steve jumped at the chance. He was so excited. I sat way up high and never went down between periods to help him. We got our brains blown out. I could see Steve dying on the bench, but I offered no help. I felt awful doing this, especially when Steven came to me after the game and said, with his eyes a little moist, "I don't think I'll pursue a coaching career, Uncle Don." I gotta admit, I got a little choked up, because it's tough to destroy a kid's dream, but it had to be done. Sometimes you have to be cruel to be kind.

* * *

With all the draft choices we got for suffering, we finally got a good club. But now the value had gone up, and we had a partner in the club who wanted to sell. The deal was that if one partner wanted to sell, all had to sell.

So I had to sell my share. The team went on with fourteen of my players and won the Eastern Conference championship of the Ontario Hockey League. I wish I'd been there to see it, but I wasn't. But I have to admit, I deserved everything I got. I made a zillion mistakes, and as I look back now, I just shake my head at the first couple of years.

But I'm kinda proud. I rode out the storm and got the ship back on an even keel. It's just unfortunate that I wasn't the captain.

* * *

One last thing about the Mississauga IceDogs. Whenever the IceDogs would visit a city for a game, they would sell out.

After Sudbury, we played in Sault Ste. Marie and the announcer said, "This is the biggest crowd for a Soo home opener in history." They all cheered because it was a big crowd, and we were losing and getting stiffed by the referees. It was always the same. I always felt that the referees were saying, "We're not going to be intimidated by this big stiff Cherry. We'll show him, and we'll show the league. We're not afraid."

I also feel that same thing happened to Dougie Gilmour in the 2009–10 season when he took over the Kingston Frontenacs. It's like they were sayin' to him, "Yeah, we know who you are, Dougie, and we're not intimidated."

I digress. We're losing in the Soo and the PA announcer says it's the biggest crowd ever to see a regular-season game there. I wonder why? We're a last-place club. You know why.

When the announcer says that, I get up and bow to the crowd. They loved it.

I did interviews before the games, after the games, and during the games. I signed autographs and I packed them in in every city in the league except one: Mississauga.

* * *

I've said in the past that trying to learn about great men and reading books about them has helped me. One such man is Lord Horatio Nelson, the English admiral whose victory at the Battle of Trafalgar changed the world for the next two hundred years.

Napoleon was all set to invade England, but after the defeat of the combined fleet of the French and Spanish at Trafalgar, he had no choice but to cancel his plans for the invasion. Without a navy to provide protection for the barges that were going to carry his troops across the English Channel, Napoleon had to bring back the army that was already lining the French shore, ready to invade England.

And the defeat of Napoleon's forces by the Duke of Wellington at Waterloo ten years later would never have happened without Nelson's victory at Trafalgar.

Nelson's reputation for being loved by his men was legendary, as is revealed by this story.

Nelson was in his flagship, the *Victory*, cruising the Caribbean when one of his sailors fell overboard. Usually, in the English navy in those days, that was the end of the sailor. He was either left to drown or rescued and charged with desertion and hanged. But Nelson's second-in-command, Thomas Hardy, said he wanted to rescue the sailor. Nelson agreed, so Hardy had a small boat lowered with a couple of men. They rowed back to the sailor and pulled him aboard.

The *Victory* had its mainsails down, waiting for Hardy's return, when suddenly, the lookout called that the Spanish fleet had just appeared on the horizon. Nelson had to make a decision: Does he remain and face certain capture or does he run up all his sails and escape?

He declares, "I will not lose Hardy," and remains at a dead stop so Hardy can catch up.

The Spanish admiral saw the *Victory* with all its sails down and couldn't believe that an English man-of-war would be sitting with its sails down waiting to get captured.

He said, "This must be a trap. The English fleet must be waiting just over the horizon. When I sail in to attack this ship, they'll spring the trap."

He stopped too. Hardy caught up to the *Victory* and Nelson sailed away.

This episode was told from ship to ship throughout the English fleet, and one more tale of how Nelson would never leave his men was added to his reputation.

Now, you're gonna say that it's a stretch to get from there to the story I'm going to tell you, because it doesn't compare with the action of Nelson. But in a sense, in my world, it does.

When I was with the Boston Bruins and we were on the road, whenever the bus arrived to take us to the rink or the airport, I was always the last one to get on the bus. The reason was that the captain, Wayne Cashman, would count the players before I got on the bus. If one of the players had slept in, Cash would come up to me in the hotel lobby and tell me a certain player wasn't there. I'd say, "Go get him," Wayne would go up to the room, hustle the guy on and nothin' was said. I would say somethin' to his roommate for leavin' the guy, though, and believe me, if the guy ever did it again, a lot was said.

One day, we'd played in Chicago and we were headin' for the airport. Wayne didn't come to me and I got on the bus. On this trip, everybody was there—Harry Sinden, the GM; Tom Johnson, the assistant GM; Paul Mooney, the president; all the reporters. We take off.

Five minutes out, Wayne comes to me and says, "Uh-oh, Grapes, I'm in trouble, and Terry's in trouble. He's not on the bus."

It's a long way from the hotel to the airport in Chicago, and I know that Terry O'Reilly is gonna miss the plane. I say, "We've got to go back."

So we do, even though all the brass are gonna be hot.

When we get back, Terry is standing in front of the hotel with his bags. He hadn't taken a cab and tried to catch up. Somehow he knew I would not leave him.

Terry got on the bus to the usual ribbing and hollerin' from the players. Stuff about sleepin' in, bein' a teacher's pet and all that sort of stuff.

Nothin' was said. Terry never said thanks. He knew. It was the right thing to do as far as I was concerned.

I tell you one thing. There was an awful good feeling among the players on that bus.

Yes, it's a stretch to compare that to risking your life with the Spanish fleet approachin', as Nelson did. But in my world, it's almost the same.

* * *

The way Sir Francis Drake played out the delicate situation with his brother, John, helped me deal with that difficult and delicate situation with my nephew, Steve, and his coaching career.

When I was a young boy, I started to read books about leaders, especially military leaders such as T. E. Lawrence, who became better known as Lawrence of Arabia; Julius Caesar; the Duke of Wellington; Winston Churchill; and Field Marshall Bernard Montgomery. I started off with historical fiction, especially the ones that had to do with battles.

The one that started me was a book called *The Golden Admiral*. It was historical, and it was written by F. Van Wyck Mason. My favourite book of all is *Seven Pillars of Wisdom* by T.E. Lawrence. It's about his battles in the Arabian desert against the Turks. When the battles with the Taliban started, this book was flying off the shelves, even though it was written ninety years ago. The reason was that the Taliban is doing to our soldiers what Lawrence did to the Turkish Army during the First World War.

My two favourite heroes are Lord Horatio Nelson and Sir Francis Drake. I would say that Drake is my top favourite. It amuses me when I see people going to seminars about how to be leaders when all they have to do is read Drake's life story. I learned a lot from his life, and I think I have every book written about him, even a book that Ron MacLean gave me called *The Secret Voyage of Sir Francis Drake*, which says that in his voyage around the world, no one knew he was actually up in the Northwest Passage and had sailed up the coast of British Columbia.

I have many favourite stories of Sir Francis, such as how he conquered the Spanish Armada. Make no mistake, I know Lord Howard was the admiral, but Drake was the leader, and when the armada arrived off the coast of England, a rider was sent to warn Drake that the armada had been sighted.

Drake was lawn bowling at the time. He continued playing the game and said, "I have time to finish the game and beat the Spanish too." The rider went back and told the admirals, and it spread through the whole country. It showed confidence. A lesson.

There was a humour lesson as well. When he was sailing around the world, Drake went into the Pacific, raiding the Spanish, and one day he came upon an island where a soldier was sleeping against a tree on the beach. Beside him in a crate was the pile of gold he was supposed to be guarding.

Sir Francis landed quietly, took the gold, then took leaves and brushed away his footprints in the sand to make it appear that nobody had been there. You can imagine the soldier waking up and thinking that spirits had taken the gold. That showed humour.

Another story showed how he loved his sailors. He wanted to attack a Spanish fort that was on the Spanish Main. It could not be conquered because all the guns were pointing towards the sea, and they were enormous. The only way you would ever be able to get to this fort and all its gold was through a swamp, and the Spanish thought that nobody could ever go through this swamp.

Except the Cameroons.

The Cameroons were half-breeds. They were half-Indian and half-Spanish. The Indians didn't like them, and the Spanish didn't like them, so they lived in this swamp and they knew it like the back of their hands. Drake went to the chief of the Cameroons and said, "Listen, you lead me through the swamp to the back of the fort, and I'll be able to conquer it. You can have anything you want."

The chief and the Cameroons hated the Spanish and killed then whenever they had a chance, so he agreed. They went through the swamp, they conquered the fort and they had a pile of gold and jewellery.

Drake was a privateer, so he's different than a pirate in that he has a letter from the king or queen allowing him to attack the ships and colonies of certain countries. In Drake's case, Elizabeth I signed the letter, and Spain was his target. As a privateer, this was the way it worked: it was the first democracy. There was a pile of treasure for the sailors, there was a pile for the officers and there was a pile for Drake. When the Cameroon chief came aboard, Drake said to him, "You can have anything you want."

The Cameroon chief pointed to Drake's sword, which had emeralds and diamonds on it. He says, "I want that sword."

Drake explained to him, "No, you can't have that sword. I won it in battle, and that was given to me by a famous Spanish admiral."

The chief said, "You promised I could have anything."

Drake's word was his bond, as usual, so he took off his sword and handed it to the chief. While he was doing that, the chief handed him a big ball of solid gold. Drake looked at it, threw it into the sailors' pile of treasure and walked away.

Do you not think those sailors would follow him to the end of the earth? They loved him.

He also showed how to handle delicate situations. As they were sailing around the world, they had about four ships, but they were in a lot of battles, so they came down to two ships, the *Golden Hind* and the *Swan*. The *Swan* was a little ship, but it was a beautiful

Me at seventeen (middle)—my Junior days with the Windsor Spitfires. That's my buddy and roommate Jimmy Robertson on the left.

Tim and Rose in Rochester, New York. Story on page 80.

Timothy, me and Cindy in Rochester, New York.

Mom in front of our house in Kingston with my dogs Dudgeon and the bulldog Topper.

During a fight in the Boston Gardens (L to R): Jim Pettie, Dwight Foster, Al Secord, John Wensink, Stan Jonathan, Bobby Miller, Don Marcotte, Rick Middleton, Mike Millbury, Jean Ratelle, Bobby Schmautz, Al Sims, Dennis O'Brien.

1969 Western Hockey League Champions, the Vancouver Canucks. Never lost a game in the playoffs. That's me with Andy Bathgate, Bob Lemieux, Bryan Hextall, Bob Barlow (pouring), Marc Reaume, Ted McCaskill, Donnie Johns (drinking from the cup) and Murray Hall (holding the bottle). Little did I know it would be my last real game.

The Barrie Flyers ready to board the train to Winnipeg to win the Memorial Cup, beating the St. Boniface Canadiens four games to one. In five games I got two goals and two assists. Thank you, hold your applause. That's my friend Ralph Willis peeking over my shoulder. We were a happy bunch.

Ricky Middleton when he won the Seventh Player Award from the Boston Gallery Gods.

Bobby Orr and Eddie Shore, the two greatest defencemen to play the game.

With Stan Jonathan when I gave him the Bruins' Seventh Player Award.

Bobby that year had 46 goals, 89 assists, 135 points and 100 minutes in penalties, +128.

Eleven 20 or more goals scorers on one team — a record never to be broken, 1977–78. They were: Wayne Cashman (24 goals); Al Sims, filling in for Brad Park (22); Bobby Schmautz (27); Greg Sheppard (23); Bobby Millar (20); Terry O'Reilly (29); Peter McNab (43); Rick Middleton (25); Stan Jonathan (27); Donnie Marcotte (20); Jean Ratelle (25).

Me and my boys.

As a Montreal Canadiens hopeful, they always made you feel first class and a member of the team, even though you never had a chance, like a confirmed minor leaguer like me. A first class organization.

Editor of *The Hockey News*, Ken Mackenzie, presenting me with the American League Coach of the Year plaque.

KINGSTON
PONIES BASEBALL CLUB

DEL CHERRY

1923: Dad led the league in hits, home runs, RBIs and batting average.

In my office at the Boston Gardens.

My 1975–76 Bruins.

one. It was perfectly made; everybody loved it, and Sir Francis's brother was captain. He loved the *Swan*. It was his favourite ship of all time, and he never stopped talking about it. But they got to a point after all the battles that they had lost so many crew that they had only enough crew left for one ship. How can Sir Francis go to his brother and say, "Look, you can't have your ship — I'm going to sink it"? How can he tell his brother that?

So what he did was, he waited until they were resting in a bay one day and he went to the *Golden Hind*'s carpenter and said, "Look, I'm going to take my brother fishing, and when I take him fishing, I want you to take your augur and drill holes all over the bottom of the *Swan*. And if you ever tell anybody, if it ever gets out that you did this, you know what will happen to you."

So Sir Francis goes over to the *Swan* in a little boat and gets his brother, John, and they row away and go fishing. The carpenter goes in and drills the hole in the bottom.

From a distance, John can see the ships, and he says, "Francis, don't you think my ship seems to be listing a little?"

Sir Francis says, "No, it looks okay to me."

Well, you know what happened. It sank, and all the crew that was on that ship came over to the *Golden Hind*; and now Drake had a strong crew.

Sometimes you have to be cruel to be kind.

* * *

I can hear what you're sayin'. "That's all well and good to have a crew that loves you. But if everybody loves you, how do you keep discipline on a ship or on a team or in a business?"

Sir Francis had that figured out too.

He was their best friend when they behaved, and he was their worst enemy when they crossed him.

On his trip around the world, the queen's favourite, Sir Thomas Doughty, was along, probably to spy on Drake for the queen. But when Doughty caused trouble, Drake arrested him, tried him, sentenced him to death and personally executed him.

Doughty was the queen's favourite, but Drake had to run his ship his way.

I'm not saying you should cut a guy's head off. I'm saying that it's great if they love you, but there must be fear too—in a ship, a team or a business.

* * *

I often think of the way my good buddy Chris Simon was treated by everybody in hockey. His suspensions were so unfair.

Think of all the short suspensions the league gives out—four games for hittin' from behind and giving concussions that put guys out for months. Think about guys that never played again after being tripped into the boards on icings. I can go on and on about suspensions that should have been.

Now think about Chris Simon, who altogether drew fifty-five games in suspensions. You know how many games his victims—if that's what you want to call them—missed through injuries because of what Chris did to them? Not a game. Not a period. Altogether, they only missed one shift! And the guy that missed the one shift didn't really have to miss that shift. They just kept him off for a shift to make it look serious.

Look at the guys Chris went after. Every one of them was a pest that deserved to be gone after.

Fifty-five games of suspensions in return for one missed shift! As far as I'm concerned, it's so unfair to a great guy and a great team player.

* * *

All the years I played and coached in the United States, I never flew the Canadian flag or had a Canadian flag decal on my car.

You might ask, "Why not? Are you not proud to be a Canadian?"

Of course I'm proud to be a Canadian, but the U.S. has given me and my family their milk and honey—education and life—and I'm not about to go around the U.S. crowing about how great Canada is.

When I played in Rochester, I sat beside a Canadian who was always saying how great Canada is. Day after day, it was the same thing.

We had a couple of Americans on the club, and the trainer was American, so one day I said, "Look, give it a rest. All of us Canadians are proud to be Canadian, and we know Canada is the best. But knock it off, pointing this out every day, day after day. And those Canadian stickers you have all over your car are an embarrassment. If you like Canada so much, why don't you go back? You won't, because you can't survive there and live as well as you do here in the United States. You should appreciate the United States for the life it has given you and quit crowing about Canada all the time."

Which brings me to the point. I'm writing this as the soccer World Cup is going full tilt, and as usual in Toronto and Mississauga and Brampton, cars are flying foreign flags.

It's great that you are proud of where you came from, or where your parents came from, or your grandparents came from, but nobody leaves their homeland unless they can't make a go of it or they're persecuted. They come to Canada where everything is free to them from the cradle to the grave. Canada gives them a great life, and all they want to do is celebrate where they came from—a place where they couldn't make a go of it. It's ridiculous.

I ask you: if Canada was a factor in the soccer world, what flag do you think these people would be flying on their cars? If you think Canada, you're dreaming. I have a few friends who play soccer for Team Canada, and they tell me that when a foreign team comes to play Canada, they see second- and third-generation kids, born and bred in Canada, boo Canada and cheer the country where their grandfathers came from.

I ask you this: the people who fly foreign flags on their cars to cheer on the country where their grandfathers come from, do you think those people flew Canadian flags when Team Canada was playing for the hockey gold in the Winter Olympics? Not a chance. I've said this before and I'll say it again: You're living here. Your family is living here. You are educated here. You take Canada's milk and honey. In my world, you should love Canada, and it should be number one in your heart.

And if not, here's the door. Don't let it hit your ass on the way out.

* * *

I first met Graham James when I flew out to Swift Current to help with a banquet to raise money for a bus. I think it was $23,000 that they needed.

The reason they needed a bus was that a year before, on December 30, 1986, the junior team, the Swift Current Broncos, were travelling in a snowstorm. They had an awful crash, and four young players were killed. Joe Sakic was on that team, and one of the players who died was the brother of Lindy Ruff, the longtime coach of the Buffalo Sabres. The Broncos' coach was Graham James.

I flew out there and did the banquet. I met James for ten seconds, shook hands with him, and when I came back, I said to Ron, "You know, Ron, there's somethin' funny about that coach out there. I only met him for ten seconds, but I looked in his eyes, and he had a funny look in his eyes."

It wasn't too long after that that Sheldon Kennedy comes out and tells all the awful things that James did to him.

I remember on television, after James had been convicted—he got three and a half years—Ron asked me what I thought of it, and I said, "He should be drawn and quartered, the son of a bitch."

Evidently, he was sitting among some convicts at the time, and they were all watching it. After I said that, they had to put him in solitary confinement to protect him.

So I thought that was the end of it.

The other day—April 5, 2010, to be exact—right after it came out that James had been pardoned, there was an article in the paper from the Canadian Press by Bruce Cheadle. He was interviewing a fellow that, way back before all this, tried out for a team that James was coaching. It was in Winnipeg. In fact, it was the Junior B team—the Fort Garry Blues in 1979–80. That was way before the sexual assaults that James committed on Sheldon Kennedy and Theoren Fleury. He assaulted this kid too.

It haunted this kid to this day. He's not a kid anymore, of course. Cheadle's article said he's a lawyer, a divorced father of a six-year-old daughter, and a longtime volunteer hockey coach. The guy blames the psychological effect of what James did to him for breaking up his marriage to "the most wonderful woman in the world."

If he had come through and spoke out like Theo and Sheldon, it would never have happened to them. So he was really upset about the whole thing. He has a guilty conscience. He has to go to a psychiatrist.

He just can't understand how a guy like Graham James can be pardoned. For the life of me, I can't either. They make this decision without the government's consent or knowledge. It's unbelievable.

The Canadian Press write-up said, "Records show that James was one of the 14,748 Canadians given a pardon is 2006."

Fourteen thousand pardons in one year! Man, that is really somethin'.

So this guy didn't want his name in the article, but he really has a guilty conscience. He said, "One day, it so enrages me that I feel it's my civic duty to go forward and say everything that I can to make sure that this never happens again.

"And then the next day I'll wake up, and the dark demons will take over; and I will worry about what will happen if I'm cross-examined and ridiculed for [not] being strong at the time. Why didn't I stop all of this? Theo and Sheldon were younger than me, and if I'd stepped up, I could have prevented all of this."

His heroes in this whole thing—because they had the guts to step up—were Sheldon and Theo, and I'm gonna quote the end of the article to show that maybe "Coach's Corner" is good for something after all, instead of just nice clothes and charm and personality.

> His other hero and unwitting saviour is CBC hockey commentator Don Cherry. When the Sheldon Kennedy story first broke in 1996, its impact was devastating. The release of Fleury's autobiography last fall had a similar impact. "My head is spinning, and I'm wondering what to do and what's going on in my life," said the man. "The demons are out front and centre and you wonder who you are and what you're supposed to be." On the Saturday following Kennedy's revelations in 1996, *Hockey Night in Canada* host Ron MacLean asked Cherry about the issue. Don said simply, as eloquently as Don Cherry would say, "I'd have drawn and quartered the son of a bitch."
>
> "For whatever reason, it was exactly what I needed to hear at that time to go on," the man recounted. "To know I wasn't wrong; I wasn't gay; I didn't invite any of this. It was anger so clearly focused on what he had done. Some might call it frontier justice, and it just couldn't have been more spot-on at the time. I'd like to say that [Cherry] saved my life because I was clearly at a dark point at that time."

* * *

I'm often asked about the code that they have in hockey. Some of the media ridicule it. I don't know why. Every business has its code that you don't know about until you're inside it—even the media probably.

So let's look at a few of the things that are part of hockey's code. This isn't all of it, but I'll give you a few examples.

The funny thing is that the first one you learn has nothing to do with hockey. When you first come into the game at the pro level, an old veteran will get you aside and say, "Look, kid, the very first thing you do when you're out drinking with the guys, you pay your round. If you can't afford to buy your round, then don't go out." The worst thing you can do is sit and drink, and then when it comes to be your round, oh well, it's time to leave. If you ever do that, you're out. That was the first important thing that was told me.

On to hockey. Never pick your spots. This is another one that was told me early on. There's a lot of guys in the world that'll fight guys their size, and even guys that are smaller, but they'll never fight a true heavyweight. Everybody knows who those guys are. If that's the kind of guy you are, you're in trouble. There was a lot of times I went into a fight, and I knew I was gonna lose. But I had to go in—and I usually did lose, because when you go against a big super heavyweight and you've got short arms, boy, you turn into a catcher. But it has to be done. Never pick your spots, because the players know it right away.

If you happen to go into a fight and you happen to get the better of the guy, and you've both served your five-minute majors, if he comes out and wants to go again, you gotta go again. You gotta answer the bell.

I remember Bobby Probert, when he was first starting out. He was fighting a guy called Todd Ewen. Bobby got cold-cocked right at the start of the fight. Down he went to his knees. He was helped to the penalty box, got in the penalty box, then, as soon as he got out, wanted to go again. As soon as I saw that, I thought, "Boy, oh boy, this Probert is gonna be a dandy."

He was. And he died way too young. He was only 45 when he collapsed on his boat and died on July 5, 2010.

A true fighter will never fight a weaker opponent or a smaller guy. I have to say, in all my career, I did it twice, and whenever I think of it, I'm still ashamed of it. One was with a guy named Rudy Migay. He had speared me, and before I knew it, I had the gloves off. He couldn't fight, and I did a number on him. I've thought about it to this day. Another guy was Bobby Ellett—and I ended up coaching him. When I was playing against him, he did the same thing as Migay—he speared me or something. I was on him so fast that when I saw a picture in the paper the next day, there I was, already on top of him, and my gloves were still in the air.

I always felt bad about those two. Never fight a smaller opponent or a weaker opponent, because you'll get the reputation of just grabbing small guys. I did it to two guys, and I still regret it.

If a guy cheap-shots one of your players, like Pittsburgh's Matt Cooke did to Marc Savard of the Bruins or like Philly's Mike Richards did on David Booth of the Panthers, you have to go at 'em right away. Right away. If it's a cheap shot, you can't wait.

You often see, when a player has been in a fight, some of the other guys on his team will go over and kick his stick and gloves towards the penalty box. Then they go to the penalty box and throw them in at the guy. I could never understand that. Our guys in Boston, we always picked up the sticks and picked up the gloves. We'd go over to the penalty box and hand them to him and give the guy a tap. That's what you should do.

If you're a true heavyweight, always act like Bobby Probert. He was the best. He is the model. Bobby would never say a word after the fight, never even look at the guy. Even if the other guy was yipping at him, he'd just smile. I loved it when, if Bob was on the ice for a commercial timeout, the DJ would play "Bad to the Bone."

Don't be like Donald Brashear—the time in 2000 with Marty McSorley, the time that caused all that trouble, when he made like he was washing his hands after the fight as if to say, "I wiped you out." Naturally, Marty had to go back at him the next chance he got, and when Brashear skated away, Marty went after him, hit him with his stick and got such a long suspension that it ended his career.

It was all because Brashear didn't follow the code.

Most of all, if you fight at all, never fight a European. First of all, they usually have a visor, so there goes your hand. Visors can break your hand easy. And let's imagine what would happen if the

European got a good shot in. You can't win. If you win the fight, you were supposed to win. If they happen to get a good one in, you'll be remembered forever.

I remember the time Brad May got knocked cold by Mats Sundin. It wasn't a fight. Sundin had cheap-shotted Brad from the side and just happened to catch him on that magic spot on the chin, and down he goes. They had to take him to the hospital.

It happened in Vancouver, and the next morning we're flying back to Toronto, and I meet a guy in the airport who was a friend of Brad's. He said, "I was in the hospital with Brad last night, and he said he was fine. But he said, 'The only thing that bothers me is that Grapes is gonna go on television next week and say Brad May has been knocked out by a European.'"

Naturally, I didn't.

Never run up the score because the other team never forgets. If you're up 6–1, and you keep your number-one power play on, you're only asking for trouble. People ask how on earth I had eleven 20-goal scorers on the Boston Bruins. It's a record never to be broken. Even the best teams now only have six. In 1976, once we got up by a big score, the third and fourth lines would go out on all the power plays and take a regular shift for the rest of the game.

Our first and second line loved to be on the power play, as they had bonuses, but it was to their credit that they still encouraged the third and fourth lines and used to holler, "Go get 'em, Power." That's a team.

Teams remember if you put out your number-one power play, and they will be ready for you the next game. Besides that, it's not the Canadian way to kick a guy when he's down. Baseball is the same way. If you're up by a big score and you're trying to steal bases, look for a ball at your head the next inning.

I was watching a baseball game last year when a rookie hit a home run for St. Louis. He flipped the bat and stood there and admired it. His first-base coach gave it to him as he came down. The first baseman gave it to him. The second baseman gave it to him. The third baseman and his own third-base coach gave it to him. Finally, the catcher stood on home plate as he headed for home, then *he* gave it to him.

When the kid got to the dugout, his manager took him aside and ripped him. The next time up, he knew he was gonna get it. He was plunked, as they say. He just accepted it. He never did a thing. He just laid the bat down and went to first base. It's the code.

In the minors, we had a different kind of code. When I was coaching in Rochester, we had a great centreman. He was a dandy centreman, and he led the team in scoring. But I could see the players didn't like him, so I called over the "straw boss," as I called him.

A straw boss in hockey was the same as he was in construction. Say you have a company, and you have a hundred labourers. You always have one guy—he never gets any more money, and he's never a supervisor, but you know if you want to get something done, you have to go to this guy.

I called over Rod Graham, the guy I considered the straw boss. I said, "Rod, we got a leading scorer here. How come the guys never hang around with him, and how come they're never friendly with him?"

Rod says, "Well, he ate all the shrimp."

I said, "Well, that's it then. Now I understand." Say no more.

I'll tell you what he meant. It was another part of the code. Down in the minors, when you don't have much money, and you're drinking, you either grab a sandwich or, if you have to be in by twelve-thirty or something, you order a sandwich to go and you take it back to your room.

But if there's no curfew, you go to a Chinese place.

Well, say there's six guys, and you each order a dish. One guy will order chop suey; one guy will get egg foo yung; one guy orders chow mein; and so on. Naturally, somebody will order shrimp. Then, when it comes, they'll all share. But this guy, instead of sharing, he ate all the shrimp. He was never, ever accepted by the guys after that.

You never throw your sweater on the dressing-room floor. You hand it to the trainer or the equipment guy. I heard a story about something that happened in the Montreal Canadiens' dressing room. After a game, a rookie took his sweater off and, instead of handing it, he threw it to the trainer. But it landed on the floor.

The entire room went quiet. Captain Jean Béliveau stood up, walked over and picked up the sweater and handed it to the trainer. All eyes went on the rookie. Not a word was spoken, but he now knew the code.

* * *

We should also talk about a few things are different now in hockey, and it's because it used to be a Canadian game, but the Americans have taken over. Like I said earlier, I like the Americans, but I don't like that we've lost things in our game because of them.

The sweaters are now called jerseys, if you can believe it, and we've sort of accepted that. But in Canada, it was always called a sweater. Remember that great story by Roch Carrier, *The Hockey Sweater*? It was about a French-Canadian kid who got a hockey sweater by mail-order from Eaton's, but they sent him a Toronto Maple Leafs sweater instead of a Montreal Canadiens sweater. The story wasn't called *The Hockey Jersey*, was it?

But the Americans call them jerseys, and we follow. For a hundred years, they were sweaters. You sweat in them. You sweat in a sweater.

Jerseys originally came from Jersey, one of the Channel Islands off the coast of France. They don't play hockey there, but the fishermen used the sweaters to stay warm out at sea. Americans used jerseys when they were playing football; then, when they finally got around to playing hockey, they used the same name. Nowadays, most kids call sweaters jerseys. Another little part of our hockey heritage is gone.

Our dressing rooms are now called locker rooms because the Americans call them locker rooms. Have you ever seen a locker in any of our hockey dressing rooms? I don't think so. They're called dressing rooms because that's where we dress. You sweat in a sweater. You dress in a dressing room. It's sad how we follow the Americans.

At one time, centre ice was called centre ice. Now it's the neutral zone, because in the States they call it the neutral zone. Remember the old joke that English-Canadians used to have about the logo on the ice at the Montreal Forum? It was the C wrapped around an H, like the logo on the Canadiens jersey (just jokin'), and people used to make fun of people who spoke English with a French accent and said the CH stood for "Centre Hice."

If you have a loaf of bread, you have one end, and you have the other end. In hockey, we used to call it "our end" and "their end." And you have the centre. The States call it neutral, so we call it neutral.

One that gets me—to show you how we follow the States—is the word *dangle*. As the older players know, we used to say, "Boy can that guy dangle!" meaning he could really skate fast. MacLean said dangling had to do with a guy stickhandling. I said, "You're wrong. It means you can skate fast."

"Oh no," said MacLean. He said I was the one who was wrong. Even the producer showed me a thing in the dictionary that said dangling had something to do with bouncing around, like earrings or something.

John Muckler, who has been in the business forever and been a Stanley Cup–winning coach, as we know, was coming in for an interview. I said, "John, what does *dangle* mean?"

He looked at me as if I was nuts. "It means you can skate fast," he said.

You won't believe where it all came from. A few years ago, a U.S. company did a commercial, and in the commercial they had two NHL players running through the bank in hockey gear, bouncing a puck on a stick. One of the bank guards said to the other guard, "Look at those guys dangle."

Now, I know it makes sense to some guys who really don't know hockey. Bumping the puck up and down on the stick it does look like dangling, but that's not the way it was. Dangle means you can skate fast.

It really ticks me off when you hear the new announcers in Canada, guys who are supposed to know what's going on, when they say, "Look at that guy dangle through them." It's sad that the Americans run the show, and we just follow along. Not me.

* * *

On July 5, 2010, I get a call from Tie Domi telling me that Bobby Probert has died. Tie left a message on my answering machine. He was all choked up. Those tough guys are the softest hearts of all.

It's ironic that he was the first guy to tell me about Bobby, after Bob and him had those beauty fights. I feel for Bobby's mother. She lost her husband at 51. He was a tough sergeant in the Windsor Police Department. Now she has lost a son at 45.

Bobby's beautiful wife, Dani, and her four kids were brave at the viewing when Ron and I went down to Windsor. Dani and I were even going over some of Bobby's bouts just to keep her spirits up. She mentioned how ticked Bob was about *The Battle of the Blades*, that CBC show where hockey players skated with top women figure skaters. Bob was told he had to wear figure skates, and he worked hard all summer to skate on 'em, then he gets to Toronto for the taping and they said, "Oh, that's okay. You can wear hockey skates." The reason they said they could use hockey skates was that Tie Domi was on the show as well and when he got there, he said, "I can't use figure skates." Bobby was really ticked at that.

MacLean, who was the host of *The Battle of the Blades*, told me Bobby was the favourite of all the crew and the women there. He was always the one who'd say, "Let's do something. How about I go out and get us some pizzas?"

I told Dani that Brian Williams, who was with Bob in Afghanistan, said that Bob was the absolute favourite of the troops over there. They loved him. One time, Brian woke up at 3 A.M. and Bob wasn't in his bed. Brian pulled back the tent flap and there was Bob, sittin' under the stars, shootin' the breeze with all the troops.

I know for a fact he was always playin' in celebrity hockey games or makin' appearances. Any good cause and he'd be there to help.

* * *

Bobby had two great fights with Troy Crowder. The first one was pretty even. The second one, he hit Troy so hard his helmet went flying off and went five feet in the air.

Ron and I went down to Detroit to see that game and I saw the linesman before the game. I told him, "If those two guys go, I don't want you jumpin' in."

The linesman said, "Are you kidding? I want to see them go too!"

That was the toughest ticket in Detroit that year. Ron and I had to sit up in peanut heaven.

Then there were the classics between Bobby and Tie Domi. The first one was pretty even, and I was told by Bob's father-in-law that the second fight was the only one Bob ever prepared for. He did it in his garage, because he was really ticked off at Tie going to the penalty box after the first fight and makin' like he was puttin' on the heavyweight belt.

Bob did pretty good on that second one. He did a number on Tie. You might break even on your first fight with Bobby, but no one ever won that second one.

Bob had so many fights in his career. He was the top gun, and every hopeful enforcer had to try him. If you could fight Bob Probert and survive, you were in. Wendel Clark and Bob were the same class guys after a fight. Just go to the box. No yappin'. No showboatin'. No hands in the air, hand-wiping or any of that stuff. If you were an enforcer comin' up and you said, "Bob, I've got to try to make it. Can we go?" Bob always said, "No problem," but there must have been times he really didn't feel like goin'.

If you wanted to go, he never turned anybody down. Although quite a few guys wish he had.

* * *

There's no doubt Bob Probert was a tough customer. The acorn didn't fall far from the tree. His father—Big Al, as everyone called him—was a tough customer and you did not want to cross this guy, as Al Strachan, who helped me write this book, found out much to his sorrow.

Al was stopped by Big Al for speeding and was told to get out of the car.

Now, before I tell you the rest of this, let me tell you a couple of stories about Al Strachan.

At times, Al—as you know if you have seen him on *Hockey Night in Canada*—can be sort of a sarcastic, smug sort of an individual with an attitude. Along with Brian Kilrea, he's the smartest guy I have ever known.

One time after a game in Quebec, we were back in the hotel and a few of us got into a conversation about metric, which I despise. Dave Hodge liked it and buried me in the argument. All of a sudden, Al, who was sitting there, started in on Hodge. He said, "Excuse me, Dave, but you haven't got your facts straight," and he proceeded to absolutely bury Dave with history and facts of metric and the way that the Liberal government had passed it through without any debate. There was nothin' left for Hodge to say.

I saw Al the next morning. Somebody had given me a Cross pen-and-pencil set the night before, and I gave it to Al and said, "Thanks for coming to my rescue. This is a gift."

Another time, I went over to London, England, with Al. I think we saw every church, every statue, every monument, every museum. He took me everywhere. We went to Nelson's flagship, the *Victory*, in Portsmouth.

Al was staying an extra week, and the night before I was going to check out, I went down to go over the bill. The man behind the counter was really snowing me. You know how these English guys are. He was very proper. I felt he was charging me too much.

Now, Al had made the arrangements for the whole thing and he just happened just happened to be walking by.

Al said, "Is there a problem?"

I says, "Well, Al, here's the bill."

He says to the guy, "This is totally unacceptable."

The guy wanted some sort of confirmation for the other rate, and Al said, "Well, do you think I carry the thing around in my back pocket? Look at my own bill. We're travelling together and we're on the same rate. Now straighten this bill out."

The guy offered to lower my rate a bit, but Al wouldn't accept that. "We're not bargaining here," he said. "The price has been agreed upon and that's what it will be, not halfway between what you want it to be and what it really is."

The guy did it. Al had that attitude. There's no doubt about it.

One night we went to see a Gilbert and Sullivan musical. The only thing I knew about Gilbert and Sullivan was that when I was in high school, some of the kids put on *HMS Pinafore*.

Al and I went to see *Iolanthe*. Al wanted to go. So we're in the balcony, and between them speaking so fast, which they do in those Gilbert and Sullivan things, and the limey accent, I had no idea what was goin' on.

So after the show, we go back to the hotel and we're having a couple of pops—some things never change—and I said, "You know, Al, I didn't even know what was going on there. Even when that guy was singin' alone and did that long song about his dream. I can't understand it."

He looked at me. And I said, "Neither can you."

He says, "Oh, yes I can."

I says, "If you understand it, then let's hear you go ahead and sing it."

By golly, if he didn't sing the whole thing! So he does have an attitude and smarts.

So now we get back to Bobby Probert's dad. Al Strachan had this attitude even when he was a young guy goin' to college in Windsor. He had bought this junker of a car—and it was a junker; it was a rust-bucket—and when he was stopped for speeding by Big Al, he gave him the same attitude.

Bobby's dad, Big Al, said, "Get outta the car."

He said, "I'm not getting out. It's my car, and I don't have to get out of it."

Big Al opened the door, put his heel through the floorboards and said, "This car is unsafe. It's now Crown property. Get out!"

Al got out of the car.

Big Al was a legend in Windsor, and like I said at the start, the acorn didn't fall to too far from the tree.

* * *

Bob was a 29-goal scorer who could fight. He'd be worth four or five million today.

After he left Detroit, he went to the Chicago Blackhawks. He thought the world of Bob Pulford, who ran almost everything in Chicago. Pully and Bob Murray, the GM, got together and gave Probert a beautiful contract at the end: $1.5 million a year for four years. Detroit, after all he did for them, was only offerin' $800,000. That's why he left Detroit. He didn't leave because there were any problems. He just got offered a ton more dough in Chicago. I don't think, for all the things he did for Detroit, they treated him very good.

When he got to Chicago, Bob Murray told Probert, "Hey, Bobby, you've got a two-way contract. You don't behave and you'll be riding the buses in the minors."

Probert said, "No, Bob. I won't be riding the buses. I'll get the keys and I'll be driving the bus."

He was a beauty. At 45, he left us too soon.

* * *

I've been in a lot of fights. I've won some and I've lost some, and I've got to admit, there really is no rush in the world like the one you get when you drop your gloves and the other guy is ready to go, too.

When you're young, it's a lot of fun, but as you get older, you get a few losses. You get a few more lumps than usual; you gain a con-science, and then you're in trouble. That's when you start to have second thoughts. You start to hesitate, and you know the old saying: He who hesitates is lost. That's so true in the fight scene.

The other reason you have a tough time in fights when you get over 30 is your hands. They really take a lickin'. You wouldn't believe the hands on Joey Kocur, the Detroit Red Wings enforcer. He didn't just try to hit you; he tried to put his hands through your head. It looks like he's had a Ping Pong ball implanted under each knuckle.

As you get older, you fight less and less, and that's why you don't see many guys over 34 fighting.

Now, with the visors and the helmets, its murder on the hands. Someday down the road, the league will bow again to the bleeding hearts and make it mandatory that you don't take off your helmet in a fight. Then we'll really see the hand injuries. I love it when I see one guy who's having trouble getting the strap loose on his helmet, and the other guy gives him time while he gets it off. He doesn't try to drill him while he's fiddling with the strap. That's honour! I love those guys.

* * *

I have never seen a player fall from grace as fast as Jonathan Cheechoo did. When he played for the San Jose Sharks, he was terrific. Him and Patrick Marleau and Joe Thornton, they had magic together.

Jonathan was traded to the Ottawa Senators along with Milan Michalek for Dany Heatley when Dany put the gun to general manager Bryan Murray's head in the summer of 2009 and said he wanted to get traded.

After just one year in Ottawa, you knew somethin' was gonna happen to Jonathan. When you only score five goals in sixty-one games, you know somethin' has to happen. Ottawa had offered him around the league, but no one wanted to pick up his $3.5-million salary. So they placed him on waivers before they sent him to Binghamton in the American Hockey League in March 2010, and there were no takers.

What a fall! Five years earlier, Jonathan Cheechoo was the winner of the Rocket Richard Trophy with 56 goals. He was terrific. Now, I know that when he did that, he was playin' with Patrick Marleau and Joe Thornton. Then he signed a big contract and he was playin' with the same guys. Nothin' different, but he dropped to 37 goals. The next year, he had 23 goals. The year after that, he had 12 goals, then in 2009–10 he had five goals.

So the Senators bought him out. They just let him go as an unconditional free agent and got nothin' back. Because they bought him out, Jonathan will get $2.3 million of the $3.5 million over two years.

What happened?

Some guys say that with the big contract, he had lost his desire to play. I believe he just lost his confidence, and when you lose your confidence, it all snowballs. You might get benched a little, and when that happens, a little more confidence goes down the drain.

I have to admit the Sharks kept him playin' with Patrick Marleau and Joe Thornton for quite a while. But when he got sent to Ottawa, he knew he was just a throw-in and that the Senators had to take him because of the salary cap. That does not help your confidence.

I know it's hard to feel sorry for a guy who's getting that type of dough for the next two years, but I do feel bad for Jonathan Cheechoo because he was always one of my favourites.

* * *

Remember earlier I said I was ashamed of myself for fighting with a smaller guy, Rudy Migay?

I was on top of him and everybody was gathered around, as they did in those days. I remember this guy reachin' over and squeezing the top of my head, that's how strong he was.

I looked up and it was a tough-lookin' guy named Murray Balfour. He was a Regina boy who played for the Regina Pats, then he moved to Ottawa-Hull in the EPHL, which was one of the Montreal farm teams. He tried to crack the lineup in Montreal, but he was sent to Rochester, and that's where I ran into him, so to speak.

I knew after the Migay thing we were gonna tangle. Sure enough, he ran our goalie, Claude Evans. I went to check him from behind, but he jumped out of the way and I fell down. Quick as a flash, he was on me and doing a number on me. He was bringin' up uppercuts, one after the other. He was on my back and I couldn't do anything. Blood was flyin' all over the place. I was almost out, but I said to myself that I was gonna give it one more shot. I grabbed the top of the net and heaved with all my might. Murray fell off to the side and I gave him, as they say, a right-hander from Port Arthur. I caught him flush on the mouth.

Boy, it felt good. But we were behind the net by then and after I did that, my fist bounced off his mouth and hit one of the posts that we had to hold up the screens. This was before they used glass. My arm exploded. Between the beating I had taken and the pain from my arm, I was almost out. A player called Steve Kraftcheck grabbed me and held me against the screen. He said, "Stop this madness." He didn't know—and nobody else knew—that if he had let go, I was goin' down.

Murray was split pretty good, but not as bad as me. Neither one of us would go to the dressing room for repairs. We sat in the penalty box with blood flowing out.

Murray did his job, and I got a beating. I deserved it. But I'm awful glad I got that one good shot in.

* * *

Murray left the Montreal organization in 1959 and went on to star with the Chicago Blackhawks. He played on a line with Red Hay and the great Bobby Hull. It was called the Million-Dollar Line.

When Chicago won the Stanley Cup in 1961, Murray had five goals and five assists in eleven games. He got a beauty for Chicago in the third game of the series, and then he scored in the third overtime of the fourth game to give the Hawks a 2–1 win.

Murray had a tragic end. He got traded to Boston, and while he was there, he broke his arm. He was sent to Hershey, the Boston farm team, and while he was recovering, the doctors found that he had lung cancer. It was tough to figure, because he never smoked, he never drank and he kept himself in good shape. Murray died in 1965 at the age of 30. A good and tough hockey player who stood up for his teammates; I really admired him.

* * *

I never, ever understood why some guys, when their team is already out of the playoffs, take such delight in being scorers.

Hey, I want to win, too, and I admire guys who play right to the end, but after you score a goal or win a game against a team that's fighting for the playoffs, do you have to go dance around like you've won the Stanley Cup?

I was out of the playoffs twice. Once, my first year, we were two and a half games out of first place and never made the playoffs, if you can believe it. The other time was the Spokane Comets. The team wasn't that bad, but the reason we were out is that we had so many five-minute majors for deliberate intent to injure that we gave up so many power-play goals that we were out of the playoffs.

We had about five or six games to go, and it was embarrassing to see a couple of guys on our team when they scored. We had this guy on our team, his name was Bill "The Destroyer" Shvetz. He says, "Look, I know we're going to try right to the end, and we're not going to give up, but do you guys have to dance around when you score a goal? And when we win a game, do you have to dance around like we won the Stanley Cup? That jumping around is starting to embarrass me. Cut it out."

He was so right. I don't mind guys being happy about winning, but when teams are in a dogfight to make the playoffs, and you happen to get the winning goal against them and they're out of the playoffs, you play it cool.

One time when I was coaching the Bruins, we were playing the Colorado Rockies in Boston, and I looked ahead. I know you shouldn't look ahead, but I did. We didn't think that they could ever beat us in the Boston Garden. Nobody ever beat us in the Boston Garden. Sure enough, they did. You'd think they'd won the Stanley Cup.

In the Boston Garden, the visiting team had to go through the Bruins' bench to get to their dressing room, if you can believe it. I stood there and called them all the names you could think of. "Where were you all in October?" I shouted. "Where were you in December? Now you won a couple of games when it doesn't matter, and you're putting on a celebration like you won the Stanley Cup. You're not even in the playoffs, you sucks."

You know what? Not one guy said a word to me, because they all knew I was right.

* * *

Hockey players all love cars, and I am a car man to the extreme. I love my cars so much that I sometimes go and sit in the car when it's raining. I like to hear the rain hit the car.

My happiest time personally is when I'm washing the car. I never can understand a guy washing his car and not drying his car off with a lovely towel. I love the feel if it. But if you don't dry it off, it's like having a new suit with dirty shoes, as far as I'm concerned.

My cars all have whitewalls. You should see me trying to get whitewall tires now. It's unbelievably difficult to get whitewalls. I like the thin ones.

I sing to my cars—my two cars that I have now. I'm a car guy.

The very first car I ever had was a 1955 Ford Custom—light blue with light-blue cloth inside. It was absolutely gorgeous. The next car was a '57 Olds. It was unbelievable. It was two blocks long. It had the "wonder bar" on the radio—you could touch it and find a station. That was quite the thing back then. And when you wanted to change the radio, you just touched a little button on the floor. The switch to change the headlights to high beam was on the floor too. It was an Olds 88. It was unbelievable. Beautiful!

My next car was a '60 Pontiac two-door. It was unbelievable. I know I keep saying they were unbelievable, and I shouldn't, but I just loved my cars. It was a Laurentian. Beautiful, black with white stars in the back. It would knock your eyes out. I never see any of them anymore. I see lots of other old cars, but I never see a '60 Pontiac two-door hardtop. Isn't that funny?

A '64 Pontiac I had next—a Parisienne. Burgundy with black cloth inside. That was the car that I wouldn't let my kids climb on or eat ice cream in. After not letting Cindy or Tim jump around in it, it was still in mint condition, and when I was going to the Boston Bruins, I was not going to let some jerk get it and ruin it, so I was going to have it burned. But two guys, Bob Kelly and Lynn Zimmerman, asked me for it and said they'd keep it great.

I gave it to Lynn Zimmerman because I knew Bob Kelly was going to the National Hockey League. He kept it in dynamite shape for thirty years.

My next car was a '74 Monte Carlo. Another beautiful car. White with black interior. My next car—this was one I really loved—was a

'76 Cadillac Seville. This was when I was in Boston. I had BRUINS
plates put on it. I think I just did that to bug Harry Sinden and the
assistant GM, Tom Johnson. It was white with red leather inside. It
would knock your socks off.

The car I got next was a 1980 Eldorado. It was black with a black
leather interior, and it was gorgeous. But it had front-wheel drive,
and I didn't like that.

The cars I drive now are my two favourites. One is a black
Lincoln, 1982—real sheepskin on the front seats. I drive that in the
winter. And now I come to my favourite car of all time, a 1983
Lincoln Mark IV—white, white leather, sheepskin front seats, red
dash, red carpets. Whitewalls, naturally.

If a guy can love a piece of steel, I love this car. I can say that
here in this book because my black car can't read. I would never
say this aloud about the white car in front of the black car. It would
get jealous.

I also have a '93 Ford F-150—flare-sided. Very, very rare.

But I'm in love with my favourite '83 Mark IV. When I'm in my
beauty, I go into my little world, my inner sanctum. I don't have a
cellphone and nobody can get at me.

* * *

I feel sorry for guys that have cars just as a matter of convenience.
They just drive them from here to there. They don't feel for them.
I can't understand it. I've always loved them.

On a Sunday afternoon in Kingston, I'd find a nice, shady spot
and I'd put that Cadillac Blue Coral on them. It would take me
eight hours to put it on, but they just shone, and I just felt so good
getting in them. It was almost like putting on a brand new suit.
They have that feel.

One time back in the 1960s, I was in the New York Rangers
training camp. Eddie Shack was a big star back then, making a lot
of money, and we were stayin' at the Foxhead Inn in Niagara Falls.

Eddie had a beautiful red Chevrolet convertible, white top. It was a beautiful car. I was thinking I'd give my right arm—well, maybe not my right arm, but my eye teeth—for a car like that.

Then one day, I came out in the morning, and it had rained all night, and he hadn't bothered to put up the convertible top, and the car was full of water.

I thought, "How can a man ever treat a car like that?"

It ruined my day.

* * *

Everybody remembers their first car and everybody remembers their first home.

I had been playin' hockey for a long time, and it seemed that Rose and I and the family had been knockin' around in apartments and rented homes all our lives. We had absolutely no furniture whatsoever. We had a TV. That was it.

We loved the city of Rochester, so we were going to settle down there and buy a house. We looked all over and finally found a place we really liked. It was in our price range and had a great address: 14 Placid Place, Rochester, New York. It was in a middle-class neighbourhood. We loved it. It was in great shape and it was kinda underpriced. We put in our bid. There were no other bids, and I'm sorry to say that unfortunately for us, we had a real-estate woman who did us wrong. We lost the place.

We kept lookin' around and we never did find another place like that, but we found a place at 181 Elm Drive—a great American-sounding address. It cost a little more, and I have to say it was not in very good shape. On the outside were wooden shingles, and people had painted over bad paint for years. It was in awful shape. It was all peeling. The inside, with all the furniture in the place, didn't look too bad.

So I borrowed $2,500 off my mother-in-law for the down payment. Can you imagine that? I've played ten years of pro hockey and I have to borrow $2,500 off my mother-in-law! We agreed to pay $18,500 for the house.

We buy it, and the sellers move out. We go over, and what a shock with the furniture and the rugs gone! The hardwood floors were a complete mess. It looked like somebody had walked around in hobnailed boots and left little holes all over the floor.

We hadn't eaten, so I went down to a hamburger joint and came back, and there's the family—Rose, Cindy, Tim and me—sitting on orange crates in the middle of this disaster, eating hamburgers.

Rose looked around, and I could see the disappointment on her face, even though she never complained about anything. Usually, when you move into a new place, it's happy times, but I could see her eyes getting a little misty.

I said, "Rose, I'll fix it. You'll see." I get up and I walk over to the wall, and I say, "Look, Rose. Under this wallpaper, it's probably good walls. I'll paint them and it will look brand new." I grab a piece of wallpaper and I pull it back, and the wall is full of holes!

I said, "That's it, Rose. I'm driving you and Cindy and Tim down to Hershey to stay with your mom. I'll stay here alone. I'll have this place looking like a show home, Rose. You've gotta believe me."

So I drive down to Hershey, leave the family there, and I'll tell you, there's one thing I can do in life. I was not much of a hockey player, but I can paint and I can restore homes. I did that when I was a young boy with a Mr. Cornwell. We specialized in it. I bought a forty-foot ladder, a scraper, tons of sandpaper, and went to work. I worked two straight weeks, every day, scraping and sanding. I finally got it done. I put two coats of paint on the outside—Revere green, which was a dark green, and white trim. It looked absolutely dynamite. It would knock your socks off. I used a trick Mr. Cornwell taught me. When he used semi-gloss paint, he used to puts lots of linseed oil in it. When you put it on, it shines beautiful.

Next was the inside. I did the walls, filled in the holes. It took me five days to fill in the holes and sand it down nice and smooth. I got it looking good and painted it a beautiful light-green inside.

Next were the floors, which were a real mess. I rented a big, heavy sander and did the floors. I made them brand new. I hung new doors—which is a hard thing to do, but I did it. I put on nice white shutters. By the way, those doors and shutters are still on the house.

I put in new shrubs and seeded the grass in front. It took me all of the month, but I have to say it was worth it. I picked up Rose in Hershey and drove up with her and the kids, and when we came up to the house, to see the look in her eyes, I'll never ever forget it.

It was one of the great moments of my life.

* * *

Ron MacLean and I do the same thing every year. We start from the first game of the playoffs, usually sometime around the second week of April, then we go on the road right to the end, which can be around June 15.

It's a long time, and we get very tired. Every year, when it starts out, I say, "How in the world am I going to find something to talk about every other day?" But somehow or other, we not only find something, but at the end of every show, I'm saying, "Wait a minute. I've got one more thing to say."

Still, by the time it gets near the end, we get kind of irritated at one another. We spend more time with each other than with our families. The travelling and getting up and the airports gets to you.

In 2009, we were travelling back and forth between Pittsburgh and Detroit. By the time you go from your hotel to the airport to get there at least an hour early, then wait for a plane that's usually late, then make the flight and wait for your luggage, then drive downtown, you might as well just drive from one city to the other. That way, you don't have to deal with airport check-ins and security. So that's what we did, and I used to see Ron take his wallet out and put it in the console of the car all the time before we started to drive.

I have a wallet, but I just keep it in my back pocket. After we'd gone back and forth, back and forth, between Detroit and Pittsburgh,

I went to get out of the car in Pittsburgh, and I couldn't stand up. My back. It was about a month later, and it was still bothering me. Then I met a trucker who said the reason was that I had that wallet in my back pocket, and it threw my back off.

We're in Pittsburgh, and we've been going for weeks and weeks. And at almost every morning skate, MacLean had said, "I wish I had one of those little pairs of binoculars that I could carry around." We usually sit up high for the skate, and you can't always see which player is which because you can't tell who they are now with their visors and their helmets.

So this one day, we've got an off-day in Pittsburgh, and I go out in the morning to one of those Army-Navy stores. I go in and I buy him a little pair of binoculars, and I'm kinda excited about giving them to him. So I go back to the hotel so I can give them to him before we go to the practice.

Now, the night before, because we'd been staying in this hotel a lot, the management had set up a suite for us near our rooms with a couple of two-fours of beer. We'd had a few beers until about two in the morning and gone to our rooms and left most of the beer behind. Unbeknownst to me, when Ron got back to his room, somebody called him from *Hockey Night in Canada*. He went back to the room with some of the crew, and they drank all the beer until about six in the morning.

But I don't know any of this, and I go back with the binoculars and phone his room. I can't get through, so I am really steamed after I've gone and done all this. I figured — and I was right — that he had gone out and got hammered and was sleeping in, but what bugged me was he didn't phone. He told me later he went to bed and he wasn't going to go to the morning skate. Yeah, sure. So now I am going to fix him. I know the security guy, and I go to him and I says, "I think there's something wrong with Ron MacLean, my partner. He would never do this if everything was okay."

He says, "Oh, Don, we can't break into a guy's room."

I says, "All right, it's up to you, but if there's something wrong with him, remember you were told."

They must have got together and thought, "Geez, he's right. If somethin' is wrong, and he told us, we could be in deep trouble."

So four of them—four security guys, and you know how big they are—go up to the room. Fortunately, MacLean didn't put the chain in the hook, so they didn't have to smash their way in. They go in, and he is sleeping. He told me later he was out cold with a hangover and a headache and these guys are standing over him shouting, "Sir! Sir! Are you all right? Are you all right?"

He said, "You couldn't imagine how awful I felt with a headache and a hangover and these four guys standing over my bed shouting, 'Are you all right? Are you all right?' Talk about embarrassing."

Beauty!

* * *

About ten years ago, when New Jersey was in the playoffs, the season was over. The Devils had won, and Ron was out drinking quite late—it sounds like he drinks a lot, doesn't it? Don't we all?

Anyhow, the next morning we're sitting in the little van that's going to drive us to the airport, and he's not there. We were supposed to fly out of LaGuardia, not Newark, and to get to Queens from New Jersey is a really tough trip.

I says, "I'm not leaving until MacLean gets here."

The other guys are saying, "Come on. Let's go. He can take a cab."

I says, "He's not taking a cab."

So, somehow or other, I talked the people at the hotel desk into giving me a key to his room. I went up, and he is out cold. Believe it or not, he had everything in order. He had his shoes in order, his clothes all laid out. It was beautiful how he did it, even though he had been out drinking the night before. So I took his shoes and put knots in the laces, then hid 'em. I hid his clothes, too. Then I stood over him, got a couple of inches from his ear, and shouted, "Come on! They're waiting for you downstairs. Hurry up!"

Well, you should have seen him banging into the walls, trying to undo the knots. I just stood back and enjoyed the moment.

Beauty!

* * *

In the 1940s, there was a Ranger defenceman called Bob Dill. He was a tough defenceman — well, he thought he was a tough defenceman. And he was always giving it to Rocket Richard. He was always calling him names and calling him dumb and stuff like that. He was really ripping him all the time and banging him around. One day, the Rocket said, "That's enough," and they got into a fight. The Rocket knocked Dill cold.

So they go to the penalty box, and when they come out, Bob Dill says, "All right, Rocket, let's go again, you so-and-so."

The Rocket knocked him cold again.

The headline in the Montreal paper the next day was DILL PICKLED! I love that one.

* * *

In the States, in all their sports, when the players are talking to the coach, they always call him Coach.

The second American we had on our team in Boston was Bobby Miller — Mike Milbury was the first — and Bobby was from Billerica, Massachusetts. In the first meeting he was at, he asked a question: "Can I do so-and-so, Coach?"

I says, "Yes, you certainly can, Player."

The next time he said something and called me Coach, I says, "Okay, Player."

He kind of looked at me funny. I said, "You're a player. I'm a coach. Your name's Bobby. Mine is Don."

* * *

It was during the playoffs a couple of years ago, and like I said before, as it goes on, we get a little punchy and we start to play little tricks on one another.

So here we were, standing in line in the airport, waiting for our ticket, and Stephen Walkom, who was the head of the referees, was in another line. Now, MacLean is always complaining about the officiating, so I says to him, "You know what? You're right about the officiating. I'm gonna go and tell Walkom what you've been saying. I'm gonna go over and tell him that he's wrong and that you think that he's wrong and that you really believe he'd better smarten up."

He says, "Oh, don't go over there. Don't start anything in the airport."

I says, "No, I've had enough. I'm going over there right now."

So I march over and get right in Walkom's face, and I says, "Look, I'm playing a joke on MacLean. You let on that you're mad and keep looking at him, and I'll point my finger at you. We'll really put on a show here."

Stevie's a good guy. He goes along with it. I'm puttin' on a show and poundin' him in the chest, and he keeps lookin' over at Ron, who is dying a thousand deaths over there. Beauty!

Well, the kicker of the whole thing was, there was a reporter standing watchin'—I won't mention his name—so the story in the paper the next day was, "Cherry is a dinosaur. Cherry confronts Steve Walkom and almost assaults him."

It was a big article about what a bad guy I was for taking on Walkom, who was just doin' his job.

* * *

I was on the other end of a trick like that once.

We had Dave Newell refereeing the Bruins one night, and it was on *Hockey Night in Canada* and they'd gone to a commercial. Now they were back, and they were just about to drop the puck. It was a faceoff in our end, and all of a sudden, Dave Newell called time.

He called time, and I'm down at the end of the bench, hollerin' at him and everythin'. All of a sudden, he starts skatin' over towards me.

I'm thinkin', "What's goin' on? This guy's comin' over here. The TV cameras are on. The game's supposed to be goin'."

So he come right over to our bench, and I thought, "What the heck?" So I go over to him and get down in the front row and I'm ready to go to war with him.

He pokes me in the chest and he says, "I just have to tell you somethin', Cherry. That's the sharpest suit you've ever worn. I've seen you wear sharp suits before, but that's the sharpest." And he's lettin' on that he's really pokin' me in the chest. "That's the sharpest suit you've ever worn, and don't you forget it."

I understand that on TV they were sayin', "There's Dave Newell, puttin' Cherry in his place and tellin' him to keep quiet or he's gonna get in deep trouble."

Well, needless to say, the players on the bench were just killin' themselves. I've gotta admit, Dave got me good.

* * *

When I started coaching the Mississauga IceDogs, the very first game of the season, we were playing the Sudbury Wolves in Sudbury. We got there, and the place was absolutely jammed. They had police controlling the crowd, and I had to have an escort. In fact, after the game, the owner of the Sudbury Wolves said, "I wanna thank Don Cherry. This is the biggest crowd we've ever had for an opener. He just paid for our whole training camp."

So there I was with a nice jacket on, sort of a light-brown plaid. I had black pants. I looked pretty good.

It was a great game. It was 4–3 with less than a minute to go. I pulled the goalie, and we rung one off the post, but unfortunately, they come down and put it in an empty net. We lose.

After the game, I have to do a thousand interviews. I sit down and do the interviews. We've just lost our first game. It was a tough loss and very emotional, but we did our best.

The next day in the paper, a woman reporter really ripped us.

She complained about the type of hockey we played. It was a 4–3 game with less than a minute to go! It was an exciting game.

Then she said, "Not only that, Cherry had a very bland jacket on."

The point I'm trying to make is that she had it in her mind that no matter what happened, she was gonna be critical. She didn't say that the crowd was goin' wild; she didn't say that I had a nice plaid jacket; she didn't say that it was the biggest crowd that the Wolves had ever had at an opener in their history; she didn't say that the crowd was so excited that I had to have a police escort out. None of that.

That's the way reporters are. Some of them have it written before the game even starts. Never let the facts get in the way of a good story.

* * *

When I was playing junior with the Barrie Flyers, my roommate, Ralph Willis, and I got a call about eleven o'clock. Our curfew was nine-thirty, but the call came in at eleven telling us to report immediately to the Barrie Arena on Dunlop Street—a lovely old building.

We had no car. It was the middle of winter. We had to walk all the way down in the middle of the night, and it was freezing cold. We're all sittin' in the dressing room. All of a sudden, Hap Emms comes in. He was the coach and he always smoked a pipe, so he sat down beside one of the guys and lit his pipe.

He says, "All right. I want to know why fellows don't like this guy." He was talking about the guy sittin' beside him.

Can you imagine that? Him sayin' that, and the guy sittin' there?

So the first guy that answers says, "I don't know, Hap. He's just one of those guys you don't like."

The next guy says, "Well, I think it's because he's a selfish hockey player."

It went on and on around the room, everybody saying somethin' bad about the guy. I never saw anything like it.

I still don't know why Hap did it. I have no idea. But he did it, and he heard this guy get told by everybody why they didn't like him. I don't think one guy said he liked him, including me.

Anyhow, the guy turned out to be a pretty good hockey player. He went and played in the Quebec league, then he came over and played for Punch Imlach in the American league with Springfield.

At the end of the first period—this was with the Indians now—he started to take his equipment off. We thought he was one of those guys who just takes off some equipment between periods, then puts it back on again. Lots of guys do that. But this guy kept taking it off and taking it off and we started to think, "What the heck is the matter with this guy?"

What happened was Bill "The Destroyer" Shvetz was playing for the Cleveland Barons, and he had drilled our teammate into the boards.

So this guy's got all his equipment off and he's standing there with nothing on, and Punch Imlach comes in and says, "What are you doing?"

He says, "I'm not playing in this league. It's nuts. I'm going back to the Quebec league."

He went in, took a shower and went home.

This guy turned into a pretty good coach, though, I must admit. He won a Memorial Cup. He worked his way up from the American Hockey League to coach the Chicago Blackhawks, and he did a very good job there. In fact, he was being considered for coach of the year.

So there we were at one of those luncheons they have during the playoffs to introduce the people who are nominated for coach of the year and stuff. I'm sorta sittin' there daydreaming after lunch, and this guy says, "I'm being considered for coach of the year, but it can't be that big a deal because Don Cherry won it."

Everybody in the place looked at me. I couldn't believe he said that! It was quite embarrassing, but that's okay. You sit in the weeds, and eventually your turn will come.

Sure enough, it's the playoffs, and his Hawks are playing in Edmonton, and they really get bombed by the Oilers. They're flying back to Chicago, and one of the reporters asked him what he was gonna do now.

He said, "We're gonna fly over the Mayo Clinic. I think I'll get the pilot to land, and we'll get twenty heart transplants."

Well, you can call a hockey player stupid. You can say he doesn't have any talent. You can call him many things, but you can never, ever say a hockey player has no heart. That's the ultimate insult.

So I do "Coach's Corner" that night. We were doin' another game, but I say that an incident happened in Chicago, and I tell everybody what this guy said about the Blackhawks.

I say, "They're gonna get beat in Chicago, and when they skate off the ice, this coach will have his hand stuck out for the players to shake. I guarantee you the players will skate right him by for insulting them like he did."

Well, right away, everybody phones the players and tells them what I said.

Sure enough, Edmonton smoked 'em, and he stood there with his hand out as they went by to the dressing room. We had the camera on him. Every guy skates by him. Naturally, this was featured on "Coach's Corner."

It's the old story: You play with the bull, you get the horn.

* * *

I'm often asked why Bobby Orr didn't stay with the Boston Bruins. He finished his career playing with the Chicago Blackhawks.

There were so many reasons, but the number one reason was Alan Eagleson.

I was there the afternoon that the split really happened. Bobby had hurt his knee, and he was in a comeback, and he was on a bike at the far end if the dressing room. I was there working on a stick for my son, Timothy, who was 14 at the time, so it was after practice and everybody else was gone.

I was just sittin' there, when all of a sudden the president of the team, Paul Mooney, come in. He was smoking a pipe, and he went up to Bobby and he says, "Bobby, can I speak to you for a minute?"

Bobby says, "Get out of here, Paul. You're trying to drive a wedge between Alan and me."

Mooney says, "No, Bobby. Just let me talk to you for about a minute. That's all."

Bobby says, "Get out of here."

So Mooney turned and walked out, and as he went out, he looked over at me and just shook his head. It was found out later he was going to offer Bobby a piece of the Boston Bruins if he'd stay with the team.

You know how much that would have been worth? Wouldn't it have been lovely if Bobby had right now been one of the owners of the Bruins? They wouldn't be where they are right now.

The Bruins had told Eagle about the offer, but Eagle didn't tell Bobby because they had a deal cooked up with his friend, Hawks owner Bill Wirtz, for Bobby to go to Chicago for $250,000.

Bobby knew he was in trouble when he got to Chicago. Bill Wirtz, at the press conference, when it was time to introduce Bobby, said, "Here's our new star, Bobby Hull."

* * *

I've always blamed Billy Reay, who was coaching the Hawks at the time, for the way Bobby was handled as a player in Chicago.

We went in there to play the first exhibition game. The ice was lousy, and he played Bobby about twenty minutes. Bobby couldn't turn because he was still coming back from another knee operation. Our players loved Bobby so much they would never dump the puck into his corner.

All Reay needed to do was be careful with Bobby and bring him along carefully until his knee got better. He could have lasted another two or three years. Instead, there he was, playing twenty minutes on bad ice in a stupid exhibition game.

I said, "He won't last till Christmas," and he didn't. It broke our hearts.

* * *

To tell you what kind of guy Bobby Orr was, when he saw that he couldn't play anymore, he wouldn't accept the money from Chicago. He gave it back.

If he had stayed with us, he could have had a piece of the Bruins. I would have known to let him skip the morning skates, like I did when he played for Team Canada '76, I was an assistant coach.

Naturally, Bobby could have had a regular shift and he could have been on the power play. But he wouldn't have killed penalties. I know that, even with the bad knees, he'd still try to block shots killing penalties. He wouldn't have had to go to morning skates on game days, and he could take it easy in practices.

Bobby and Brad Park were fantastic together. He would have lasted another two or three years.

When I look back and think of all those things we missed because of Alan Eagleson, I think Eagleson should hide his head in shame.

* * *

Bobby Orr was what we called a room-service guy. On the road, he never left his room because he would be swamped with people comin' after him, so he'd order room service.

He always walked around his room wearing a T-shirt and shorts. He had his pants on a hanger, and he wouldn't sit around in them because he didn't want them to get wrinkled. That's how meticulous he was.

He'd play cards with John Bucyk all day, but if it was a game day, he'd leave about two o'clock in the afternoon for a seven o'clock game. He'd get half-dressed, and he had a stick with a whole bunch of pucks taped to it and he'd carry that around all afternoon. It was almost like a baseball player with that lead donut on the bat in the on-deck circle.

He was like a caged tiger.

* * *

When I was coaching the Bruins, lots of teams used to call up a tough guy from the minors when we'd come to town because we were the toughest team in the league, bar none.

One guy that Detroit brought up was John Hilworth. We had a guy named Clayton Pachal at the same time as we had Stan Jonathan. Well, Clayton Pachal was a rookie, but at the time, Stan Jonathan wore a helmet, and they looked like twins. They lined up over in the far corner, and Hilworth thought he was lined up against Jonathan; but instead, he was lined up against Pachal. So he started the fight with Clayton, and Clayton got his clock cleaned — Hilworth did a pretty good number on him. He was struttin' around.

So the next period, I started Stan Jonathan. It just happened that way, so Hilworth thought he was going to give it to Clayton again. Stan carved him to pieces. I can still see that look on Hilworth's face: "What the heck happened here?"

* * *

That was in the Detroit Olympia, and it was in a tough section of town — out on Grand River Avenue, if you know Detroit.

The night before we played, they'd had a tennis match there, and a guy and his wife stayed around for a drink, waiting for the traffic to clear. Then the guy told his wife to wait while he went out to get the car.

He never came back. He was murdered, and he had less than four dollars on him. It was a tough neighbourhood.

The crowd would pick up asphalt as they walked in and throw it at the visiting players' bench. I used to try to have fun with the crowd, but one time, I heard something solid hit near me. I looked down, and someone had thrown a live rifle bullet. Needless to say, I never encouraged the crowd after that.

* * *

When we're on the road, Ron MacLean and I always go to the morning skates.

I've always wondered why it is that every team, as soon as they go on the ice, skate counter-clockwise. I mentioned it to Ron, and he had some idea that it was because they were left-hand shots or something like that. He didn't know.

Isn't it strange? Starting way back when I was in junior, I've never known it any other way.

I don't know what the answer is, but it seems kinda strange. I suppose a psychiatrist could figure it out.

* * *

A lot of people ask me how morning skates started. They started back in the fifties. There used to be morning meetings only, but a few guys started to go out if they had their skates sharpened, to try them out. Then a couple of guys started to bring pucks and sticks and fool around. More and more guys on the ice, fooling around. Next came sweatsuits, then equipment, and it got so, in the seventies, there were full practices for three-quarters of an hour. It was ridiculous.

The routine is the home team goes on at 10 A.M., off at 11:15 A.M. sharp. I remember one time in Detroit, six of the guys stayed on till 11:16, and six of our guys went and kicked them off the ice.

Some guys hate the morning skate. On the road, the team does it to get the guys out of bed, but everyone goes on the ice at home. Except my Bruins. If you wanted to skate, okay; if not, fix your sticks and stay for the short meeting and go home. The game is the thing. Some teams left their game in the morning skate. Funny thing, this year, in the playoff finals, it was mostly the Black Aces who skated on the morning of a game. They're finally wising up. I always, as a head coach, went on with the Black Aces in the playoffs. I would stay till the end with them and then take them for lunch. I would work them hard. One day Harry got a call from the league complaining that I was chewing the ice up too much on the day of a game. Nowadays the head coach usually doesn't go to the morning skate on the day of a game, but I wanted them to feel part of the club. I knew how they felt because I was a Black Ace.

* * *

You'll see guys, when they're foolin' around taking shots before the practice starts, hit the post on purpose. They like to hear the ring.

Remember the French Connection line of Gilbert Perreault, Richard Martin and René Robert? Well, when I coached the Colorado Rockies, René Robert was on the team, and that was his habit. In the morning skates, he'd always ring it off the post.

I said to him, "René, you shouldn't do that because when you're in a game and you gotta react real fast, you'll shoot at the same spot."

He just laughed at me because he had scored about 250 goals by that time. But I'm telling you, it's the truth, and one game, he hit four goalposts.

It only stands to reason: if you do it time after time after time, when the puck comes to you in a game, you're gonna shoot for the same spot. I know it sounds good when you hear that clang, but when the game is on, you react the same way and hit the post.

But René put nearly thirty in the net for us one year, so I couldn't complain too much. But you know, I bet he coulda had forty.

* * *

A lot of people used to complain that when you were watching a game in the Boston Garden, you never knew how many shots the teams had. There was no shot clock like there was in other buildings.

When I first went there, they had one. I'd be behind the bench, and I could hear Phil Esposito all the time: "Look, the guy never gave us a shot there" and "Look at that. They didn't count that shot." He was more interested in the shots than in the goals. It really bothered him. Another thing, too: The Boston crowd was strange. If the other team came in and got a couple of shots and we didn't have any, when we got our first, it was a big joke. They'd give a big, sarcastic cheer.

I told Harry that between the crowd and Phil countin' the shots, the shot clock had to go. I said, "Harry, if you don't get that thing out of there, I'm gonna tear it off the wall myself."

Hey, Harry just wanted to win.

So he took it out, and until the last year of the Boston Garden, there was never a shot clock in there. That's the reason why.

* * *

I know it's hard to believe, but all the time I played junior and all through my professional hockey career, you were not allowed to drink water during the practices or during the games. In those hot arenas, in those hot woollen sweaters we used to wear in those days, we'd lose eight to ten pounds a game. The goalie would lose a lot more than that.

And if the coach ever caught us drinking water, we were done. In the practices, we used to get so dry that we'd actually take the snow off our skate blades and put it in our mouths.

One day on the bench, I was absolutely dying for a drink of water, and I thought I was gonna be very clever, so I asked the trainer for an ice bag. I took the ice bag and I drank water out of the ice bag. The coach saw me, and after that, he'd put hot stuff—hot sauce or liniment or something—in the ice bags so we couldn't drink out of them.

The first guy I ever saw drinking between periods was Jim McKenny. He drank a Coke in Rochester. Then, when we started playing the Russians in the seventies, it came out that they always used to drink something, and that they had cases of Coke in their dressing room. After that, things changed.

I guess the Russians were right. You go to an NHL practice today, and they stop every fifteen minutes so the guys can have a drink, and all the bottles are lined up on the boards. Every guy has his own bottle.

When you think of all those years, until the Russians came along, that we used to dehydrate, it's amazing. And we didn't really need to do it!

But I'll tell you one thing: after we'd lost those eight to ten pounds in practice, we'd go to the bar, and we'd put those eight to ten pounds back on pretty fast. The tastiest thing in the world is an ice-cold beer after you've lost all that weight in a game.

* * *

One of the guys who used to work with *Hockey Night in Canada*, I don't want to say he was cheap, but one day, he said he lost his tie at the hotel. He went down to the desk and the manager said, "Well, go down and see if it's in the lost and found."

When he went down, he didn't find his tie, but he found three others that he took.

So, at every hotel we went into after that, he'd say he'd left his tie behind on the last trip. Then he'd go down and pick up two or three ties from the lost and found.

* * *

On *Hockey Night in Canada,* we go for a commercial when the game ends, then we come back for the three stars. In the arena, people wait around for it.

For years, the three stars of the game were introduced in order—first, second, third. They'd announce the first star of the game, and he'd skate out. Then people started leaving before the second and third stars had been announced.

So I said to Ron Harrison, who was the executive producer at the time, "Ronnie, if you had Miss America, do you think they'd start off with the winner? No, they build up to it. Here's number three. Here's number two. And now, here's the winner. They build up to it. So what you have to do is play it smart. Introduce the stars three, two, one."

That's what they do now. I could never figure out why they did it the other way.

* * *

One of the cruellest things that ever happened to me was when I was playing. I had hurt my shoulder, and we were in training camp and I was trying to make the team. I had a real bad cut. I'd go to bed at night with that shoulder, and the cut was still bleeding. I was having an awful time, and I was trying to let on I could shoot the puck, but really, I couldn't shoot because of that cut on the shoulder.

So this guy calls Milt Schmidt, who was the coach. He says, "Hey Milt! This guy's got a worse shot than me." The guy's name was Bill Quackenbush.

He was an all-star defenceman, and he won the Lady Byng—as a defenceman, if you can believe it. He had one penalty all season, so that ought to tell you something.

They call Larry Zeidel, who cut guys up with his stick, cruel. And my buddy Connie "Mad Dog" Madigan, he was cruel. But I never forgot how a man could be so cruel as to see that a kid was having a tough time with an injured shoulder and to make fun of him.

There's different kinds of cruel. And you know what? I'll take Connie Madigan's cruel and Larry Zeidel's cruel over Bill Quackenbush's cruel any day.

* * *

Zeidel got me one time too. It's in Hershey, I'm playing for the Springfield Indians, and Pete Conacher, a great hockey player at the time, he gets a great goal.

Well, I pull a Dale Hunter. When Conacher went to turn after he scored, I drove him into the boards. Well, Larry come in, cross-checked me headfirst right into the boards, and when he cross-checked me into the boards, he broke his stick.

I got up. I started to chase him because he wasn't a good fighter, he was a good stick man. He started yelling, "Don, I lost my head! I lost my head!"

I said, "If I get a hold of you, you're *really* going to lose your head."

I finished the game, but I had a concussion and I had to go to the hospital. I had to spend the night in the hospital, and it was one of those deals where they keep you up all night, 'cause if you go to sleep with a concussion, you might not wake up.

So about ten o'clock in the morning, the Springfield bus drives up. Out comes our coach, Pat Egan. He comes in the room and he says, "Okay, let's go."

The nurse says, "Wait a minute! Wait a minute! This man can't be moved. He's concussed." First time I'd heard that word.

Egan says, "Concussed be damned. He's playing this afternoon in Cleveland." He turns to me and says, "Get dressed. Let's get going."

I got dressed and I played in Cleveland.

* * *

Darryl Sittler still holds the record with ten points in a game, and I have to admit he did it against the Boston Bruins.

It wasn't an easy feat. The goalie who was in was Dave Reece, and his record was 7–4–2. He was a pretty good goalie. We were a first-place club at the time, and I think they were a third-place club; but it was one if those nights where every time Sittler shot, it would go in. It could be from behind the net or off a skate, but it would go in. He had six goals and four assists.

We had Gerry Cheevers on the bench, and I was thinking of showing Reece some mercy, but the reason I didn't send in Cheevers was that he had just come back from the World Hockey Association and he hadn't practised for a couple of weeks. I looked down at him when he was sitting on the bench, and he put a towel over his head, so that's how much he wanted to go in.

Poor Davey Reece. He never played another minute in the National Hockey League.

But there's one thing: he got his name in the record book, and Darryl Sittler keeps his name alive. When Sittler goes around to banquets, he always gets asked about that night, and he says, "The sad thing is that Dave Reece, who I scored my ten points against, tried to commit suicide after that. He jumped in front of a subway train. But he survived. The train went between his legs."

An oldie, but a goodie.

* * *

Pat Egan was the coach of the Springfield Indians. He was the guy I broke my stick over in practice in the movie.

I was one of the Black Aces. He had the puck and was coming at me, and I knew he was gonna jump at me and try to hurt me. But I beat him to it and broke my stick over him. Naturally, I got sent to Three Rivers the next day.

But he was a colourful guy, I gotta admit. He played eleven years in the National Hockey League, and he was a tough little guy. Even when I broke my stick over him, he got up. He was built like a gorilla.

One time, we were driving along the New York Thruway, and a partridge hit the front window of the bus. What a mess. It smashed both windows, and the driver was Paul Lemay. How he ever kept control of that bus and stopped it from going off the road and getting us all killed was beyond me, but he kept the bus on the road.

Pat Egan got the remains of the partridge, took it to the hotel we were staying at and had the guy cook it for dinner that night. He was a strange guy.

By the way, the bus driver was "All the way with Paul Lemay."

* * *

Every year, the Bruins used to have to make a long road trip while the circus came into Boston Garden. They had all their wagons and equipment behind the building, and there was a ramp right there where you walk into the building. It would take you two minutes.

But Paul Mooney, the president of the Bruins, was so mean, he wouldn't let the circus people use that ramp. He made them walk all the way around the building to the front entrance on Causeway Street and come in that way and take an elevator up. It took them about twenty minutes.

Mooney had a lovely new car. I can't remember what kind it was, but it was a lovely green car. It was a beauty, and he used to park it near the ramp. The day that the circus was pulling out, they took all the elephant manure and piled it all over his car. It seeped in and ruined the car.

It didn't pay to tick off the circus guys.

* * *

In the Boston dressing room after a game one night, I went into the room. We had won. It's no problem. We're goin' on the road the next day and I say the usual stuff, somethin' like "Plane leaves at ten. Get your sticks ready." Everybody usually takes six sticks on the road with them.

I see one of my favourites—a friend and veteran—fire his stick against the wall and knock down all the other sticks. I figure it was an accident, but then he turns and stares at me.

I say, "What the heck is wrong with you?"

He mumbles something, and I go ballistic. I can't let him get away with this, whether he's a friend or not, because he's a leader on the club too. I said, "You act like everybody else on the club, and if you don't like it, get your skates and get out of here. If you're on that plane tomorrow, you're no better than the rest of us. Act like the rest of us."

Now I'm driving home with Rose on Route 114—a two-lane highway out in the boondocks—on a cold and freezing night as only the area around Boston can be. I look to my left, and who do I see driving alongside of me? My buddy that I had just given heck to. He's just furious, and he points to the side of the road for me to pull over.

I've cooled down by now, but I know this is not going to be nice. We both pull over and he gets out and comes to my window and really lights into me. I don't want to push this too far, so I ask him, "Why did you throw your sticks?"

He tells me I benched him during the game.

Now, I don't remember benchin' him, but sometimes, with penalties and power plays, things get mixed up and you forget a guy. Maybe it did happen. I don't remember it, but I can't back down. I'm absolutely freezin', but steam is actually comin' off him, he's so hot.

Finally, he says, "Is that it?"

I says, "That's it."

He was on the plane the next day. No problem. A leader cannot have insubordination and survive. I later made him a captain of the Boston Bruins, and he was the best captain I ever knew.

* * *

On a trip to Vancouver with the Boston Bruins, we landed at Seattle and had to wait for our connection to Vancouver.

A few players come up to me and said, "Hey Grapes, how about us takin' a bus and not flyin'? We could get a couple of cases of beer on the bus and kind of get-together. It would be a lot of fun."

I had a bad feeling. I didn't think management would be very happy about it, but I went along with it. I got the bus and we got the beer and the guys ordered some food—some chips and sandwiches and stuff like that. Wayne Cashman got pig's knuckles. I couldn't believe it.

It started out pretty good. I'm sittin' up at the front and things are getting' a little rowdy, but not bad. Nothing serious. Then I hear voices from a couple of guys who weren't dressing and weren't happy. You gotta understand, when guys aren't playin', they're unhappy, and I guess misery loves company—they stick together. Now they've had a few pops and they had a little bit of false courage.

Every so often, I hear, "Oh yeah, blame it on us. Blame it in us," just loud enough so I can hear it.

That's it! I get up and march down the aisle. Some of the guys are asleep, with their legs across the aisle. I'm throwin' them out of the way to get to the back where these guys are, and I grab a beer bottle on the way. The two wise guys are sitting at the back, wide-eyed, seeing this maniac coming towards them with a beer bottle in his hand, firing bodies all over the place.

I stand over them and I say, "Say one more word and I'll put this bottle right through your head."

Not a word. So I said it again. "Go ahead. Say one more word!" Again, nothin'.

Then one of my centres, a little guy, gets up—and he's had a few—and he says, "Wait a minute, Grapes."

I says, "Sit down, you little midget, or you'll get the same thing."

I said to Danny, the trainer, "When we get to the hotel, you go in and get the keys and you stand at the door of the bus. As the guys get off, you hand them their keys." Then I told the guys, "You do not leave your rooms until the skate tomorrow morning. You get in your room, and you stay there or you will be very sorry."

I go to the bar that night, and yes, I saw a veteran sitting all by himself in a booth, drinking. I didn't say a word, but right then, his days were numbered. I made his life a living hell until he couldn't take it any longer, and finally, he went in and told Harry Sinden he was quitting.

I can still see Harry storming down the stairs from his office in the Boston Garden. He got to the boards and he was leaning over, yelling, "What the hell is going on? Twenty games to go in the season and one of our best defencemen quits. How does that happen?"

I said, "Gee, Harry, I wouldn't know. I guess now we'll have to bring up Mike Milbury."

The sad thing is that everybody on the team loved this guy, but the ship is the thing. You don't pull your weight, you upset the ship, you have to go. Over the side. No exceptions.

The two wise guys in the bus were shipped out shortly after, and the guy in the bar was gone.

The coach has a way of making players look good, and the coach has a way of making players look bad. Nobody was a wise guy after that, and although I didn't have many rules, nobody broke the ones I had.

* * *

I was an awful guy to deal with after a game if we lost, especially in the Boston Garden, because the fans in there could get tough when we'd lose.

When we'd drive home, I'd be steaming, and Rose would have to get Kleenex to clean off the windows.

The cars used to be parked inside the Garden with the keys in them. The parking attendants would park them for us. One time, we'd lost, and I was in an awful mood, and I said, "Get in the car! Let's go."

Rose said, "Wait a minute!"

I said, "Never mind waiting a minute. Get in the car. Let's go." I'm ticked off. So she gets in the car and never says another word. As we get to the Mystic River Bridge, I says, "There's money in the glove compartment. Give me a couple of quarters."

She says, "There's no money in there."

I says, "How do you know?"

She says, "Because this isn't our car, dummy."

* * *

I always loved some of those beautiful old arenas, and one of the most beautiful, in my opinion, was the old Quebec Coliseum— the Colisée, as they call it.

I was there when it first opened up, with the Barrie Flyers on our march to the Memorial Cup. We had to go in there and play the Citadelles. We lost the first game, and somebody wrote, "The only reason the Barrie Flyers lost the first game was that their heads were too big to fit inside the Quebec Coliseum." We were a pretty good team. We won the next three games, and we were on our way. But that's not what I remember the Quebec Coliseum for.

I remember it for a game when I was with the Rochester Americans. It happened on a Sunday afternoon. I had a fight with somebody—I think it was Bugsy Watson. In those days, there was only one penalty box. We all used to sit together, with the police between us.

So we have our fight, and I go into the penalty box first. Then, as the other guy is stepping in, I drill him right between the eyes.

Well, that made the cops look bad, and they didn't like that, so I was grabbed by the cops. One cop was on one arm, and the other one on the other. Now there was a big schmozzle. The benches had cleared, and all the players were out on the ice, and as I'm being held, I notice Jean-Guy Gendron. He's looking at me, and he can't reach me. But I see him going around the outside of the crowd to my left, trying to work his way towards me, and I know exactly what he wants to do. The more I try to get away, the tighter the cops hold on. He takes his stick and he corks me right over the head. You could see it clearly on television because he used white tape on his stick, and it stands out.

Finally, they let me go. I'm being escorted off the ice—and in those days, the French girls had purses, and they had heavy bottles of makeup in them. Some girl threw her purse at me, and it had four bottles of makeup in it. It was really heavy. I picked it up, and I fired it back. There was this great, big guy standing there. He was about six foot three or six-four and he was a television announcer. He was bald, and he was looking the other way. And I can see this purse sailing up towards him, and I'm thinking, "Oh my goodness. It's going to hit him right in the back of his bald head."

It did. It hit him right in the head, and down he goes.

They hustled me off, and there I was in the dressing room, thinking, "Oh, no. I killed him." Well, I didn't kill him, but either way, I'm thinking I'm gonna get a long suspension.

But this happened with about two minutes to go in the game, and the league president, Jack Riley, and his assistant, Jack Button, had both been at the game, but they decided they shouldn't miss church. So they left just a few minutes before all the trouble. They're in the cab, going to church, and the taxi driver has the game on the radio, and they hear that a riot has broken out!

Jack Riley told me a couple of years later that the only reason they didn't suspend me was that they hadn't seen it because they were on their way to church, so they had to watch it on television.

That was before videotape; in those days, they used film, which wasn't always clear, but when Riley and Button watched that film, they saw me get hit over the head by Gendron with his white tape on his stick, so they didn't suspend me.

That's my fondest memory of the Quebec Coliseum. It's a great old building.

Oh. I forgot. We won the Calder Cup there too. That was pretty good.

* * *

I played in every professional league that ever existed. I played in the American Hockey League; I played one game in the National Hockey League; I played in the Central Hockey League; and I played in the Western Hockey League. I also played in the Eastern Professional Hockey League. A lot of people ask me if I thought I'd be able to play in the NHL today if I was playing now. Well, figure it out. In those days, there were six teams in the NHL; there were six in the AHL; six in the CHL; six in the WHL; and six in the EPHL. That's thirty teams. There's thirty teams in the NHL today.

That means everybody that was playing professional hockey back in those days would be in the National Hockey League today.

Talk about being born at the wrong time.

* * *

My son, Tim, is the Greater Toronto scout for the Ontario Hockey League. He rates all the young kids. I sometimes go with him for fun, but when I owned the Mississauga IceDogs, I didn't have any choice. I had to scout, and one day, I went down to Welland to scout a kid by the name of Jamie Tardif.

We drove all the way to Welland, and there was all kinds of scouts there, and Jamie Tardif got kicked out in the first thirty seconds for hitting from behind. All the scouts left, and Tim says, "Let's go, Dad."

I says, "No, I can't go, Tim. What will all the other players on both sides think? I leave, and these guys will think they're nothing."

So I stayed through the whole game. It didn't mean a thing.

All the rest of the scouts drove over to St. Catharines and saw some other guys that could have helped us, but I had to stand there the whole time because I cannot leave.

It's the same thing today when I start a game with Tim. I can't leave, because it's an insult to them if I leave.

So this game in Welland, I stuck it out to the end, and about a month later, I was walking through the airport and I ran into the coach of one of the teams.

He says, "You can't believe how both teams thought the world of you for staying at that game and not leaving."

So, ever since that day, when I start a game, I always stick it out, no matter the score, because I know how I would feel if someone was there to scout just one player and left. I always put myself in their place and think how they'd feel, and I always stick it out.

* * *

When Tim and I go on our scouting trips, I always buy $20 worth of tickets on the 50-50 draw. The way the 50-50 works is that the club gets half the money and the winner gets the other half.

One night, they'd sold $1,400 worth of tickets and I win. I've won $700, but what am I going to do? I can't have them announce that I've won the money and kept it. So I give the money back to the club.

Two games later, I buy my $20 worth of tickets again. I win again. This time, it's $800. Tim is really chucklin' at this. Again, I can't keep the money so I give it back to the club.

Three games later, it's a big one. They sell three grand in tickets! I always give my $20 worth of tickets to Tim because he can see the numbers better than me. Now they start callin' out the number, and Tim's lookin' at the tickets. I keep lookin' straight ahead. I'm hopin' I'm not winnin'. I see Tim's eyes lookin' at me.

I look at him. I say, "You're kiddin'."

He says, "No. You've won it again, Dad."

I had to give the $1,500 back. Tim was chucklin' all the way home. He was really havin' a big laugh.

* * *

The Boston Bruins always had a long road trip when the circus was in town, and one time, we flew all the way from Los Angeles to Montreal. We got in about four in the afternoon, so we must have left LA early, because there's a three-hour time difference.

So I said to the guys, "You wanna go for a skate, just to get a bit of the jet lag out and have a sweat and a shower?"

They said they did, so we went down to the Forum for an easy optional practice. They all showed up, and I could tell they were gonna have some fun, so I just let them go out and skate. So they started to fool around a bit. Some of them started to wrestle. Some guys let on they were fighting. Terry O'Reilly and Mike Milbury were on their knees playing "patty-cake, patty-cake baker's man." Everybody was just having fun.

Unbeknownst to me, there happened to be a photographer from *La Presse* way up high in the stands. We didn't know he was there. *La Presse* is a French newspaper in Montreal that is almost totally dedicated to the Canadiens and hockey. This guy took all the pictures of the guys having their fun practice.

The next day, Harry Sinden flew in from Boston, and as he was going through the airport, he saw *La Presse*. They had a two-page spread full of at least thirty pictures of the Bruins fooling around in practice.

Harry was not amused.

* * *

I'm often asked what it feels like to be fired as a coach.

You get vibes, and it really is funny. You sense when you're in trouble.

All of a sudden, the PR guy is not quite as friendly as he used to be, or hanging around as much. The trainers don't come into your office as often. The secretaries aren't phoning you quite as often as they usually do. They realize that if they hang around with you too much, then maybe it looks like they should go, too, because they're friends of yours.

I don't know whether it was by accident or not, but it seemed strange. For four years in a row, my Boston Bruins equipment bag had COACH DON CHERRY embroidered on the side. My fifth and last year there, I got my equipment bag, and it just had COACH.

* * *

I went to the training camp for every NHL team at some point. There were only six teams in the NHL in those days, and over my sixteen years in the minors, I went to every team's camp at least once. Unfortunately for me, I was destined to be a minor-leaguer. In fact, when I became an assistant coach for Team Canada '76, Sam Pollock, the general manager in Montreal, was the GM of Team Canada, and he remembered that I had passed through their organization. He kept a record of every player who ever attended training camp, and he had written a comment about every one of them.

So when we were working together in 1976 at the Canada Cup, Sam went back in his book and looked back at 1961. It read, "Donald S. Cherry. Confirmed minor-leaguer."

I can't argue with that.

I was at every training camp, and the classiest one of all of them was the Montreal Canadiens.

First of all, we lived at the Queen's Hotel. Granted, four of us lived in each room, but it was still classy. We'd have our dinner at night in the dining room, and there would be a string quartet playing.

The dressing rooms were just so classy, too, and they did a wonderful thing that no other organization did. It was a small thing, but it meant a lot to us minor leaguers. They put us in the same dressing room as all the stars. Dickie Moore was sitting next to me. Across was Boom Boom Geoffrion.

They give you good equipment, not old equipment with holes in it. You really thought you were going to make the Montreal Canadiens.

First class all the way.

* * *

After my training camp with the Montreal Canadiens, I was sold to Spokane—sold, I think, but maybe traded for a roll of tape—never to be heard of again for sixteen years.

Now, fast-forward to 1976, and once again the Montreal Forum is the home rink. It's the Canada Cup, and we had a pretty good roster of guys in charge of the team. Scotty Bowman was the coach. I was an assistant coach, along with Al MacNeil and Bobby Kromm. Alan Eagleson ran the show. Jean Béliveau, Sammy Pollock and Toe Blake were all there helping out as well.

To me, Toe Blake is the greatest hockey guy who ever lived, and I'll tell you why. Just look at his record. As a player, he was on that super line with Elmer Lach and Rocket Richard on that Canadiens team that won all those Stanley Cups. They called it the Punch Line, for obvious reasons. Toe himself was called the Old Lamplighter because he was always scoring goals and lighting the red light.

The Team Canada '76 position was almost an honorary thing with Toe. He never really said much. He never attended meetings or those stupid dinners we had to go to because Eagleson had arranged them. But with Toe just being there, it was really something. He'd sit there and watch every practice, and for some reason or other, he took a shine to me. That was very unusual, because not many people take a shine to me.

He'd be sitting alone up in the stands, and I'd go up and listen to his stories. What a waste, because no one else was around.

I think if there was one other person around, he wouldn't have said a word, because actually, he was kinda shy, which is hard to believe. When he coached, they called him "The Bear." He was gruff and sometimes mean to the players, but they loved him. If you crossed him, it was the end, so they were in fear of him. But it was one of those deals that they respected him so much that they loved him.

One day, he took me to his bar. It was an old tavern that served only men. It had seen better days, and in fact, it was torn down a few years later. One of the greatest experiences of my life was in this old tavern. What happened was one day, Toe said, "I've gotta go close the tavern tonight. Would you like to come along?"

Sure I would. So we went along, and I went in there. There was nobody in the place, and it was just closing up. Toe was washing the glasses, putting them in the water, stacking the glasses and that. Around the walls of the tavern, you couldn't believe the pictures—pictures of all the old players like Eddie Shore, Sprague Cleghorn, Bill Cowley, Maurice "Rocket" Richard. You went back in time just looking at them all. The whole place was full of them. They were all over the walls, and I often wonder what happened to those pictures.

So as Toe was washing away, I started asking him about some of these guys. You had to be kind of careful; you couldn't push him on anything or he'd clam up.

"Well, how about Bill Cowley? What kind of player was he?" Well, Toe talked about Bill Cowley, what a great skater he was. He went on and on.

"Eddie Shore. Tell me about Eddie Shore. Was he as tough as they said?"

"Boy, was he tough. I'd tell you how tough he was." And then he talked about Eddie Shore in his day.

I went on to Elmer Lach. "Tell me about Elmer Lach. He was your linemate. What was it like playing with him?"

"Well, all you had to do was get in the open and Elmer would find you."

He went on and on. It was one of the greatest experiences of my life.

Then I said to him, "Toe, all the coaches have drills. Go this way. Go that way. Do circles. Do this. Do that. But that year when I came to the Montreal training camp, you just divided the players into teams.

"There would be eighteen players on each team back in those days, and you'd have two teams. You'd start the practice just like a game—take shots to warm up a little and to warm up the goalie, then drop the puck and let 'em go."

He says, "Don, all that other stuff is just show. If the guys are in the National Hockey League, they don't have to do drills to learn how to come out of their end. Game conditions are so much better. They have to scrimmage, but you have to do it at top speed. If they're not doing it at top speed, and they're just going through the motions, then you're wasting your time.

"You should have seen some of the practices we had back then. It was better than some of the games."

That was the secret of his success, he said. The guys used to scrimmage all the time. He must have done something right. He won more Stanley Cup than any other coach until Scotty Bowman passed him in 2002, and Scotty always said that he could never have done it without all the advice and help that Toe Blake gave him.

As far as I'm concerned, Toe is the greatest coach and the greatest hockey guy of all time.

* * *

One thing really bothered me in this year's playoffs. It happened the day we lost that beautiful Trooper Larry Rudd of the Royal Canadian Dragoons. We had lost four Ontario boys in Afghanistan in that month—May 2010. I see a headline in USA Today and it says, CANADA—SAFE HAVEN FOR DESERTERS AND DEFECTORS. It proceeded to tell how all the deserters can come here and live safely.

One guy said, "I would rather go to jail than go and fight in a war." I guess we're just one step up from jail. That's what those defectors think of us.

The article said that these defectors were being helped by other defectors in Canada from the Vietnam War. But that's okay. That's fine. If the government wants these people in Canada, that's fine. But what really hurts is that it made us sound like were Sweden or Switzerland, who stand up for nothing and have never been in a war. We really sounded like a bunch of pacifists up here, while in reality, we'd lost more troops per capita in Afghanistan than the United States at the time.

It's a sad thing that we're known in the world as a country that gives a haven to these deserters and we're depicted as a pacifist nation.

* * *

Gary Doak was a defenceman who played for me on the Boston Bruins. Now, Doak was the most intense person I have ever met. He was up for every game—three hours before the game.

We were playing in Philadelphia, and Kate Smith was singing "God Bless America" just before the game started. Halfway through, Doakie couldn't take it anymore. He was whizzing around the rink, halfway through the national anthem.

When we were in Montreal in the finals, we were in the dressing room after the warmup, and the trainer comes up to me and he says, "Grapes, you gotta get out there. Doakie won't come off the ice. He keeps warming up and the police are coming to get him."

I go out, and he's all by himself, whirling around, and the police are standing by the door, waiting for him. I got him to come off the ice before they did anything.

When certain things happened, we called it the Gary Doak Syndrome. It would be somethin' like this: Bobby Schmautz was like the straw boss on the team. If anything was going wrong with anybody on the team, you could rest assured that Bobby would come up and tell me.

So one day he comes up and he says, "Don, you gotta do something about Doakie."

I says, "Why? What's wrong?"

Schmautzie says, "He doesn't like his pants, and Danny, the trainer, won't give him a new pair."

So I called Danny in, and Danny says, "Don, he's nuts. This guy is nuts. He always wants this, and he always wants that. It's always somethin'."

I said, "Danny, just give him the pants to keep him happy."

So he gives him the pants, and about a week later Schmautzie comes in and he says, "Grapes, I got something to ask you. Doakie wants his old pants back. He doesn't like the new ones. Can he have them back?"

Here's another one. The stick companies used to have representatives that would come around.

They worked for Sher-Wood, Victoriaville, CCM, Northland—companies like that. They'd go and see all the guys that were using their sticks. The guys might ask for a bigger curve or somethin', or give their complaints. They might even say everythin' was fine. That rarely happened.

The representative for Sher-Wood was a real nice guy. He was French-Canadian, and he had lost an eye playing hockey. So, he worked for the company, and he knew what he was doin'. He'd played the game.

Now, you must realize that every player in hockey wants a stiff and light stick. The stiffer and lighter, the better. Every time these stick guys would talk to the players, the players would say, "Could I get it a little stiffer and a little lighter?"

After he goes around our room one day, the Sher-Wood rep comes to me and he says, "That's it for me. I'm quitting. I've had it."

I said, "What the heck happened?"

He says, "I go to Gary Doak and he says his sticks are too light and too stiff!"

The Gary Doak Syndrome.

* * *

There were two places the Boston Bruins always had trouble winning.

You'd think one of them would be Montreal, but it wasn't. Montreal was pretty good to us. In 1976–77, the year the Canadiens only lost one game at home, we were the guys that beat 'em that one game. They only lost eight all year, and we beat them three times. We didn't have a problem with Montreal in the regular season. In the playoffs, maybe, but not in the regular season.

We'd always had trouble in Toronto, and it went back for years. The reason we had trouble there was that three-quarters of the team came from around Toronto. They were always ticked off that they couldn't go home and visit their folks. Then friends would come downtown to visit 'em and they'd stay out. There was always discord when we were in Toronto. Before I got there, I think the Bruins got beat 10–0 one night.

Anyhow, we go in and I come up with this one. I say, "Look, here's the deal. We have an optional skate tomorrow at eleven-fifteen. Be there if you want. It's optional. Go home and visit if you want.

"You guys that are stayin' here, I don't want you to stay out late. Be in by eleven-thirty or midnight. But listen, Harry knows what I'm doin' here, so you guys had better be ready for Saturday night. That's all I'm askin'. My ass is on the line here, helpin' you out."

Well, you shoulda seen the games in Toronto from then on. I tell ya, except for that one game when Sittler got his ten points against Davey Reece, we could hardly wait to get to Toronto. It was like the seventh game of the Stanley Cup.

The Leafs couldn't understand why, when we'd win the game, the guys were all so happy. It was because as long as we won, they could keep on doin' it and they knew that.

It was the same thing in LA. For years, we'd get there on a Friday and they'd go out and have a good time and the whole deal. Then they'd never ever win a game. I said almost the same thing to 'em as I said in Toronto. I said, "Look, you guys can go out and have some fun, but I want you in by midnight for sure. I don't mind if you get a little glow on, but I don't want anybody gettin' hammered, and this time, I'll be kinda watchin'.

"But after the game, all I'm saying to ya is the bus leaves at ten Sunday morning and I'm only askin' that you don't do anything in the hotel. That's all I ask."

They knew what I meant. Go out and have a good time. From that time on, when we went into LA, we played great and after the game, the Kings were like the Leafs. They couldn't understand why we were jumpin' around so much.

A guilty conscience is the greatest motivator of all.

* * *

Bobby Schmautz was one of my favourites. He was a tough little guy that, I said before, I used as my straw boss. Even though he was tough, he was awful short.

We were always kiddin' one another, and one time, he was kiddin' me about bein' too heavy.

I said, "Well, that's true, Schmautzie, but I can lose weight and you can't grow a foot." I thought that was a pretty good comeback.

So one day, we're in Minnesota, the night before a game. We're having a pop or two, and in a bar, mostly serious, and I see something I didn't like: Schmautzie drinkin' from a mug full of vodka with just ice in it. A couple of beers, I don't mind. Hard stuff bothers me.

I says, "Schmautzie, be careful here. Don't push me too far."

Well, sure enough, he did push me too far. He drank too much and he comes in that night and broke a stained-glass window as well as some other stuff. It cost him about $2,000 in damages. I don't think the stuff was worth that much, but that's what they do in hotels. You do things like that and you pay the price.

I made him pay the price as well. He was dying the next night in the game. Absolutely dyin'. And I kept double-shiftin' him. All night long, it was, "Schmautzie up next. Schmautzie up next." He was throwin' up at the end of the bench. I was so cruel to him. But I never suspended guys and I never fined them. I just kept double-shiftin' him. We were up 4–0 or 5–0, so it didn't matter. I wouldn't put him on the power play because that would be too easy, but I made him kill penalties. Even a couple of players said, "Geez, Grapes, give him a break. He's gonna die."

He's killin' a penalty and goes out to the point because he knew he still had to do the job. He blocks a shot and gets a breakaway. Now he dekes the goalie, puts the puck in and collapses in the corner. He's so sick and so tired he can't get up, and the guys had to help him get up and get to the bench.

As they get him there and he sits down, I said, "Schmautzie, next shift."

* * *

Darryl Sly was my defence partner with the Rochester Americans. Could he skate! I'm telling you, only Bobby Orr could skate better than him. He was so powerful, his legs would go like pistons. If he had been hungrier, he could have been in the NHL for a long time, but he had a great arrangement going.

He made three times as much as me. He made $15,000 a year. I made $5,200. He put every cent of his money away, and he lived on his wife Sylvia's salary. She was a nurse. Later, he took that money back to Collingwood and bought a Chrysler dealership, Blue Mountain Chrysler, for a song because Chrysler was really down at that time.

He carried me for six years. When we were out there together, I'd say, "Stand up, Darryl. Stand up." Then they'd dump it into our end, and I'd say, "Go back and get it, Darryl," and he would. That's how fast he was.

I took care of the front of the net and he took care of the puck.

We used to sit beside each other, and one day, he played a pretty good trick on me. But I got in trouble because of it.

We're sitting there one day after the morning skate, and Joe Crozier comes in for one of his talks. Now, we're anxious to get home. We've already finished our morning skate, and we've got a game tonight, and we wanna get out of there. But we're sitting there, and Joe is going on and on and on. He's talking about how we gotta play good tonight and how it's an important game tonight. And on and on.

Now, I'm one of those guys that always stared at the coach all the time. The whole time he was talking, I stared at him. Darryl, on the other hand, was one of these guys who'd rest his head in his hands and look down at the floor. So Joe is going on and on, and all of a sudden, while I'm looking at Joe, Darryl Sly snores. Well, I burst out laughing! And to make it worse, I can't stop laughing. It was one of those deals like when the teacher gives you heck and you can't stop laughing.

Joe's really mad. He storms out, then a couple of minutes later the trainer comes in and says, "Joe wants to see you in his office." Naturally.

Well, I couldn't tell him what had happened. He's giving me heck and saying, "What are you doing to me?"

Well, I can't tell him that Darryl had snored, so I'm standing there, and Joe's going on and on now giving me a long lecture.

And Darryl? He'd gone home. He got me pretty good on that one.

* * *

Ron MacLean gets these great ideas. I go along with them because he works so hard on them.

So we're having a couple of pints after the game, and he says, "I've got a great idea. I want you to do *The Phantom of the Opera*."

This is how I remember Wayne Cashman, a warrior in front of the net,
at a time when defencemen could really dish out punishment.
But as you can see, Cash could really dish it out, too.

Looking beautiful at the Boston Gardens.

Making a point in Boston Gardens.

With Ron and the most winning junior coach of all time, Brian Kilrea, at the prospects game in London.

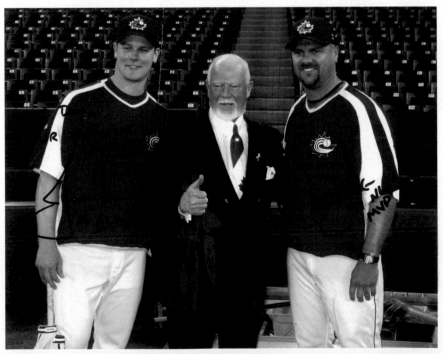

I have to admit, I was proud and honoured to stand with these two great MVP Canadians, Justin Morneau and Larry Walker.

2003 CHL Top Prospects Game, Team Cherry Wins 4–3

Players: Marc-André Fleury (G), Kevin Nastiuk (G), Mike Egener (D), Kevin Klein (D), Frank Rediker (D), Brent Seabrook (D), Aaron Dawson (D), Steve Bernier (F), Dustin Brown (Captain, D), Jeremy Colliton (F), Dan Fritsche (F), Ryan Getzlaf (F), Nathan Horton (F), Jean-François Jacques (F), Kamil Freps (F), Corry Perry (F), Antony Stewart (F), Petr Vrana (F). Staff: Don Cherry, Head Coach; Brian Kilrea and Bert O'Brien, Coaches; Russ Hammond and Brian Millar (Trainers).

That's Bobby Orr leaving on the right.

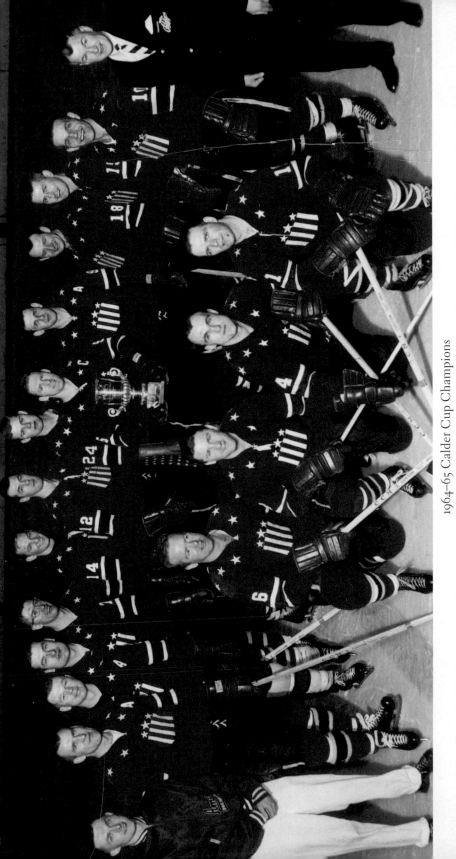

1964–65 Calder Cup Champions

Standing (L to R): Ken Carson (Trainer), Gerry Enman, me, Duane Rupp, Al Abour, Jim Pappin, Ed Litzenberger, Gary Smith, Larry Hillman (with the cup), Dick Gamble, Bronco Horvath, Billy Harris, Stan Smrke, Joe Crozier (Coach). Kneeling: Red Armstrong, Rudy Migay, Darryl Sly, Les Duff.

My 1972–73 Rochester Americans
Back row (L to R): Sam Paolini, Gerry Sillers, Larry McKillop, Bob Thompson, Bob Malcolm, Dave Hrechkosy, Ron Fogal, Bob Kelly, Wayne Morusyk, Rick Pagnutti, Barry Merrell, Herman Karp, Lorne Rombough, Nate Agnello. Front row (L to R): John Den Hamer, Gaye Cooley, John Bednarski, Guy Borrowes, Rod Graham, Don Cherry, Bob Ellett, Red Armstrong, Gene Sobchuk, Lynn Zimmerman, Terry Collins. Not present for photo: Jeff Hunt.

1ST Place Overall Rochester Americans—a great bunch of guys (1973–74)
Back Row (L to R): Wayne Morusyk, Ron Dussiaume, Art Stratton, Gary Bredin, Bob Malcolm, John Wensink, Bill Knibbs, Jean Gauthier, François Ouimet, Larry McKillop, PR and Asst. GM John Den Hamer, Trainer Nate Angelo. Front Row (L to R): Bob Sneddon, Bob Ellett, Rod Graham, Barry Merrell, Coach Don Cherry, Murray Kuntz, Dick Mattiusi, Doug Ferguson, Lynn Zimmerman.

If you look closely, that's me coaching the Rochester Americans in the AHL at the Boston Gardens against the Boston Braves. I'm between two hotdog vendors. I know what you're thinkin'. Notice I'm not standin' on the back of the bench. My back was so bad I had to hold onto a wall. Great for ten-hour bus trips.

Long-time friends
Mel and Bev Price,
and Frick and Frack.

At the ACC for the Leafs' season opener for the 2009–2010 season with my friends and the 48th Highlanders. Lianne Harrower, my make-up lady who makes me look so good, and my buddy David Sealy, my floor director who tries to tell me what to do.

I just look at him, and he says, "Yeah. I really wanna do it."

I says, "What are you talking about?"

He says, "Well, we'll go up in the United Center. We'll get the organ, if they'll let us have the organ, and we'll rent a cape, and we'll rent a mask."

So I'm looking at him as if he's nuts, but I'm no chicken, and I say, "Okay, if that's what you want to do."

So sure enough, that's what we do. We get up there. He gets all the equipment. He arranges for this cape and this mask. He works at it, and he convinces Mark Punga, the cameraman, and Sherali Najak, the producer, and we work at it.

"Louder," he's yelling at me. "Louder." Then it's "Too fast. Too fast. More feelin,' put your heart in it." So I go along with it, and I put up with all the abuse because I know he's really got his heart set on it, and he really worked hard on it—well, I did, too; but this is his baby. He really thinks they're masterpieces. That's all he talks about.

So we work for about three or four hours on it. We finally get it done. We used it that night. I thought it was pretty good. Ron thought it was wonderful. A masterpiece.

The next day Ron could hardly wait to hear the boss Scott Moore's reaction to his masterpiece. The boss phoned Sherali and Ron, all excited, asked, "What did he say? What did he say?"

He said, "You're not going to run that thing again are you?"

You shoulda seen the Ron's face. I just howled.

* * *

The original organ in the Chicago Stadium was legendary. The pipes for it were wrapped in cement, and they ran along the ceiling. They couldn't be saved when the Hawks moved to the United Center.

The new building is a nice, big building, there's no doubt about it. But I think Michael Jordan described the United Center best when he said, "This building has no soul."

I'm afraid the old Chicago Stadium is just a dream now, and the magic is gone.

* * *

The National Hockey League came up with a great idea: in the finals every year, they bring in the five top prospects that have been ranked by Central Scouting and will be coming into the league. Then we put 'em on *Hockey Night in Canada*.

This year, 2010, we had a vintage group: Taylor Hall, Tyler Seguin, Cam Fowler, Erik Gudbranson and Brett Connolly.

About 90 per cent of these top prospects make the National Hockey League. It's funny to see them come in with their new suits on, their hair cut short, their shoes shining, the whole deal.

Actually, it started back in 1993 in Montreal. *Hockey Night in Canada* had promised the kids that they would go on at the end of the second period. We're sitting in the studio before the game, just Ron and me, and the kids come in just to say hello.

Ron says, "The plans have changed. We can't get you on. We don't have the time. I'm really sorry."

I said, "What are you? Nuts? We don't have the time? These guys are all excited. They wanna be on national television."

He says, "Well, we don't have the time."

I says, "Oh yes, we do. They'll go in 'Coach's Corner.'"

So we had the very first group come on. It was Chris Gratton, Chris Pronger and Todd Harvey. We had them, and that started the whole thing.

Then, in the Montreal *Gazette*, one of the columnists wrote something like, "This proves that Don Cherry is a bigot and a racist, because they didn't have the two French-Canadians on." Well, what happened was the Canadiens had taken the top two French-Canadian prospects, Alexandre Daigle and Jocelyn Thibault, and were introducing them at centre ice the same time as I was doing "Coach's Corner" with the other three.

Now we do it every year, and it's a great tradition. Dave Keon Jr., who works for the league, takes them around. He takes them into the dressing rooms. They meet all the guys on the teams, and they meet the guys who were in their shoes years ago. This year, for instance, they met Chris Pronger, Jonathan Toews and Patrick Kane. They get a good feel for the game and for the NHL. It's a heck of a good idea.

* * *

People wonder sometimes what happens to a player who signs a big contract, then goes in the tank. You see it all the time in all sports. Their mind changes.

Even the kids right out of junior have to watch it. If they're a first-rounder, they get three years at $900,000 a year. With incentives, it goes over $1 million. You're 18, and you're a millionaire and everybody's tellin' you how great you are.

To make it in the NHL, you have to keep the same mindset you had when you were a junior. You've got to be hungry. But a lot of them change.

It's the same with boxers. Look at Mike Tyson. He makes millions upon millions, then he goes to Japan and gets flattened by Buster Douglas, a guy who's not even in the top ten. Tyson had a lot of money but he didn't train.

I think my hero, Jack Dempsey, said it best when he lost the championship and he knew he hadn't trained as hard as he should have. He loved the great life and he had married a movie star. When she asked him what had happened when he lost, he said he didn't train as hard. She asked him why he hadn't, and Jack said, "It's tough to run at 5 A.M. when you're wearing silk shorts."

* * *

The biggest award that could be given to an athlete back in the sixties was the Hickok Belt. It was a belt worth $25,000, with diamonds and rubies in it. Phil Rizzuto, the New York Yankees shortstop, won the first one in 1950, and for twenty years after that, they always had the presentation dinner in Rochester. All the top athletes were there, and in 1967, hockey was represented by Bobby Orr. Basketball was represented. Everybody was there. All the top athletes in every sport, and all the top entertainers. I remember the winner was Carl Yastrzemski.

I guess it was because the dinner was in Rochester that they invited the Rochester Americans. We were from the American Hockey League and they didn't even put us on the main floor. They put us in another room to watch it on television. Third class. So we went there, and we were in this room and Joe Crozier, the general manager and coach, was supposed to speak for hockey. But he saw all these top athletes and top entertainers like Henny Youngman. It must have cost a small fortune to get all these people there. So as soon as Joe saw that, he bailed. He comes to me—and I've had about two or three pops, and I've never spoke in public in my life before.

He says, "Cherry, you're speakin' for hockey."

I says, "What? Are you nuts? I've never spoke in front of people."

He says, "You are. You're the guy."

So what else was I gonna do?

So if you're gonna be one of the speakers, before you do, you go into a thing called the green room. And all the celebrities are in there. It was long and narrow and kinda dark. I was standin' at the back all by myself. Nobody knew the Rochester Americans, let alone me. All the top guys were there, and all their floater friends, and they're all standing around the bar. And here I am at the back of the room in the dark, terrified.

All of a sudden, the back door opens and in comes this tall man dressed in black. White tie. White shirt. Slicked-back hair—straight back. Big cigar. He comes to me, standing at the back, and he says, "Hello, son. How are you?"

So I turned around and it was Jack Dempsey! Jack Dempsey! My hero, the greatest heavyweight champion of all time.

He puts his hand out and he says, "How are you doin', son?"

I says, "I'm fine, Mr. Dempsey."

So you know what he says to me? He says, "What is this dinner, anyhow?"

I explained to him this is for the Hickok Award. It's a big belt with all the special athletes and all that. I guess he was a special guest. I said, "You know what they've got for you, Mr. Dempsey? They've got diamond cuff links."

I said to myself, "Don't stand there now with your tongue in your mouth and not say anything. Speak up." I was pretty shy back in those days.

So I said to him, "You know, Mr. Dempsey, when you did your exhibition tour in Canada, my dad was your second."

He said, "Oh, I remember doing that tour."

I said, "Well, he said you were the nicest guy and kind to everybody up there. He thought you were a great guy, and so do I."

He said, "Well, that's very nice, son." Thank you.

All of a sudden, the floaters and everybody looked back there in the dark, and here was Jack Dempsey. I think he liked talkin' to me 'cause I was just an ordinary guy with a short brush cut and all that. All of a sudden, they saw him and the horde come towards him. He says, "Well, it has been nice talkin' to you, son." Thank you.

He knew that from then on, his life wouldn't be his own. They'd be pushin' and shovin'. I'll always remember, he looked back and waved goodbye.

What a thrill! I often think back that if I hadn't agreed to speak, I would never have met Jack Dempsey.

So I did my best. I got up. I didn't even know how to pronounce Yastrzemski and I had to congratulate him for winnin'. So I just called him Carl.

We were in another room, watchin' the thing on television. Henny Youngman was so funny, people were cryin' for mercy. Remember he used to have that violin and he'd do a little *hmm-hmm*, then he'd say somethin'? Well, he had the people with tears in their eyes. I know it's an old line now, but he was the one who said it first, and it was the first time we heard it: "Now you take my wife. Please."

Another one was "Knock knock."

"Who's there?"

"It's the Boston Strangler."

"It's for you, dear."

It's the only time I've ever seen where guys were laying on the table laughin'. He was the funniest guy I've ever heard at a banquet. He was killin' me.

So that was the Hickok Award. It was the biggest thing in sports at the time, but it's gone now. They stopped it after 1976.

To this day I can still feel Jack Dempsey putting his hand on my shoulder and saying, "How ya doin' son?" It seems like a dream, and I say to myself, "Did it really happen?"

It did. Honest.

* * *

There's no doubt that the best guy at banquets today is Dennis Hull. He is absolutely the best, as far as I'm concerned.

Him and I started out together. I needed the money at the time. I'd just come from being coach of the Colorado Rockies. It was about 1980. We used to do the dog-and-pony act or whatever you'd call it. We met in Montreal one time and he flew in from somewhere — Chicago, I guess — and he'd just had a hemorrhoid operation. He was still laughin' and jokin' at that.

So I was at a banquet just recently, and a guy come up and says, "Do you remember you and Dennis Hull hitch-hikin' into town?"

And I remember now, the limo broke down, and him and I were out hitch-hikin'.

Anyhow, we used to go into little towns and villages and do our best. We'd go and we'd get there in the morning and we'd go and meet everybody in the factory. And we'd meet the mayor and have to meet his kids. We really earned our money.

I was doin' a speech—and you always spoke *before* Dennis—
and I was dyin'. I really was dyin'. And he was laughin' down there.

I said, "Wait till you get up here."

Well, he got up and he was dyin', too, and that's when he started
to laugh. That's when he got that laugh that he has now. If you've
ever been to a banquet with him, when he laughs, everybody
laughs. He's the absolute best.

He tells a lot of stories about his brother, Bobby, and he told me
a story one time that Bobby had been asked to go to the Bing
Crosby golf tournament, an annual tournament. Bobby said he'd
go, but when he saw all the people that were gonna be there, all
the singers and entertainers, he said, "I'm not goin' there." He just
said, "I'm not goin'."

So Dennis said, "Well, I'll go."

People knew Bobby, but they didn't know Dennis at all, so they
kept him to right near the end. Just before Dennis spoke, a lady
sang. She was pretty big. She was an opera singer, and when she
finished, she got a great ovation.

So out wanders Dennis, this little guy that nobody has heard of,
and there's deathly silence and he says, "Ha! I guess you thought it
was over, eh? When the fat lady sang?"

Well, it brought down the house. The only problem was that the
opera lady threatened to sue him.

* * *

I used to love to go down to Fenway Park in Boston. My son and I,
we just loved goin' down. The grass was almost emerald green. It
was just beautiful. I loved the baseball announcer, Sherm Feller,
just the way he used to talk.

They had everything classy there. The subway was fallin' apart
in Boston, but you get to Fenway and it's great. The Green
Monster. You're right on top of the ball players. It's like you're in
the game.

One Saturday afternoon, Tim and I went there to see the Yankees, and Billy Martin was their manager. Reggie Jackson was acting like the jerk that he usually is, and they were changin' pitchers. Jackson was talkin' with the fans, then he was layin' with his arms on the fence, talkin' with the Red Sox pitchers in the bullpen, just shootin' the breeze. He was laid back and all that, and he was doin' the same thing when he was goin' up to bat.

I said to Tim, "Tim, Billy Martin is not gonna put up with this. You watch: something's gonna happen."

Sure enough—the only time I think it's ever happened—Billy Martin called time and he sent out a ballplayer called Paul Blair and went to Reggie Jackson and said, "You're out."

Jackson said, "What? Me?"

And Martin said, "Hey, you're out. Get in the dugout."

He goes in the dugout and they had a pushin' match. Pushin' and rasslin'. What a show they put on.

I just loved Billy Martin as a manager. He was a tough so-and-so, and a colourful guy. And a great guy to watch when you'd go to a ball game.

How come baseball managers can go out and argue with umpires and hockey coaches are fined big dough and given a penalty for arguing with refs? Prima donnas.

* * *

I did a few commercials for Quiznos sandwiches. They were pretty good. We did one with Tie Domi where he was tellin' me how he was gonna score forty goals or somethin' like that. Then he drops the tray and I say, "Not with those hands." And he gets mad at me.

Quiznos ran a contest one time. It was gonna be for $25,000. They were gonna fly the winner out to Las Vegas and play one hand of blackjack for $25,000. They said, "Don Cherry will fly with you."

So this lady from Winnipeg wins the trip for a shot at the $25,000. My son, Tim, and I and the lady fly out there, and they set it all up and we go to the hotel, and they said, "Oh no, you can't play for $25,000. You can play one hand for $12,500 and another one for $12,500."

So I thought I was just there to sit there and give her a little support. I'm just sittin' there watchin', and unbeknownst to me, she had no idea how to play blackjack. I said to Tim, "I hope she doesn't get a twelve or something like that."

Sure enough, she gets the cards and she gets twelve. She looks at me! She looks at me and I have to make the decision! I look at Tim and I start to sweat. If I tell her to get a hit and she gets another face card, she loses. She didn't know. They'd just tell her she lost, then she'd blame it on me because I was the one who told her what to do and she lost.

I said, "I can't believe this. What are you going to do?"

She said, "I don't know. What do I do?"

If I tell her to hit and she breaks, she's gonna blame me.

Everybody else looks the other way, so I have to make the decision. I'm sweatin' bullets, but I tell her to take a hit.

She got a six. She won. She didn't even know that she won.

Now the dealer is dealin' again, and she's lookin' in her purse and sayin' she doesn't have enough money. If she loses this hand, I'm gonna be the bad guy.

She's got a face card up and a five in the hole, and he's got a six or something. She looks at me again.

I'm still sweating bullets here. I say, "Stay."

So now the dealer, he deals himself an eight and he breaks. I was so nervous, my face was purple.

So here's a woman that won $25,000 and did not know what she was doin'. If she'd have lost, it would have got all over Winnipeg that I had lost her the $25,000.

Everybody went to dinner. I was so upset over the whole thing I had to go to bed—after a few pops, naturally.

* * *

Nowadays, the plus-minus statistics are published for the public, and everyone can see them. But before they started doing that, the teams had their own guys who kept track of them, or the league sent them out, but only to the teams.

I always got the plus-minus statistics, but I never ever let the players see them. What was the point? If the guy was a big plus, he'd get complacent. If the guy was a big minus, he'd put more pressure on himself and feel bad. So it didn't make any sense to me.

One day, I made a mistake while I was in Colorado. I got the plus-minus report from the league, and I left it on my desk by accident. I usually just crumpled it up and threw it away. I didn't even want the trainer to see it.

We had a great guy, a defenceman, Mike Christie. He was born in Big Spring, Texas, by the way. I don't know where he learned his hockey, but he was a great guy. One time, him and Danny Gare from Buffalo were standing there, waiting for a decision from the referee. You know how they stand and wait for the referee to explain?

So him and Danny started goin' back and forth at one another, and it ended up that they were throwin' 'em while they were waitin' for the referee.

Anyway, the day I left the stats on my desk, he was standin' there waitin' for me. He had nothing to do and he happened to turn this plus-minus sheet around. I come in, and he was almost in tears. "Minus-38! Minus-38? I never realized how bad I was. Minus-38! That damn Hardy Astrom, he lets in a goal every time I step on the ice."

That was the one time I ever let anybody see the plus-minus. I felt bad.

I'll tell you why I felt that way.

Sometimes, doin' the faceoff in your end, you put a line on with a certain defence and they're always in their end. They're always against the good lines. The other way around, if the faceoff is in the other end, you put the offensive guys on, and if you have the last change, you've always got them out against the weaker line and the weaker defence.

So you really have to put it in perspective. Don't get carried away with plus-minuses—unless you're Bobby Orr, who had the highest plus in history, as we know. He was plus-128. When I tell guys that, they don't believe it because now, most of the time, the guy who leads the NHL is between plus-40 and plus-50.

Can you imagine? Plus-128! By the way, as I've said many times, he had 46 goals, 89 assists, plus-128, fought a lot that year, hit a lot that year and blocked a lot of shots. What more can you do?

* * *

I must admit that I am a sauna addict. I have to have a sauna every day.

We have actually checked into hotels during the playoffs and MacLean has asked, "Is there a sauna in the place?"

He actually doesn't like them. But if the guy says no, he says, "Well, we have to check out."

We've got in cabs and gone around until we find a hotel with a sauna. I can't feel good unless I have a sauna.

* * *

Eddie Shore was a very rich man. He invested in the Ice Follies and made a lot of money. So he was very wise, but not a very nice guy. He did things to hockey players that should never have been done, but we all wanted to play so bad, we'd put up with it.

He'd been a great player himself in the NHL's early days. He was born in 1902 and he was on the first Boston Bruins team to win the Stanley Cup, in 1929. He won the Hart Trophy four times and the Bruins thought so much of him that near the end of his career, they let him manage and play for the Springfield Indians while he was still playing for the Bruins in the NHL.

One time, he said to me, "Mr. Cherry, if you can visualize it, in reality, your manoeuvrability is nil." I thought that was pretty good. He also once said, "You know, Mr. Cherry, a hockey stick, in most players' hands, is a scientific tool. In your hands, it's a blunt instrument."

One time, there was a practice, and Eddie was talking to me and giving me lectures as usual—yelling at me, as he always did, calling me Mr. Cherry. So anyway, he's givin' me heck, and at the end of the practice, he says, "Cherry and Duane Rupp (another Black Ace), you can stay on."

If you can believe it, he made us skate around and around and around. He even turned the rink lights low so he would save electricity. Rupp and I skated around and around that day for four and a half hours. Four and a half hours! A lot of people think your legs get tired. No, your back gets tired.

He kept comin' out of his office to check on us all the time. The guys brought us some tea with honey to keep us both goin'. So when it was all over, I went up to him and I said, "Eddie, why did I deserve that?"

He said, "When I was talkin' to you, you looked away and looked at the clock."

What happened was, there was a big clock in the arena, and it was right behind his head. I guess my eyes strayed to the clock, and for that, I went four and a half hours!

Another time—a player tells me; I wasn't there—he was walking out of the arena, and it was dark and he heard this voice hollerin' at him, "Young man! Young man! Would you please move that ladder?"

He's looking around and he can't see anybody. Finally, he looks up, and there in the rafters is Eddie! In the dark! He had been changin' light bulbs with a big, tall ladder and the ladder had slipped. There's Eddie hanging from the girder with one arm. Who knows how long he had been there?

You have to give Eddie credit, though. When he got on the ice, he was really unbelievable. He was really somethin' to see. He was so good that he said he'd show us somethin'. He took the laces out of his skates and skated backwards as fast as most of us could skate frontwards. He could even tap dance. I can only imagine just how wonderful he was as a player.

But as a coach and manager and owner, he was dictator. And not just to us.

One time, we thought we'd scored a goal in a game in Springfield. The goal judge put the red light on, and the referee—now, this is the American Hockey League—overruled the goal judge and called it no goal.

Eddie went down and got the mike—for the public-address system, so that the entire crowd can hear it, if you can believe it!—and started chastising the referee. He told both goal judges to leave, and said that from now on, he wasn't going to have goal judges in the building. He said, "What's the sense of having goal judges if the referee is going to overrule them?"

* * *

I was involved in the first goal ever scored by a goalie in the National Hockey League—sort of, as they say.

I was coaching in Colorado, and we were playing the Islanders. Billy Smith was in the net for them and we had a delayed penalty. So Rob Ramage, who was on the point playing the right side, he goes in, and for some reason, he's behind Billy Smith. Somebody took a shot and Billy Smith deflected it, but he didn't have possession, so the play kept going. The puck went to Ramage and he put it back to the right point—but that's where *he* should have been!

Unfortunately, nobody had filled in for him.

I can see the puck goin' down the ice, but it's a 3–2 game and I won't look. Wilf Paiement was lookin' at it.

I said, "Is it goin' in, Wilf?"

He says, "Yeah. Tie game."

Rob Ramage put it in his own net, but Billy Smith was the last guy to touch it, so he became the first goalie to score a goal.

It wasn't really a goal like the one Ron Hextall scored later on when he shot the puck himself. But they counted it.

* * *

When I played for the Sudbury Wolves in junior, we had a trainer, an American guy, who was a wise guy. I knew they were gonna shave him 'cause he was a rookie, so I went to him and I said, "Look, whatever they do, go along with it. They're gonna do somethin'. Don't fight it, because the more you fight, the more they'll get determined and they'll hurt you."

He thought he knew it all. He was a baseball guy. He went on to be a pretty good baseball trainer afterwards. But no, he had to fight them and he was still fightin' them when unfortunately, they broke his arm.

And you know what? After they broke his arm, they still shaved him.

It was pretty brutal back in those days.

* * *

One time when I was playin' for Springfield, we were training in Niagara Falls and we had the son of a famous hockey player who'd played for Montreal. And he thought that because his father was famous, he was a famous hockey player too. He wasn't, but he put on the airs and acted like he knew everything. I knew this kid was in trouble.

Sure enough, I was in the room (and I didn't do it—not that I'm chicken or anything, I just didn't believe in it) when they grabbed him. Again, he fought, which is a big mistake. You're better off to just go along with it. They were rasslin' around, and there were hot-water radiators in the room, that's how old the building was. In the process of rasslin' with them, his behind went up against the hot radiator. It burnt his behind, and you could see the marks where he had been up against the radiator.

They got him down—and he's cryin' now with pain—and they took some of that stuff that football players put under their eyes, only it was blue, and put it all over his body. All over his body! And you couldn't get it out, even with a shower. The more water you put on it, the more it seemed to sink in.

He was just married and he had to go home like that.

I was the last guy out. He was over in the corner of the shower, trying to get the stuff off with hot water. The rink was empty. Everybody had gone and he was crying.

It was a sad sight. They were tough.

* * *

I never did believe in hazing like that, but not everybody got it. It seemed that if you were a good guy, the players would leave you alone, but if you were a wise-ass rookie, you'd get it. It's funny, too, that none of the real tough rookies were ever hazed.

The first year I coached the Bruins, they hazed two rookies. I saw it. They tied the rookies up, blindfolded them, got big pails, put spaghetti in the pails, put their feet in it and told them that the pails were full of worms. The guys went crazy. There were other things I won't mention they did in the hazing that were even more disgusting.

That was the last hazing for the Bruins while I was there.

I never liked hazing, except once while in Rochester in my last year. We had a young guy come down from the NHL and he thought he was too good for us. It was obvious from the way he acted and the things he said. He was the most obnoxious little jerk I ever met.

He had only one good thing going for him: he had lovely hair and he was so proud of it. The guys held him down and shaved the front of his head. He looked like Sky Low Low, the midget wrestler, if you remember him. The guy cried and was going to have us arrested for assault.

Today, the rookie initiations are a lot more civilized. The team goes out for dinner and the bill goes to the rookie—or rookies, if they're lucky. It can still be $3,000 apiece. In fact, some of the bills got so high that Gretzky put a limit on it after a while.

I'm glad the brutal hazing is over. I actually saw it affect players. Most guys shook it off, but a few guys were never the same again.

P.S. on the hazing: When shaving a guy down around his privates, somebody has to do the job. One time, after a hazing, we were having a few pops and I kidded a guy and said, "Hey Jim, I notice you really enjoy shaving these guys. You're always at the front of the line to do the job. I guess you like fooling around with guys down there."

He went wild.

* * *

I'm asked a lot who was the scariest guy that I coached—and I had some beauties, I'll tell you. I could go through the list: Bobby Schmautz, Terry O'Reilly, Al Secord, Stan Jonathan, John Wensink, Wayne Cashman. But the guy that nobody really fooled with was a guy that played for me in Colorado, Wilf Paiement.

This guy had those eyes like Schmautzie, and I'll tell you, you didn't fool with this guy. He was the nicest guy off the ice, as a tough guy usually is, but nobody fooled with him. There was a pest called Dennis Polonich, played for Detroit. He made the mistake of bothering Wilf, and Wilf carved him pretty bad. They had a lawsuit, and I hear it cost him a ton of dough.

* * *

One time when I was coachin' the Bruins, they traded for a great big guy with a beard. They traded for him from Colorado. He kept tellin' me, "That Paiement, I'm gonna get him."

So we played Colorado and I put him on the wing when Paiement was out, and he never even looked at Paiement. He knew what he was doing.

I was disgusted with the guy. He had been yappin' to the guys about what he was gonna do to Paiement, and the next day, he was in the showers and he hollers, "Hey, Grapes! Listen, I know you don't like beards. I'll shave mine off if I'm stayin'."

I said, "You keep your beard on," and all the guys laughed.

* * *

I've seen a lot of fights and I've seen a lot of guys hurt and I've seen a lot of guys carried off. But I've never forgotten a fight that John Wensink had against the Halifax Voyageurs when Al MacNeil, a Stanley Cup winner, was the coach. It was in Rochester and one of my good friends, Rod Graham from Kingston, was in a fight with a guy. They were goin' at it pretty good and Rod got the guy down, hurt the guy pretty good, and both of the linesmen got tied up with this fight.

So a big guy, about six foot two or three, comes up and grabs Wensink from behind. John turned around and did a number on him! It was so bad, I was rooted. My toes actually curled. I thought he'd killed the guy. They had to carry the guy off. It was so bad that, after the game, a detective came, put John in handcuffs, took him in a room and questioned him. The detective told me after that while they were questioning him, John was eating a sandwich that was left over from the press room.

I was terrified, 'cause I thought Wensink had killed that one guy, and the guy that Graham had fought was badly hurt too. So after the game, I go to the emergency ward at the hospital and they're both lying side by side. One guy could hardly speak, and neither could the other guy. It was the most brutal beating I've ever seen on both of them.

So I felt like having a drink, and I go to the Downtowner in Rochester. The general manager of St. Louis is there. Now, the Blues still own John and he's sayin', "That's the way to fight."

I said, "I don't know. I think John went too far this time. I'm backin' him up, naturally, in the paper, but there's a time that you've got to stop."

He says, "No way. That's the way to fight."

So I pick up the paper the next day and there's the general manager saying, "Yes, it was a brutal beating. John has to learn when to take it easy and not be so aggressive."

I'm thinking, "The night before, he's telling me what a great thing it was."

Some people in hockey are strange. I must have made him think twice about that.

* * *

John Wensink and I are in the rink and the lights are turned down. In the American league, they turn the lights down when here's not a game. Not off, just down.

I'm with John in front of the net, saying, "You gotta stand in front of the net like this, John, and take the guy like this."

I'm pushing him a bit to show him what to do, and you know how you get into one of those deals where you push a guy a little too hard and he pushes you back? You start to get into it. And it's "Oh yeah?" and "Oh yeah?"

So we're banging back and forth and I'm spearing him and he's knockin' me down, and unbeknownst to us, the Richmond Robins had come in for the game the next night. They're standing in the dark, watching the coach and one of the players on the other team beat each other up in front of the net.

They never had a chance that next night.

* * *

When I had my *Grapevine* television show, I happened to have Rick Tocchet and Marty McSorley on at the same time. In between shows, Marty was sittin' at the one end of the bar. It was a fake bar, but he was sittin' at the one end, talkin' to somebody, and I was sittin' at the other end, shootin' the breeze and waitin' for the show to start with Rick. He was with Philadelphia at the time.

During the conversation, I happened to say, "Did you ever go with Marty?"

He said, "Naw, we got Brownie to take care of him." He was talkin' about Dave Brown.

Somehow, Marty heard him. Or he thought he heard somethin', and he came down. How he could hear with the noise goin' on, I don't know.

He says, "What'd you say?"

"Aw, nuthin'."

"What'd you say? Do you want to go right here?"

So they went back in the kitchen—and they were big guys. I'm standin' there, and I said, "Look you guys, you can't do it here. Wouldn't that be nice? I invite you and you're gonna do that? You're gonna make me look bad." I had to say somethin'."

So Marty said, "I won't forget this."

Tocchet said, "Aw, shove it in your ear."

And that was the end of it. Two great guys.

Later on, they became teammates with the Los Angeles Kings and became good friends. The only disagreement they had there was when Marty stopped Rick from punching out another LA player, Dmitri Khristich, after he had played another one of his lazy, no-hit games.

* * *

Another tough guy was Bob "Battleship" Kelly. This was in warmup. As everybody knows, each team has about twenty or twenty-five pucks, and you take shots. This was in Rochester, and somehow or other, our shots all went out into the stands and we didn't have any more pucks.

Battleship Kelly went down into the other team's end—I think it was Baltimore—pushed their goalie out of the way and took six of their pucks and skated back with them. Now, that's tough!

* * *

I loved goin' to public school in Kingston, and the reason I loved goin' was because they played baseball, and most of all, we played hockey. It was just great.

The fire hydrant was right next to the rink, and the firemen were great guys. They'd flood the ice for us, but it had to be shovelled first—and it got so it was always the same three guys who did the shovellin': Ed Birchall, Les Ulman and myself. Nobody else would help, but they'd all take advantage of the rink.

So we complained to the assistant principal, and he got up in the assembly, and I guess he was gonna try to embarrass us. He said, "There's three young boys here who have a complaint. Would one of them like to come up and express their complaint?"

Well, none of us had ever spoken in public before, and none of us had ever got up and addressed the assembly. When none of us made a move, everyone laughed.

I said to myself, "Laugh at us, will ya?" So I got up and I walked up to the front of the assembly hall. I was awful nervous. But I lambasted the whole school as a lazy bunch of nobodies and I said, "If you don't wanna work, stay off the ice," and I kept goin and goin'.

Finally, the vice-principal had to come up to me, and I remember his exact words: "That will be enough, Donald."

* * *

It didn't help. Les and Ed and I still did all the work. We even painted the red and blue lines. One morning, the three of us were up early, about 6 A.M. We got the ice cleared, and I was painting the red line with a bucket of red paint.

We'd been workin' on the ice for quite a while when two guys and two girls come up and started to make fun of us. The two girls were wearing lovely white parkas. They were hollerin', "Hey, Cherry. That line is crooked."

I never said a word. I kept goin' and they're still yellin': "Hey Cherry, you got a crooked line there. Smarten up."

I'm going along and I'm gettin' closer to them. Now I was right near them and I loaded up the brush with red paint and fired it at 'em. Got 'em all! Splattered 'em all with red paint, and I said, "How's the line now?"

Needless to say, they were bawling and crying. They ran into the school shouting and screaming. Also needless to say, I was brought into the principal's office and strapped. I guess I deserved it, but somehow, in my young mind, it wasn't fair. Here we are, up at 6 A.M., doing a good job getting everything ready. These wise guys come along and make fun of us, then use the ice. To me, they just asked for it. And I get strapped!

Little did I know then that this attitude would get me into a lot of grief in the future. But what the hell? I got them pretty good, and to see them bawling, it was worth the strapping.

* * *

Captain Jack Cherry was my grandfather, and I'm very proud of his life. When he was 17, he joined the Canadian militia to defend the country against the Fenians.

It wasn't really a war, because war was never declared. But the Fenians were Irish-Americans who kept attacking Canada from the United States to try to get the British out of Ireland. It may not have been called a war, but we were under attack from armed raiders. So, to the people in it, it was a war.

The raids went on from 1866 to 1871 before the Fenians were defeated.

Two years later, my grandfather joined the Northwest Mounted Police.

Joseph "Buffalo Joe" Healy is the co-coordinator of the Royal Canadian Mounted Police gravesite database. He helps maintain the RCMP's history and has a website that honours former Mounties. In May 2008, he started a "Vet of the Month" feature, and his selection to start the program was Captain Jack.

Here is how Buffalo Joe described it:

To commemorate the 135th anniversary of the RCMP on May 23rd, 2008, we take time to remember a man who was among the first to join the North West Mounted Police (NWMP) in 1874 and who rode in the March West. With so many others, he faced the unknown challenges of the Canadian west and did his duty as a Mounted Policeman. He's our first Vet of the Month.

Our Vet was born and raised in Kingston, Ontario. At 19 years of age, he successfully joined the NWMP. One can speculate about his desire to join the NWMP; he may have been seeking work or perhaps he wanted to travel or perhaps he heard about the opening of the Canadian west and was looking for adventure.

He enlisted in the NWMP at Kingston on March 28th, 1874, as Regimental #0165. Soon after in Toronto, it is known that Commissioner French warned the early recruits of the dangers that lay ahead. He said: " . . . I plainly told them that they would have, and must expect, plenty of hardship; they might be wet day after day, and have to lie in wet clothes; that they might be a day or two without food, and that I feared they would often be without water, and I called on any present who were not prepared to take their chances of these privations to fall out . . . There were plenty of good men to take their places."

Our young and gritty recruit did not quit. Within three months, he was squadded into "F" Division—the last Troop in the column of men which formed the March West. He rode a bay steed and he resolutely completed the journey from Fort Dufferin, Manitoba to present day Alberta, a distance of over 900 miles.

Our Vet's Police Service Record is sparse. However, we are still able to gain a glimpse into his career and garner a sense of his personality from the details that are available. Also, we can place him in context as much is known about the difficulties faced by both the early pioneers and the police patrols who sought to tame the West.

Accounts tell of the exhaustion of the NWMP men as they plodded westward. They worked without proper food, equipment or rest. Uniforms were ill-fitted and of poor quality offering little protection from the unpredictable weather. Whenever they could sleep it was on ant-infested ground.

In addition to foul weather, bugs and flies tormented both horse and rider. Stories are told whereby horses had to be destroyed by their police owners because of the unendurable torture suffered due to clouds of flies which got into the animals' nostrils and eyes. Indeed men suffered as well, and neither doctors nor dentists were available to ease pain and cure illness. Such were the conditions faced by our recruit.

Strict military discipline was not a strong attribute of most of the early NWMP recruits. Our Vet certainly fell into that category and very likely he found the adjustment into police ranks very difficult and testy. Early in his career, he had several charges brought against him by Senior Officers.

In July, 1874, he was charged with: "Not complying with an order" and fined $3.00. In August, 1874, he faced three more disciplinary charges, including: "Insolence," ($2.00 fine), "Disobedience of an order by riding in a wagon" ($2.00 fine) and "Neglect of duty in allowing a horse to get away" (fine $10.00). In September, 1874, he was again cited for another "Disobedience of an order" and fined $15.00. Given that he was making [75 cents] a day, one can see that he had trouble saving any of his earnings. As the fines increased, it also seems that our constable changed his ways as there were no more disciplinary matters noted in his record.

He served in the NWMP for three years and 44 days before taking his discharge, at Fort Macleod as "time expired" on May 11th, 1877. In the NWMP, at that time, all members served for a specific period of time and if they were not interested in further service, then their "time expired" and they were discharged accordingly. Upon his discharge at age 22, he appeared slight of build and stood at 5'11" tall. His eyes were grey, his hair was brown and his complexion was described as "fresh." One can get a fairly good visual image of our Vet from this description.

Vet of the month is Sub/Constable John T. Cherry, [a] brave and gritty figure.

I'm not sure how old he was, because in these old accounts, the numbers don't always add up and in those days, they never made you show proof of age.

One story in particular got me. Captain Jack, although he was offered 180 acres of land in Manitoba, returned to Kingston and became a sailor, then a captain of a ship, the *Holcomb*, and for twenty-two years he sailed the St. Lawrence River. When he died in 1920, the *Kingston Whig-Standard* devoted a long story to him, with the headline, DISTINGUISHED CAPTAIN SUCCUMBS. The write-up said he never lost a shop or had a wreck in twenty-two years.

One night, in a hurricane, Captain Jack got caught in open waters. He raced for safety in a bay and dropped anchor. Between the current and the wind, the *Holcomb* was spinning around in circles on the anchor chain all night. It was a harrowing experience, because they never knew if the chain would break and they would be wrecked on the shore.

Now, here is the strange part of this story: my dad never told me of my grandfather being in the Fenian raids or that he was in the Northwest Mounted Police, and he only said in passing he was the captain of a ship. I only found out when the CBC did a story on me for a show called *Who Do You Think You Are?* and went back into my family's history.

* * *

My other grandfather, Private Richard Palmountain, volunteered for the army at 36 years old and was at Vimy. Also serving in the First World War was Sergeant Thomas William Mackenzie, a relative of mine on my mother's side. He was in the First Brigade, Canadian Field Artillery. He was killed on November 7, 1918, just four days before the armistice on November 11.

Imagine, he survived the whole war, then was killed with just four days to go. Sergeant Mackenzie won the Military Medal and bar. He was 28 years old when he was killed and is buried in France.

* * *

One day, my mother saw me comin' down the street and she said, "Why don't you walk like your father? Your father walks with his back straight, head up high. He has sort of a swagger to him. When you walk, it looks like you're saying, 'Here's my head. My ass is coming.'"

When you're a kid, it kinda hurts when your mother talks to you like that, so I exaggerated it from then on. I walked straight up with my head back and it was more than a swagger, it was an arrogant swagger.

I tick off some people, I guess, the way I walk, but it got to be a habit. No matter what I did, I would take my time, and as a matter of fact, when I walk through airports or I walk through shoppin' malls with MacLean, he's always ten feet ahead of me because I have to walk this way. My mother instilled it in me.

But she lived to regret it. The day I was getting my confirmation, and the bishop was there at St. Luke's Church, my name was called and I swaggered. You're supposed to walk kinda humble, but I swaggered up to the bishop as if I was sayin', "Here's me."

My mother said afterwards, "Why did you have to walk that way to meet the bishop? You looked like an arrogant little so-and-so. I could have kicked you right in the bum."

I said, "Maw, that's the way you wanted me to walk, and that's the way I walk."

* * *

My best friend growing up in Kingston was a Kingstonian, naturally, named Mel Price. Mel grew up a couple of blocks from me, but I didn't know him when we were young. In those days, you had a couple of close friends and that was it. As we grew up, I went away from Kingston to Barrie to play for the Flyers, and Mel joined the army at 16. He was in the Airborne, the best and toughest group on any service. Every week, the regiment had a contest to pick the sharpest soldier. The prize was a weekend pass. Mel won fifty-one weeks out of fifty-two. He was the guy they always called on when they wanted to put on a show because he looked the sharpest—and *was* the sharpest.

One year at the CNE, he was the soldier who was going to show the crowd what it was like to be a paratrooper. He stood on a platform two hundred feet up, with a cable running to the ground. Mel was going to strap on to the cable and slide down and land like a paratrooper.

Well, he jumped off the tower and he's zipping along, but suddenly, it got stuck halfway down. He's dangling a hundred feet above crowd. People were afraid for his life, but he treated it like a true paratrooper. All he thought about was how embarrassing this was for the Airborne.

I first met Mel when I was 21 and working in construction for the Kingston PUC, the Public Utilities Commission. He had got out of the army and was a low labourer like me. We were part of the strong-back-and-weak-minds detail. We were on the jackhammer.

It was tough work, and to this day, both of us have trouble with our ears. There was no ear protection back in those days, and we did eight hours a day on the jackhammer.

When we would break for lunch, our gloves would stay on the gun like they were hands. They would not move. We'd just pull our hands out and when we came back from lunch, the gloves would be there, ready to go.

One time, we had our own little truck with the compressor for the guns, and we would go from job to job, doing the hard work. I was havin' a ball. Life was tough, but I was young, never thinkin' of the future, doin' construction in the summer and playin' hockey in the winter. I thought I was gonna play forever. Mel was a little better than I was. Even though we both started out as labourers, Mel rose steadily through the ranks. He became a lineman, then he was a lead man, then a foreman, then a supervisor and then the head guy.

I, on the other hand, sailed through life happy and dumb. I never thought of the future. I was going to play forever.

* * *

Rose and I had a grand time with Mel and Bev, his lovely wife. Our big night—and players today would laugh at this—was Saturday night, when we'd sit in the parlour at his grandmother's house and have a few pops. Mel would make tuna sandwiches with tomatoes and he'd put them in a steamer. We had a simple life, but we had a lot of fun.

One of our fun nights was when we'd get our paycheques on Friday night. On the way home, we'd always stop for a few in the tavern. We called it a tavern, but technically, it was a "beverage room," and at that time, it was for men only. In there, all you ever heard was laughter, and all you saw was smoke. They used to close it at six o'clock so everybody would go home for their supper, then they'd open again at seven-thirty. They had another room for the women so they could enjoy themselves as well. It was the "ladies and escorts" room. It was the same size as the other room, but that wasn't enough. The women's libbers said, "No. You cannot have something for men only. We have to be involved." You know how governments are. They have to be politically correct, so they stopped all the fun and abolished the men-only rooms.

Maybe that's when I started to dislike political correctness.

* * *

Mel followed a different route than I did. He was a go-getter. Mel was going to get ahead. In his off-hours, he used to renovate homes. He turned himself into a plumber, an electrician and a carpenter.

Mel was with me when I got involved in one of those episodes that all hockey players go through when they go back to their hometown after the season. It's usually from a guy who wanted to be a hockey player and didn't make it, and was jealous. If you were drinking with one of these guys, after a few pops, he'd show his true colours.

I was just back from one of my seasons with Rochester, and Mel says, "Do you want to go to the Shamrock and have a few pops?"

It was a tavern, and off we go, happy-go-lucky, and we sit down. I was shootin' the breeze, tellin' him all about the championship with the Rochester Americans and how great I was, and he was filling me in on all the gossip that was goin' on with the PUC. We were havin' a grand time talking about those years on the jackhammers, having a lot of fun.

A couple of guys were pullin' up their chairs. They were usually Mel's friends. I noticed this one guy, when it was his turn to buy the round, conveniently had to make a phone call or had to go to the washroom. Well, in hockey, this is a no-no. You're called on this pronto, but we're among friends and I didn't want to spoil the session. I'm not happy—it goes against my hockey tradition—but what the hell? I'll let it go.

This guy wanted to be a hockey player, but he didn't make it, and sure enough, he starts the routine. "Well, you might be a hockey player, but I've got my own plumbing company. I'm making a lot of dough." And he goes on and on about how much dough he had. Then he says, "I'm solid, but what are you gonna do when you're through with hockey?"

I don't want any trouble. I just say, "Who knows?"

He goes on. "You don't have an education. You don't have a trade. You've really got nothing. So you're a hockey player. Big deal. I'm so glad I didn't become a hockey player like you. I'm making a ton of dough."

I'd had enough. I said, "Oh yeah? If you've got all this dough put away, how come you haven't bought a round since you sat down, you cheap bastard? Every time it's your turn to buy, you disappear for some reason.

"So here's what I'm telling you, buddy. I'm gonna go to the washroom. If you're here when I come back, I'm gonna put your head through that wall. Got it?"

Mel is a real nice guy, and he's very upset. He follows me to the washroom and he says, "Don, that wasn't a very nice thing. I didn't mind paying for his rounds."

Mel is a nice guy, like Ron MacLean. He would say nothing. They just don't understand the way of the world. It's an insult to do that.

Mel said, "That's all right for you, Don, but when you leave to go back to hockey, I'm still here and these are my friends."

I said, "Well, Mel, that's just too bad, because in my world, everybody pays his own way and if that guy is still there when we get back, I'm gonna put his head through the wall."

He wasn't there. I was disappointed.

Mel and I don't see each other as much as we'd like to. We see each other once in a while when I go to my cottage in the summer. I often think about the jackhammer days, laughing and joking in the taverns, tuna burgers and a few pops. Life was so simple and so much fun. I miss those days.

* * *

Mr. Cornwell was our neighbour when I was a teenager. He was a painter and a decorator, and he worked alone. His speciality was Victorian homes in Kingston. There were many of them, and they were owned by very rich people who were very fussy.

One summer, when I was 16, he asked me if I would be his assistant. That was quite an honour because before, he had always worked alone. So that summer, Mr. Cornwell and I worked together. I would do the bull work like sanding, scraping old wallpaper off the walls and filling in the cracks. On the painting, I would do the primer coat and he would do the details. He was an artist.

The people who owned these homes were very particular in their taste. One room we worked on for two weeks. It was light green, and I thought it was beautiful. The lady of the house, her name was Mrs. Wolfe, came in and took one look and said, "Do it again."

We did it again. We were not upset, because we knew these people. They just wanted what they wanted. That's the way the rich are. The rich are different than you and I.

Mr. Cornwell did first-class work. That's why he was hired by these people. But he worked when he felt like it. If we were working outside and he didn't feel like working, he'd look at the sky, find a cloud and say, "Donald, it looks like rain. We'll have to take the day off." But even taking all these days off, we were still making really good money because Mr. Cornwell was so good.

One Saturday, I was supposed to be working, but Mr. Cornwell had seen a cloud and we took the day off. I went back to bed.

My father came home from work at noon, as he did on Saturday mornings.

I must admit, I'd gotten used to going over to Mr. Cornwell's to go to work and having him bring up the cloud issue. It got so I was happy not to work, because I could go back to bed.

But this Saturday, I heard my dad come in and start talking to my mom.

"Did Donald go to work today?"

"No."

"Why not?"

"Something about rain."

I looked out the window, and the sun was shining. It was a lovely day. I knew I was in trouble.

After lunch, Dad says, "I want you to change jobs."

I says, "But why, Dad? I'm makin' good money."

"Tomorrow, I want you to go see a person I know, Abe Jelly. He's got a job for you on the railroad."

There was no sense in arguing, so the next day, I go down to Abe Jelly's apartment. He was the foreman and he tells me to report to the Cataraqui section at 7 A.M. I show up at six-thirty at the shack. It's all covered inside with chains, jacks, iron bars, picks and shovels. I can see I'm a long way from Mrs. Wolfe's house.

The other workers started appearing, and the only way I can describe them is to say that if you happened to see the movie *Deliverance*, where the mountain men attacked Burt Reynolds and his crew, you know what I mean. These guys were tall and thin, and they had come out of the woods north of Kingston. They were the spitting image of the guys in *Deliverance*. They had the plaid shirts with the sleeves rolled up. They chewed tobacco and smoked, and they were still half in the bag from drinkin' the night before. I don't think their shirts had been washed in weeks. They were skinny and tough as nails, and they looked at me, this punk kid standing there in this freshly washed white T-shirt, with disdain.

I was now a member of the notorious section gang, one step away from the chain gangs in the southern U.S., only these guys looked a lot meaner and tougher, particularly this one guy who stared at me with hatred. I couldn't figure it out. He had only seen me for a minute. Nobody said anythin' to me. They just looked at me. Mr. Jelly came in and just said, "Let's go."

We climbed aboard one of those little carts that you see on the railroads, sixteen of us, and away we go.

We go and we go. It's bakin' hot and we're out in the middle of nowhere. No trees. No nothin'. With our picks and shovels, our jacks and chains, and what I call the killer iron bars, we start. It's a tough go, and the only break we get is to get a drink, or when a train goes by. I always envied those guys who were on the back of the caboose who would wave to us as the train pulled away.

I'm sweating tons and drinkin' lots of water. Mr. Jelly says, "I'd take it easy on that, kid." Nobody ever called me by name. Just "kid."

Well, I didn't listen to his advice. I drank and drank and died that night with cramps.

I feel lousy the next mornin', but I gotta go in. I don't have any choice. I gotta go in or they would all have had a laugh at me if I didn't. The next day, it's the same thing. And the next day. I was so tired when I got home, I would fall asleep with my clothes on.

Mom would ask, "What's the matter? Why are you so tired?"

I'd just say, "Oh, no reason."

When we were comin' in at the end of the day on that little car, I could see yellow spots before my eyes. My bike had broke, so to get to and from work, I had to borrow my brother's bike, which was much smaller. I had my work boots on, and when I turned, my boots hit the fender and I fell off. I was so tired, I just lay there. A fellow came running up to help me. He thought I was hurt. I wasn't hurt. I was just exhausted and embarrassed.

But I started to get the hang of it a little. I was still bad, but I passed. Barely.

I think the workers disliked me because they knew my dad had got me the job and I wasn't earning my keep. I guess I can't blame them. I probably would feel the same way in their position.

We worked every weekday and then we had to work a half-day on Saturday. We were supposed to have an easy time with the work on Saturday, but you know what the work was? It was unloading ties from a boxcar. Those ties were soaked in creosote, so the ants and termites wouldn't get in them and eat them once they were laid down. That creosote would burn your arms if you started to sweat.

And if you've ever been in a boxcar in summer, you know that the temperature goes up over 100 degrees Fahrenheit. And this was supposed to be our easy day. Oh, Mr. Cornwell, where are you?

I'm surviving. Not very good, but I'm surviving.

For some reason, the guy that looked at me with hatred in my first minute keeps givin' me little barbs with no let-up. He looked like Ichabod Crane. One day, we're havin' lunch and he starts again. He says, "I hear you're gonna be a hockey player. You don't look like a hockey player to me. I could run you into the ground."

I'm thinkin', "Now wait a minute. This guy is always smokin'. He's always chewin' tobacco. It runs down the side of his mouth." I've been running because I'm goin' to the Boston Bruins rookie camp, so I said, "All right, let's go."

He says, "I'll give you a twenty-yard head start."

So I take off and I thought I was really smokin' along. I look over my shoulder and he's comin' on like Roger Bannister. With those big, long strides, he buried me. I ran until my lungs burned, but I have to admit, I was helpless. He ran me into the ground! And he wasn't even breathin' hard.

Needless to say, they all laughed and I was even lower in their eyes than ever, if that was possible.

One day, we were changin' ties. To change a tie, you have a pick with a short blade on the end. You dig into the tie and you pull it up. You have to have a knack to do it, and of course, I haven't got the knack and I just can't get it.

My tormentor saw this. He came over and pushed me aside and said, "Get out of the way. You can't send a boy to do a man's job."

Now, I could be laughed at and I could be treated with disdain. In fact, as I look back, I don't blame them. But there are certain people in the world, you don't push. People like that are very dangerous people when they are pushed. I'm one of them, and he didn't read me right.

He had his pick down on the ground, and I knew I had him. I put my pick about two feet from his head. I said, "Say another word and I'll put this pick through your head."

With his pick on the ground, he couldn't defend himself. He started to say somethin', and I pulled my pick back a little farther to cock it and I said, "Go ahead."

It was a strange scene. The workers didn't say a word. They just gathered around in a circle. I think they were anxious to see somethin' happen. There was just the two of us and silence.

Finally, I said, "Go ahead. I'll put it right in your head."

He turned around and walked away.

I suppose you're thinking I was relieved. Not a bit. Not one bit.

I'd like to say that after that, I got treated with more respect. But I didn't. They still treated me with disdain, but they didn't mess with me anymore.

It was still a tough go, and to make it worse, I had to always keep my eye on this guy.

They were a tough group. They were called candy dancers. I didn't know why.

Let me describe the scene to you. There are sixteen guys with iron bars, about seven feet long, in their hands. They're lined up eight to a rail on each side. We had to straighten the rails. Mr. Jelly would be down the rails and would look to see if they were straight. He would direct us with a yell. These guys would start chanting, and on a certain word of the chant, we would all pull in unison. I guess it was like sailors when they're pulling on ropes. It was a strange scene— these guys, tough as nails, from the woods north of Kingston, singing a song.

Of course, I wasn't allowed to sing the song. Boy, I would have liked to.

I found out later that they were originally called gandy dancers because the picks and bars and stuff were made by the Gandy company. They were called dancers because of the singing and chanting. Over the years, gandy dancers became candy dancers.

They were a tough group. I started admiring them in a way, for their toughness. Even my tormentor, he had somethin'. They worked hard and they lived hard and they had an air about them.

I loved their swagger. I admired them because they could face this tough life day after day and never weaken.

One day, my mother was in my Uncle Bill's car and they were stopped at a railroad crossing. A crew of candy dancers was just down the tracks and my Uncle Bill said, "That's what Donald does."

Mom took one look and exploded. "He works like that? A 16-year-old boy with those men?" Mom ripped into Dad that night. How could he let his son do a job like that with those men? Dad only smiled. I had only two weeks to go before I went back to school, but Mom made sure I was finished on the railroad that week.

I went back to Mr. Jelly's apartment, and I tell him this is goin' to be my last week.

He said, "Okay, kid."

That's all he said. "Okay, kid." I don't think he ever knew my name.

My last day was on Friday. I didn't work Saturday morning. Nobody cared. Nobody said goodbye. I didn't expect it. So I get on my bike to go home. I come around a corner of the shack and who is in my way but my tormentor. He was leaning against the shed and he was lighting a cigarette. I'm thinkin', "Oh no. He was just waitin' for the last day to get me."

Fear was in the pit of my stomach. I actually felt sick to my stomach. But I laid my bike down, and he just cupped his hands around his cigarette to light it. He took a puff and through the smoke, just looked up at me and nodded.

He took another drag on his cigarette, took one last look, and walked around the corner of the building.

* * *

The Old North Church, I was a member there. That was where they hung the lantern to say the British were coming during the American Revolution—Paul Revere and all that. I used to go to communion early before our morning skate, and one Sunday, I was the only guy there. So when the minister come out, I said, "You don't have to have this service only for me."

He said, "No, we're not doing the service for you. We're doing it for the glory of God."

* * *

Some people wonder if I was disappointed by the movie about me, *Keep Your Head Up, Kid.* Well, there were one or two things.

Nothing's ever perfect, but I think that one of the biggest disappointments was about the music. When Randy Bachman said we could use some of his music, I was so happy. I had fought for him. The way I felt, we had to have a Canadian. I was on top of the world. We were gonna get "Takin' Care of Business" and "You Ain't Seen Nothin' Yet," but the big one that we wanted was the old Guess Who song, "No Time." I just love that song.

It was all set. That scene in the movie when we only had about a month to get the hockey team together and I sat out in the car, the music was gonna be, "No time left for you . . ." You know how it goes. So they shoot the scene, and it costs them thousands. We'd already given Randy Bachman $25,000 for about thirty seconds of "Takin' Care of Business." Not bad, eh?

I was all set to see Jared Keeso, who was playin' me in the movie, drivin' along in that old convertible of mine singing, "No time left for you . . ." So they shoot the scene, and I'm all excited, and after they shoot the scene we get a call from Randy Bachman's lawyer or agent, whatever he is. "You can't use 'No Time.'"

After all the thousands and thousands we've spent on the scene, he calls and says, "No, we don't think we want you to use it."

What a shame. It would have been perfect.

* * *

This is a story that happened to me on a plane when I was travellin' with *Hockey Night in Canada*. We were kind of in the middle, and we were all spread out. And in those days, if you remember, it was so ridiculous, you could smoke in the back of the plane.

I'm sitting there on the aisle, and all of a sudden this guy comes over and stands beside me, and he's smokin'. He's not supposed to be smokin' in that part of the plane, but he is, and boy, does he look like a weird guy! Kinda thin and tall. White as a ghost. He looked like he'd been on drugs or somethin'.

He's talkin' to me, all the time standing over me and blowin' smoke in my face. You could see he's lookin' for trouble. The stewardess was tellin' him to stop smokin' there and to get out of the aisle. He wouldn't. He just laughed at her.

Now he sits on the armrest and he's givin' me a hard time. I'm just lookin' at him. Now he stands up and he turns the cigarette in his hand and he's got the lit end pointin' right at my face. I know what he's gonna do. I know he's gonna try and stick the cigarette in my face, and if he tries that, I'm gonna have to drill him.

But I can't be the guy who starts anything, so what am I gonna do? I'm really sweatin'. I don't want a cigarette in the eye.

All of a sudden, I see two beefy hands reach over and grab him. Now everybody in the whole plane is terrified because this guy has taken over the plane. Behind us, you can hear this scuffle goin' on and thumps. Then it's quiet. But everybody is lookin' straight ahead because they don't wanna be involved—includin' me.

But I can't take it anymore. I let on I'm goin' to the washroom, and I go to the back of the plane, and there, sitting between two big tough-lookin' guys, is the guy that had been botherin' me. There's blood running from his nose.

Now he's just sitting there quietly. One of the big guys winked at me. I just went to the washroom.

Two or three years later, I'm in the airport and these two big guys come up to me and one says, "Grapes, do you remember the time that guy in the plane had the cigarette goin' in your eye?" Of course I did. He says, "We were the two guys who stopped him."

I says, "Thank goodness. How come you were on the plane?"

He says, "Well, we're detectives from Barrie, and we were flyin' to Chicago to pick up a prisoner and bring him back. We just happened to see this guy givin' you a hard time and thought we'd help."

I said, "Thank you, guys. You'll never know how scared I was."

Ya can't beat the police, especially Barrie's finest, and ya never know what you're gonna run into when you're out in public.

* * *

I've often mentioned that after my hockey career ended, I was in the doldrums with no job, no trade and no education. Then I got a chance as a coach, and one of the people who really helped me the most at that time was Dennis Ball, the chief scout of the New York Rangers.

Emile Francis, the Rangers' GM, helped me as well, because he liked my attitude of being the first person in the building every morning. I'd get there between seven o'clock and seven-thirty. For some reason, Dennis took a shine to me at the New York camp, and I know for sure that he influenced Emile. It was Dennis who got me the players. These players were the ones who didn't make the cut in Providence, the Rangers' number one farm team in the AHL. I got the leftovers. But Dennis made sure I got some pretty good players.

I wanted that Battleship Bob Kelly so bad I could taste it, but Dennis said I couldn't have him. Then later, when he phoned me and said, "Do you want Battleship Kelly?" I could've kissed him.

If it hadn't been for Emile Francis, who sent me nine players, I don't know what I would have done. Sure, he had to send them somewhere, but why send them to me? I'm sure it was because of Dennis. Dennis and Emile, they saved my bacon.

Thank you, Dennis. God love ya.

* * *

But the guy who helped me the most at that down period of my life and picked me up out of the pits was a guy by the name of Bob Clark. He was a lawyer in Rochester. He bought the Americans and hired me as general manager and coach. He trusted me and had confidence in me. He didn't panic when we were about eight days away from the season and didn't have enough players; he let me wait until Emile was starting to make cuts in the National Hockey League.

Bob Clark was also the guy who had me coach at the high school in Pittsford, New York, when I was unemployed. That's where I learned about coaching, and I was just as nervous changing lines with the high school team as I was when I went professional. That's where I learned how to do it.

I realize all that now, but sometimes you get carried away. I went to the National Hockey League and coached Bobby Orr and became a big star and was named coach of the year. A big shot, or so I thought I was. I'm ashamed to admit it, but I kinda forgot some of the guys in Rochester.

Then I got what was a great break when I look back on it. I got asked by Dave Andrews, who was the commissioner of the American Hockey League, if I would go down to Hershey and speak at the all-star banquet. First of all, I refused; then I said, "Hey, wait a minute. When I was a hockey player, that's where I spent a lot of my time." So I did go down and I spoke.

I thank God for this, because Bob Clark was in the audience, and I really spoke directly to him and told him how much I loved him and how he was the guy who pulled me out of my unemployment, and without him I wouldn't have had all the success that had come to me.

To this day, I think that's one of the biggest breaks I ever had, and I had really never said that before. I said it in front of all those people, and he was there. He came up afterwards and thanked me.

To this day, I am so happy I did that, because if it wasn't for Bob Clark, I really don't know what I'd be doin' today.

Sad to say, Bob died soon after that banquet.

* * *

I usually don't do this. This isn't a story that really happened to me, but it's a story that Ron MacLean told me after he had been talking to Dan Bylsma, the Stanley Cup–winning coach of the Pittsburgh Penguins.

Bylsma was a college guy, and one time, when he was playing for Greensboro in the East Coast Hockey League, there was another U.S. college guy on the team by the name of Davis Payne. The coach was Jeff Brubaker, who had been a real brawler in the NHL. He could really fight. Brubaker said to Bylsma and Payne, "Look, if you guys want to make the National Hockey League, you gotta be tougher. I'm gonna show you a few tricks."

So they drop the gloves and he's showing them a few tricks, and he's pushing them harder and harder. Finally, Davis Payne just cold-cocks Brubaker. He punches him right in the nose and bloodies his nose.

Brubaker stopped, paused and said, "God, that was good. That really was good. I just love it. I'd forgotten how great that felt."

That's the way fighters are. Even though they really get caught, they're so excited and feelin' so good that they really don't feel a thing.

My apologies to Dan, but I had to tell that story that MacLean told me. It's a dandy, and I know just how Jeff felt.

* * *

When I became GM and coach of the Rochester Americans, like I told you before, the team had eight owners. And they all had their opinions.

They were very distinguished businessmen who were in the

game of hockey because they loved the game. And they did take a chance buying the club. The previous owners, the Vancouver Canucks, had lost a ton of dough.

They knew the ins and outs of business, but not the ins and outs of owning a hockey team. Let me give you an illustration.

I had given them a budget for the club's salaries. We had a young defenceman that Boston had loaned us named Wayne Morusyk. He broke his ankle a month into the season, and I had to get another defenceman. Naturally, the salary of the defenceman I got was added to the payroll.

The owners, except for Bob Clark, were upset that I didn't keep to my budget. They said I was over the budget that I had set. They could not understand.

So I said to one of them, Joe Fox, the guy who owned Champion Knitwear, "Look, if you have a factory and you have a budget for the factory and one of your machines breaks down, you have to replace it and it's added to the budget for your factory, right? It's the same in hockey. Think of the players as machines that will break and you have to replace them."

Joe Fox said, "Yeah. That makes sense to me. I was just askin'."

* * *

Even though the Rochester franchise had been around since 1950, it was really on the ropes when Bob Clark and eight partners bought it.

The American Hockey League was gonna shut the team down for a couple of years to see if there was any interest. That's when Bob Clark and the others bought it, and I became coach and GM. And boy, we came back with a vengeance. The crowds came back so strong that when I looked up from the bench, I could not see cement. All I could see was human beings. All the seats were filled. They were all sitting in the aisles. They were standing at the back. The place was just jammed.

I got to know a city official pretty good, and he let us get away with this because, in the corner of the rink, there were spots for about twenty people, and that was his spot. There were mesh screens at the ends of the rink in those days, no glass, and you were right by the goalie. You were right in the action and you could hear the players shoutin' and stuff. That was the official's spot, so he used to just let us pack 'em into that building.

I know it was dangerous, but we had to make some money.

One day, one of the owners come along during a game. I won't mention any names, but it wasn't Bob Clark. This guy sees the city official and his friends and he says, "Why are you fellows standing here?"

The guy says, "Well, Don Cherry said we could."

He says, "I don't care what Don Cherry said. You can't stand here. Now move!"

The city official says, "I can't stand here, and my friends can't stand here?"

"No, you can't. Now move!"

The city official says, "Well, if I have to move, a lot more people are gonna move."

It cost us about two thousand fans a game.

* * *

It's July 5, 2010, and I'm sittin' at home, watching vintage hockey on Leafs TV. Yes, I watch hockey in the summer. I know some of you are saying "Get a life," but hockey *is* my life.

Joe Bowen, one of my favourite announcers, is interviewing Jim Pappin, one of my favourite hockey players and a teammate of mine in Rochester before he went to the Leafs. These two are discussing Jimmy's goal, the one that was the winning goal for the Leafs in 1967, the last time they won the Stanley Cup.

Everybody remembers George Armstrong's goal, but that wasn't the winning goal. He scored into the empty net and made it 3–1, and everyone remembers that one because it was in the last minute of the game.

Pappin's winner was sort of a fluky goal, I gotta admit. He threw a backhand in front of the net, and it hit a defenceman's skate and went in, so they never show that one.

Bowen said, "You seemed to score a lot of important goals in your career."

Jimmy listed off a few of them, and he said, "One time in Rochester, I got the winner because we won 3–0 and I got a hat trick."

That brought back memories.

Jimmy was a swell guy and a terrific hockey player, but he was very sulky. If he was in the open and the centreman had the puck, and Jimmy wanted the puck and the centreman didn't give it to him, I don't care if it was a three-on-one or a two-on-nothin', he'd go offside. Then he'd immediately go and sit on the bench and sulk. He'd go offside on purpose!

He was hard to manage, but what a hockey player. He'd fit perfectly in today's hockey. Imagine, he's six foot two, 200 pounds. He could skate, he was mean, he could score goals. He'd be worth about five million bucks a year now.

One year when he was with Rochester, we were in the playoffs against Cleveland, and it's a dogfight. They had a great player/coach called Fred Glover. He was a tough hockey player.

Jimmy was in one of his sulky moods, so Joe Crozier, our GM and coach, came to me and said, "I'm roomin' you with Pappin to straighten him out."

I said, "Wait a minute, Joe. I've been roomin' now for six years with Darryl Sly, and now you want me to room with Pappin and straighten him out? You're never gonna straighten this guy out. He's as sharp as a tack. It's ridiculous."

Joe says, "Nevertheless, you room with him and straighten him out."

So I'm in the room with Pappin, and it's just before our afternoon nap. He knows something's goin' on, so he says, "What's up?"

I says, "Can you believe it? Joe wants me to room with you to straighten you out. And besides, what a joke, me roomin' with you. You're not goin' that good. We don't need ya."

So it goes back and forth, and he's getting' madder and madder. He says, "I'll bet you twenty bucks I get at least two goals tonight."

Now, this is a lot of money in those days—we only got four bucks a day meal money—but I says, "You're on."

You shoulda seen the goals! The first two were screechers—him comin' down that right side and lettin' shots go into the top corner. The third goal, he gets a breakaway. He dekes to the left; he dekes to the right; he dekes to the goalie, whose jockstrap is still flyin' when Pappin just slides it home.

Now everybody jumps on him. This is the playoffs, and we're up 3–0 and he's in the middle of this crowd of guys all celebratin', and he looks over at the bench, sees me and gives me the finger!

He didn't mention *that* to Joe Bowen.

P.S.: He took the twenty bucks.

* * *

Jimmy was a tough guy to cross, I'll tell you. If you crossed him, or if he got ticked off, he was capable of doin' anything.

When we were in the playoffs, Crozier often took us to Batavia Downs, the harness racing track, just to get us away, and get us, as they say, bonding. It must have been a pretty good idea, because we won.

Jimmy had just bought a beautiful Cadillac. It wasn't new, but it was a beauty, and he had taken it in and had it painted baby blue. He loved it.

So we go to Batavia Downs, and as we're parking, another guy parks alongside us, opens his door and bangs Jimmy's door with his door.

Jimmy says, "No one get out of the car!"

So we stay where we are and the guy who banged his door into

Jimmy's car goes away. Jimmy gets out to take a look, and sure enough, his brand new paint job has been scratched.

He caved in the whole side of the guy's car with his foot.

* * *

Another time, we were playin' for Rochester and we drive up to Springfield, which was run by Eddie Shore. We get there about five-thirty, but Eddie Shore is so cheap, he won't let us into the building until six because he doesn't wanna turn the lights on. He tells us we have to sit for half an hour.

Now, Eddie used to have one of those beautiful 1967 Cadillacs with the big fins. At six, as we're getting out of the car with Jimmy, he says, "Just a minute." And he walked over and kicked in the side of Shore's car.

I was so scared of Shore from the days when I used to play for him, I ran into the building.

* * *

I struggled in the minors for more than twenty years, and I'm sorry to admit that I went through life with a chip on my shoulder the size of a log, always daring people to knock it off. It's a tough way to live, but in the world of the minors, the one I lived in, that was the attitude you had to have, or you'd get trampled.

I went nine years earning $4,500 a year. Never a raise in nine years. And in the tenth year, they cut my salary to $4,200! Eventually, after a few more years, I got up to $5,200.

Then, when I went to the Rochester Americans near the end of my career, the GM was Jack Riley, a good guy. He called me in and said, "Don, I'm raising your salary from $5,200 to $6,000." Holy smokes! Thanks, Jack. What a guy.

About twenty years later, Jack told me the only reason he did that was that he didn't have the nerve to sign a long-term veteran for

$5,200 when the lowest rookie from the Leafs was making $6,000.

I said, "Hey Jack, I don't care. I really appreciated it back then anyway."

Back in those days in the minors, you were only as good as your last shift. There were so many guys just waiting to take your job. In the American Hockey League, guys were fighting to get up to the NHL, and guys were fighting to get back after coming down from the NHL.

Me, I was just stayin' in the middle.

It was survival of the fittest, so you needed the chip-on-the-shoulder attitude. Today, it's called having an edge. It helped me survive. The problem with that was I carried it off the ice, too.

* * *

It was July 3, 2010, at about six-thirty in the morning. I was sitting alone at my cottage, having coffee, and I happened to notice a pamphlet at the bottom of my desk. It had been there for as long as I could remember—must have been twenty-five years. It had been sent by a guy named Jacques Lamiey who for some reason had been on a crusade to get me the Order of Canada. I finally had to put my foot down and tell him to stop. He was very, very hurt and I never heard from him again.

I opened up the pamphlet, and for the first time, I saw two write-ups of the game I played against the Montreal Canadiens in the 1955 playoffs, my one and only game in the National Hockey League. They were from the Montreal *Gazette*, and where Jacques got them, I don't know. Naturally, I had never seen them because the Bruins left by train right after the game, and we would have been back in Boston by the time the paper hit the streets.

In one of the stories, they talked about Rocket Richard getting a washing machine for being the second-leading scorer in the NHL in the 1954–55 season. They had a picture of him, and he was quite happy. Can you imagine giving one of those players today a washing machine for finishing second in the league in scoring?

The guy who did win the scoring title was Bernie Geoffrion. They booed him in the Forum because he passed Richard in the last couple of games in the season whie the Rocket was suspended. They never forgave him for taking the scoring title from the Rocket when it was his one and only chance.

Above the write-up there was a picture of me getting ready to cross-check Jean Béliveau as he was smacking Big John Henderson, our Boston goalie, to try to get the puck. Here's the cutline on that picture: "Don Cherry, rookie Boston defenceman up from Hershey in the American Hockey League for the playoffs, was a last-minute starter for the Bruins in place of Warren Godfrey whose injured wrist finally conked out on him. Cherry, who played a sound game, raised a welt on Béliveau's forehead when he charged the centre-man into the crossbar on the goal after Le Gros Bill took a couple of whacks at Henderson trying to dislodge the puck from his pads."

The other write-up was a column by the famous Dink Carroll of the *Gazette*. Dink wrote, "The Bruins uncovered a young defence-man called Don Cherry who looks like a good prospect. Harold 'Baldy' Cotton, the Bruins' chief scout said yes, they were counting on Cherry for next year."

Reading those write-ups for the first time really affected me. I just sat there staring into space thinking, "How could I have screwed up such a promising career?" How did I screw it up? I remember it was the happiest and most exciting time of my life. The coach, Milt Schmidt, started me. I played a regular shift and I played a pretty good game. The players accepted me on the train back to Boston. Best of all, my mom saw the game. She travelled from Kingston to see me play.

The world was my oyster, as they say. How was I to know that would be my one and only game in the NHL and I would spend twenty years in the minors?

I'm not complaining. As I look back, I was just asking for it with my up-yours attitude, and I paid the price. I'm just telling you how

I felt that early July morning when I saw the *Gazette* write-ups and how bright my future looked in hockey.

I can see those words now. "Sound game." "Good prospect." I can see the quote from Baldy Cotton saying, "Counting on Cherry for next year."

Damn.

It's so true. The cruellest words in the English language are "What might have been."

* * *

You know what bugs me about Ron MacLean? He always seems to be in good humour, which really ticks me off.

We have our routine, and we always follow it. There was only one time we almost didn't. It was about fifteen years ago and we were in Chicago. Ron was on the set, goin' through his notes, and we'd been goin' at it pretty good now for about a month and a half. I wasn't feeling too good, and in a moment of weakness, I suggested to Ron that we take it easy that night.

He looked up with look of pure shock on his face. He couldn't believe I would even consider not doin' a session that night!

"What?" he says. "Not have a cold pop in that great bar in the Drake Hotel?"

Of course he was right, and we did go to that bar in the Drake Hotel.

Of all my time in the business, that was my one moment of weakness. That was fifteen years ago, and MacLean has never let me forget it.

* * *

It was impossible to avoid watching the love affair between our left-wing media and soccer's World Cup in 2010. They kept telling us how much sexier soccer is than hockey, taking shots at hockey all the way through. There were stories suggesting that maybe Canada should rethink its passion for hockey as our number one sport. One writer said that we should take up soccer so you wouldn't have to take your kids to freezing arenas at 6 A.M. to practice. There were all kinds of stories about how soccer is so much better than hockey.

Why is it that the Canadian media dislike hockey so much? Could it be that the people in hockey are right-wing, God-fearing, middle-class taxpayers, the silent majority in this country? I will admit that they'll soon be the silent minority, but that's another story.

The media is relentless in its attacks on hockey, especially at the kids' level. Coaches are sued by parents, and it's a headline every time. It's a wonder we have any coaches at all. They are a great bunch of guys—and so dedicated. Every knock against hockey that comes up makes a big headline. And let's face it, folks, the only thing we're the best in the world at is hockey. So naturally, the left-wingers in the media never give it any credit.

Look at the NHL draft this year, 2010. The top five players taken in the draft were from the Canadian Hockey League. Nothing said at all. But can you imagine what would have happened if the top five had been from Europe? Or from America? Oh boy, you'd have seen the biggest headlines since World War II ended. We'd get roasted by the left-wing media.

It is so true of Canadians. We always eat our own.

And as far as soccer is concerned, it has been said that more people play soccer than any other sport in the country. It also has been said that more people eat rice than any other food in the world. The reason? It's the only thing available.

* * *

People often ask which Blue it is that people see at the start of "Coach's Corner" on *Hockey Night in Canada*.

Well, that's my first—and greatly loved—Blue, the apple of my eye. That Blue was with me from when I was an unemployed labourer, to coach and GM of the Rochester Americans, to coach of the Boston Bruins to coach of the Colorado Rockies, to being an unemployed coach, to *Hockey Night in Canada*. She was with me the whole way.

Then I got my second Blue, and she was with me eleven years. I have to admit, she wasn't one bit like my first Blue.

Now I have my third Blue. He's as tough as nails. One time, he tangled with a porcupine up at the cottage. I was away on the play-offs, and my wife, Luba, phoned me and told me that Blue's face was full of porcupine quills.

I said, "Of course you took him to the vet," because that's what everybody does up near Kingston when your dog tangles with a porcupine.

She says, "No, I just sat him down and pulled them out."

I said, "What did he do?"

She said, "He just sat there."

When he goes to the vetcrinarian, he walks in as if he owns it. When he gets a shot, there's not a quiver. One of the young girls who works at the vet's asked the vet how come, when all the un-neutered males come in, they pee on everything, but when Blue comes in—and he's not neutered—he never pees on anything.

Dr. Smith said, "Blue knows who he is."

Luba and Blue are always together. They sleep together. If Luba is in another room and raises her voice, Blue is there in a flash. He looks around as if to say, "Hey! What's goin' on here?" Luba and I never take vacations together because Luba does not want to leave Blue alone. He has never been in a kennel. He's the love of her life.

He really is the kindest dog I've ever known. If a young bird falls in the back yard and starts running around, he'll just go up and look at it and sniff it. He has never killed anything in his life.

At our cottage, a neighbour had a little Jack Russell terrier that would take on anything and would kill every snake it saw. Blue, on the other hand, rescued them.

Luba hates snakes, as most of us do, and hit one with a shovel and threw it in the water. Blue doesn't swim, but he went down, waded in the water, grabbed the snake, brought it to the land and let it go. He's the only dog in the world that rescues snakes.

He is so kind and tough, he reminds me of Bobby Probert. Bobby was as tough as they come, afraid of nothin' and one of the kindest men you would ever meet. He didn't have to act tough.

He was like Blue. Bobby knew who he was.

* * *

I know Luba and her friends think that I'm a little nuts when it comes to those two Mark VIs, my two Lincolns I have had since 1983.

Luba always says, "I wish you would get a new car for those long trips. It bothers me that you're in such an old car."

I say to Luba, "I appreciate what you say, but these cars are not old, they're classics. All other cars, compared to my beauties, are nothin'."

I must admit, I don't like anybody in my Mark VIs.

Let me explain. I live in a land of turmoil. Telephones. Faxes. Emails. Calls from the CBC. I carry no cell phone, and when I get in my cars, it's my little inner sanctum. I'm in my own little world. Nobody can get at me.

If you remember that segment that was on the *Rick Mercer Report*, there was a piece where he wanted to talk to my tailor. He said, "We'll drive over in your car with a camera in the back and we'll have a conversation."

I said, "No way," but he kept at me and at me, so I relented. To a point. I told him he could get in the front, but there would be no camera guy in the back. He agreed, but even so, I still wasn't happy.

One day, a situation came up where I had to drive a guy in my car. We're driving along, and I'm not really thrilled about it, and he says, "Do you hear that noise in your engine?"

I said, "No, I don't. There is no noise in my engine, and I resent you saying that there is a noise in my beauty."

He says, "Now wait a minute. You resent me trying to help you? You would rather be stuck in a parking lot with a car that doesn't start than have me try to help you?"

I said, "That's right. First of all, my beauty has never let me down in twenty-eight years. And she really doesn't like somebody saying she has a noise in her engine."

Now, I know that you're probably thinkin' I'm nuts about those cars, but I also know that some guys who are reading this agree with me 100 per cent.

I feel my beauties are like me. Big. A little heavy. Ostentatious. Gettin' old but still runnin'. And lookin' good.

* * *

It makes me laugh the way some of the young hockey players today sign their autographs. I have people come up to me with a sweater that has been signed by a bunch of players on a team and I say, "Tell me, whose signature is that?"

They say, "Gee, I don't know whose it is. Let me look at the number." That's the only way they can tell whose autograph it is.

One day, on the set of *Hockey Night in Canada*, I was signing some sweaters and I saw a signature. I had no idea whose it was.

I asked somebody, and he said it was this young player. So I went to the player and I said, "Why don't you sign your name so that people can tell whose autograph it is?"

He said he was told it was cool to sign his name the way he signed it.

Now, hardly anybody in the world signs his name more than Bobby Orr. But when he signs it, you know it's Bobby Orr. Same thing for Gordie Howe. Wayne Gretzky. Bobby Hull. If these superstars can sign their names so that you can make out who it is, why can't the other guys?

I guess they want to give the impression that they're very busy people and they don't have time for this nonsense. And I guess that they want to give the impression that they sign so many they have to hurry.

Then again, maybe they just don't care.

* * *

Before the 2009–10 season, I met Matt Duchene at the Hershey Arena. He was there for a card show, and they were taking pictures for his NHL hockey card.

He was Colorado's first pick, the third overall, and he had played for the Brampton Battalion. I told him he was going to make the Colorado Avalanche, that he was going to be a star, that he was going to be a crowd favourite, and that he was going to be the top scorer among all the rookies.

Check the record. It all came true, and usually, that's enough to win the Calder Trophy as the league's best rookie. But Tyler Myers, the Buffalo Sabres' great young defenceman, had an outstanding year and won it.

I first met Matt at the prospects game in Oshawa. As we were going out for the warmup, he said, "Mr. Cherry, 'Coach's Corner' saved my grandfather's life."

Here's the story.

A few years ago in eastern Canada, we had the most murderous snowstorm in decades. It closed roads. Power lines were down. It was awful.

During the storm, Matt's grandparents, who owned a dairy farm, were in the living room watching the Leafs on *Hockey Night in Canada*. Grandmother Duchene said, "Listen to those cows. They're ready for milking. Get out there and get it done."

So Grandfather Duchene starts to put on his coat, but says, "Wait a minute! 'Coach's Corner' is coming on. I'm watching this."

So he takes his coat off and sits down. They're both watching "Coach's Corner" when they hear a loud crash. They ran outside and saw the roof of the barn had collapsed under the weight of all the snow. It had killed most of the cows.

Matt said his grandfather would have been right in the middle and would have been killed.

When Matt told me this, everybody laughed when I said, "Well, Matt, I guess 'Coach's Corner' is good for somethin' after all."

* * *

How many times have you heard me say this on "Coach's Corner"? If you're not sure you're going to be picked in the first or second round of the June draft, stay home!

Don't go and be embarrassed.

I felt so sorry for the Brunelle family at the 2010 draft in Los Angeles. There was a big picture of them in the *Toronto Sun*, taken after Jonathan, a winger for Drummondville in the Quebec league, didn't get drafted. The mom, dad and sister are all there; the mother's almost in tears, and Jonathan has his head in his hands, bent over and staring at the floor. And the father, I can see he doesn't know what to say.

You've gone all that way to Los Angeles. You've paid for a hotel. All your friends know you're there and they're watching. You think you're gonna get drafted, but . . .

It's bad enough not getting drafted, but now all the world knows, and there's this picture in the *Toronto Sun*. The world is cruel.

* * *

John McFarland of the Sudbury Wolves was projected to go in the first round, but at the end of the first round he wasn't drafted. Naturally, the TV cameras go to him after every pick to see his disappointment. They only do one round on the first day, and as McFarland gets up to leave, a TV reporter comes up to him and says, "How does it feels not to be drafted after you were projected to go in the first round?"

How do you think the kid feels? But it's a good story, so never mind the kid's feelings.

Actually, John went to Florida in the second round, thirty-third. He couldn't have gone to a better organization, but the hurt of the Brunelle family choked me up. How must they have felt? Pick after pick going by, and they were thinking every time Jonathan's name must be the next one to be called, so they sit there. Jonathan was ranked 105th among North American skaters by Central Scouting, but he never did get drafted. That's why the family were in the last row: so nobody would notice them.

Jonathan showed a lot of heart. Guys that don't get drafted in their draft year go back to junior more determined and motivated to show everybody they were wrong. Their embarrassment after their draft year is always on their minds, and it spurs them on. You watch: Jonathan Brunelle will show everybody next year.

* * *

At one time, when the juniors drafted, it was set it up just like the NHL draft. Thank goodness they don't do that anymore. They do it by telephone now and stopped that foolishness.

The draft was in Barrie one year when I was with the IceDogs, my daughter Cindy noticed the family of a kid who was expecting to get drafted waiting in the arena. The draft had almost ended and they had sat there, pick after pick. I don't think they even went to the washroom in the whole eight hours for fear of missing a pick.

The kid hadn't been drafted, and it was right down to the wire. I went to our governor, Trevor Whiffen, and I said, "Trevor, draft that kid."

He says, "I can't, Grapes. It's closed."

So I asked him to go down and ask David Branch, the commissioner of the Ontario Hockey League, if we could have one more pick as a favour. Trevor did, and Branch goes to the microphone and he says, "Excuse me. We were wrong. There's one more pick to go and it goes to the Mississauga IceDogs."

I've forgotten the kid's name, but we chose him, and you should have seen the kid. You should have seen the family. It was like he had been drafted first overall. They were all jumping around, kissing one another.

I went down and welcomed him to the club and told him to get ready for training camp. I looked at the mom, and the mom had tears in her eyes. It's always the moms who take it the worst.

The kid was okay at camp. He was one of the last cuts. He was a goalie and he wasn't bad. When I told him he didn't make it, he knew, but you could see in his eyes that he was grateful. He said, "Thanks, Grapes, for just giving me the chance."

* * *

The ironic thing about kids hoping that they'll get drafted, even in the late rounds, is that the NHL clubs really don't want the late drafts at training camp. They just get in the way of the high draft picks. It's cruel, but that's the way it is.

So it really means nothing to go to the draft, only the opportunity to be hurt and humiliated. If you're reading this and you may be drafted, listen to me. Unless you're going to get picked in the first or second round, don't go. I know what I'm talking about. You know how I know? Because I've been there.

* * *

Sometimes in hockey, there are moves that really don't make sense to me. For instance, in the 2010 midget draft, the Barrie Colts of the OHL picked the son of Warren Rychel, who is the GM and part owner of the Memorial Cup champion Windsor Spitfires. In fact, the Spits won it in 2009 as well.

As everybody knows, any coach, GM or owner would like his

son to play for his own team. Naturally. So it's usually a given that you pass on a kid who is the son of another team's GM, coach or owner.

I know there's bad blood between the Spits and the Colts because of the blindside hit by Zack Kassian that injured Matt Kennedy and gave him a concussion in a game on January 18, 2010. But Kassian paid a heavy price with his suspension, and I know the Barrie organization was ticked that Warren did some juggling with the draft, but to draft Warren's kid, I think, was a little too much. This is family. And why antagonize a guy like Rychel? Even though Barrie may be able to trade Rychel's son to Windsor, these guys won't forget.

* * *

One day when I was with the IceDogs, I get a call from our governor, Trevor Whiffen, and he says, "Did you hear what Dino Ciccarelli is going to do?"

Now, Dino is the owner and GM of the Sarnia Sting of the OHL, and he's going to draft Dale Hunter's son. Dale is the owner and coach of the London Knights. There's very bad blood between Dino and Dale. The Hunters and the Ciccarellis don't send Christmas cards to each other.

Dale is going ballistic, and what he wants the IceDogs to do is trade him our second-round pick so he can take his own kid before Dino does. It really made no difference to us, so I made the trade and Dale picked his son. Naturally, the kid flourished under Dale.

Later, I had a guy come up to me and say, "That was great, Don, what you did for Dale."

I said, "Oh no. It wasn't that great. I just didn't have time to go to Dino's funeral, and I didn't have time to visit Dale in prison."

* * *

The Greater Toronto Hockey League is being sued by two parents because their kids did not make the team they were trying out for. The parents claim it hurt their children's self-esteem and they were humiliated.

That's a great lesson for the kids, isn't it? If you fail, don't dig down and try harder and show everybody that they made a mistake cutting you. Blame it on the coach and the league, and file a suit. Later on in life, if these kids go to college and they fail, their parents will say, "Don't blame yourself and try harder to pass next time. Blame the professor."

If you're a lawyer and you lose the case, don't blame yourself. Blame the judge. If you're a salesman and don't make the sale, blame the customer.

Talk about parents working hard to make their kids into losers. But that's the way it is now, even in hockey. If a kids' team makes the playoffs and loses, they all get a trophy and a certificate for participating. So it doesn't matter, it seems, whether you win or lose, just compete.

That's not the way it is in life. In the game of life and the world of hard knocks, you don't get anything for competing. You have to win.

That's why I always loved construction. You don't carry your weight, you're gone.

But today, I really believe this is Canada's attitude, our socialist attitude. The government has to take care of me from the cradle to the grave. Everybody expects his pound of flesh. Everybody expects his rights and demands his rights. In the old days, people came to this country without a dime, then worked at as many jobs as they could get and never asked the government for a penny. And they were very successful.

They were the backbone of the country. I'm afraid that now I see that Canadian spirit slowly seeping away. Our attitude now is, "Ask not what I can do for my country; ask what my country can do for me."

But I digress, as they say.

This is what happens with these types of parents, in my opinion: when they have tryouts, the coaches see what kind of parents these kids have. The parents looked like trouble, and the coaches could see trouble coming if the kid didn't get on the power play or get enough ice time. Parents don't realize how their acts reflect on the kids.

I've been at games where a father has put on an act, giving the coach a hard time, and I've heard scouts say, "Whose dad it that?" When they find out, they just stroke the kid off their lists. A kid with a father like that is known as a two-for-one deal. A scout said to me, "If I ever recommended a kid to my coach and the father gave him a hard time like that, I would be gone."

So the kids pay for the sins of the fathers, and I know this happens all the time. It's too bad. Usually the kid is a good guy, but nobody wants a two-for-one and aggravation like that.

* * *

When I played for Eddie Shore in Springfield, he would really get upset if you got hurt and couldn't practise or play. He would go into a tirade and say we were all soft and tell us how he would play with injuries.

He told us about the time in New York, when he fell into the goalpost before the game. The goalposts didn't move in those days, and Eddie broke three ribs. He ended up in the hospital, but checked himself out, took a train to Montreal and scored the winning goal.

He told us about the time he played against the Montreal Maroons, and they were really after him. He told us he had three teeth knocked out, and had cuts on his face. His nose was broken and so was his cheekbone. But he played the next game.

When we would get stitches, he would laugh and say, "Well, I had over a thousand stitches. I had my jaw broken five times and all my teeth knocked out. I had broken ribs, my ear torn off and my nose broken fourteen times."

He told us another story. He had a cut on the back of his leg and they put eighteen stitches in. He went back out to play, the stitches broke and everywhere he skated, he left a trail of blood.

We thought, "Boy, does this guy ever lay it on really thick." We thought it was all a joke until we talked to a guy who had been one of Shore's teammates. He hated Shore, but when we told him the stories, he said, "I hate to tell you, boys, but they're all true—and more."

And may I say, despite all his injuries, Eddie Shore won the Hart Trophy four times.

* * *

I've seen guys play through injuries and pain. Bobby Orr was one. He had to have his knees iced down after every game. I played with a guy called Gerry Ehman with the Rochester Americans. He had a chronic groin injury. When he was young, he had a groin injury and they froze it. After that, he had to have it taped every game.

I've seen hockey players play with injuries that in most sports would put them out for a month. In fact, Dr. Vincent Nardiello, who was the doctor for the New York Athletic Commission, said that hockey players were the toughest team-sports athletes of all. The only athletes he saw who were tougher were bull riders in the rodeo.

But for overcoming pain and a chronic injury, I'd have to give the award to Wayne Cashman. With his bad back, he was always in pain, but he would never miss a game. And Wayne was a crash-banger who took no prisoners, which made it even worse.

Wayne would always come late to the games. With his bad back, he couldn't sit around in the dressing room. It was so bad that he never took a treatment because it wouldn't do any good.

Cash always disappeared after warmup, just before the games. I never made a big deal of it until one day, I happened to walk into the stick room, which was just off the dressing room. Here was

Cash, fully dressed and ready to go on the ice, with the trainer tying up his skates for him. His back was so bad he couldn't bend over to do up his skates.

I never said a word. I just walked off shaking my head.

I had to keep him going. If he sat on the bench too long, his back would seize up on him. If we had a lot of penalties, I would have to have him kill some penalties, even though he wasn't a penalty killer.

I noticed that every once in a while, when he went to go over the boards, he would wince. I swear I could feel my own back hurt just watching him. I knew his back was killing him.

Once in a while, I would say, "How's your back? Really, Cash, how is it?"

All he would say was, "Okay."

I'm at home after the morning skate on the day of a game, and I get a call from my trainer. He says, "Cash is in the hospital. They have him in traction."

I told him to tell one of the young guys to dress and that he would play that night.

I go to the rink, and who's there early for a change? It's Cash. He made sure he was there early so he would play.

I said to the trainer, "Danny, what's going on? I thought you said Cash was in traction."

He says, "I don't know, Grapes. He showed up around four-thirty. He checked himself out of the hospital. He asked me if I'd told you he was in the hospital, and when I said I did, he was ticked that I'd told you. He got down here early so you wouldn't scratch him from the lineup."

The team doctor who put Cash in the hospital was really upset, but I know one thing: I'm not goin' to be the guy who tells Cash he's not playin' tonight. I value my life too much.

But I'm in a dilemma. I can't let him miss too many shifts or his back will freeze up on him. But it doesn't seem right that I should give him regular shifts with his back bein' the way it is. So I decide

I'm gonna give him regular shifts and put him on every power play until his back gives out on him and he has to quit.

We win the game. He gets two goals and has a fight.

After the game, I walked up to Cash and I asked him, "Cash, seriously now, really, how's your back?"

He said, "Okay."

* * *

It really is a shame that Paul Henderson is not in the Hall of Fame. I know Paul says that there are a lot more deserving players than him, but that's the way Paul is. He would never, ever say he belongs in the Hall.

I know there are some people who are always ready to jump on something like this and say, "A player doesn't deserve to be in the Hall for one goal." And I'm sure everybody remembers the goal that he scored against Vladislav Tretiak to win the greatest series ever—the 1972 Summit Series—for Canada.

But people don't realize that Paul got two more winning goals for Canada. He should have been, as far as I'm concerned, the MVP of the series.

Let's take a look at his NHL record. Thirteen years in the NHL. He played 707 games. He had 477 points—that's a point every other game. And look what he did in the playoffs when it really counts: 25 points in 56 games. Not too shabby.

There's no goal—except maybe Bobby Orr's goal to win the Stanley Cup in overtime against St. Louis in 1970—that people remembered for so long.

Everybody remembers where they were when Paul scored that goal. I was with a bunch of players in Rochester, and we were all sitting around in the dressing room, listening to it on the radio. When Paul scored that goal, we all leaped up and jumped around.

The thing I don't understand is that they put Tretiak in the Hall of Fame. He's the guy who didn't come through for the Russians and lost the game.

But the guy who scored the goal and won the game, he's the guy that's out.

It doesn't make any sense to me.

* * *

Walter Gretzky and I have a theory that I think is great: a smaller puck for the smaller player. Think about it: kids could handle the puck a ton better and shoot it quicker and faster. It would be so much fun to watch them stickhandle. I also like the idea of making them play on half the ice, with the nets on the side boards. The reason: the kids get more involved, stickhandling, shooting, and goalies get to make saves. It makes sense. Other sports have the equipment geared to the smaller player, and so should hockey. Does it make sense for a kid to handle a puck the same size as Sidney Crosby? I know the kids would usually have more fun. It will never happen because it makes too much sense. And besides, what would Walter Gretzky and I know?

Walter and I, one time a few years ago, were invited to an exhibition game between some youngsters to raise money for a lacrosse league. After the game, Walter and I were walking out and a kid came running up to us and said, "Who's the best hockey player ever: Bobby Orr or Wayne Gretzky?" Now, how am I ever going to get out of this one?

I said, "Wayne Gretzky is the greatest player playing today."

Walter didn't say anything; we just kept walking. Finally, he said, "You know, Don, you'd make a good politician."

As I look back in my life and at my teammates in hockey, I see now that we were not prepared for life after hockey like they are now. We had our teammates, and that was it. If you had friends outside of hockey, you were out as far as the rest of the team was concerned; you were thought of as sort of an oddball. In junior, for instance, you never, ever hung around with your schoolmates if you went to school. You went to school, practised or played your games, went to a show that night, and in bed by 10 P.M. And you always hung out with a teammate. And then on to pro, same thing: no friends outside of hockey, isolated from the real world—and, I must admit, too much drinking.

I remember when I went to my first pro camp. I did not have a beer with the boys. They tolerated it and did not brush me off, because I was a rookie, but with all that time on our hands, I'm afraid I got into the suds. Here was the time I could have been preparing for life after hockey. But no, I fell right into the routine of practice, then lunch. I will say it was not too often that we'd drink in the afternoon. We definitely did not get drunk before a game—maybe a few beers. We thought of a guy who got drunk right before a game as a drunk, not a good guy, and we made sure he didn't last. But for sixteen years I sailed along the way, and it was the same with the wives—they very rarely made friends outside of the hockey wives, and when we had a party, very rarely was there anybody outside of hockey.

Travel was so simple in American Hockey League after a game: get on the bus, hotel room key given to you, back on the bus again the next morning. Simple life. Even when I became GM and coach in Rochester, I kept my involvement with the league to a minimum. I had an assistant GM and PR guys to take care of the league stuff. I concentrated on the players—getting good character guys, no floaters, maybe not as talented, but guys you could depend on and then make it enjoyable for them to play. I had played for so many coaches who for some reason did everything they could to tick the players off and make life miserable. I could never figure that out. I'd do anything for them; and if a jerk took advantage, I'd get rid of him. Simple.

I could never understand the logic, all those years, of the way we travelled after a game in the AHL. We'd play the game, get on the bus, all pumped up because of the game. Get on the bus, have a few pops, play cards, and about 3 A.M. we'd stop and have to go into one of those motels in the mountains that hasn't been open in months. Rooms freezing, sheets damp, can't get to sleep till 4 A.M., and then they'd start banging on the doors at seven-thirty for everyone to get up. You'd wait till the last minute to get up because the room would be freezing. Get on the bus—no breakfast, groggy and pissed, another four hours to go. It made no sense. So when I became GM and coach of Rochester, I said, "Take your choice, we can do it that way or we can do it *this* way: I'll put beer on the bus, you can keep your per diem and I'll put sandwiches on the bus, and we'll go all the way." They voted 100 per cent for all the way, just as I knew they would.

So I would have sandwiches—different kinds, naturally—delivered to the bus driver. I would personally put the beer on ice in garbage cans while the warmup was on. It was heaven for a hockey player. It's the only time all the players packed their bags quickly, showered quickly, got their bags on the bus quickly. We were gone and on our way in record time. Then the guys could play cards, play music, have a few beers and the sandwiches were passed out by a rookie. We were lucky; life was good. Usually, the buses are a mess after these trips. One morning, they saw me picking up the trash. After that, when the players left in the morning, the bus was spotless. They had all pitched in and picked up the trash, and if we got a new guy, he was told, "Help pick it up."

We were a team. The players are the sharpest guys in the world—street smart. Some of them have been on their own since they were 16. So they knew I had saved the cost of a night at the hotel. They would never say anything, but I told them the money I saved on the motel, we'd use for a party. They knew I like shirts and ties, but I knew it would be tough to tell them to wear shirts and ties on trips like that. But you know what? They all wore shirts and ties— wrinkled, I must say, but looking good. People only saw us when we walked in to the enemy's arena. Didn't matter, we felt good about ourselves and we were a first place club.

I loved those guys I coached in Rochester.

* * *

I am going to go back here to something I said on *Hockey Night in Canada. Hockey Night,* once in a while, shows the hockey players walking into the arena before the game—one of my favourite parts. One night, we did a game near the end of the season between Ottawa and Tampa. In comes one of my favourite hockey players, Mike Fisher, and he's in a godawful black jacket a lobsterman wears when he's fishing, and a black toque. In the hallway, there's a Tampa guy dressed just like him. I say, "Let me show you the difference between two suck teams, Ottawa and Tampa, who are not going to make the playoffs, and two first-place teams, and one of them is going to be a Stanley Cup winner." We show the guys walking into the game between Pittsburgh and Washington, and here comes Billy Guerin, Sidney Crosby and Jordan Staal for Pittsburgh, and Mike Green, John Erskine and Max Bradley for Washington, looking like fashion plates. I said, "See, kids? There's the difference: you dress first class, you play first class, like Pittsburgh and Washington. You dress third class, you play third class, like Tampa and Ottawa. You know what? Ottawa and Tampa look like a bunch of thugs." The owner of Tampa phoned the NHL and complained, and Ottawa phoned the NHL and the CBC—not Bryan Murray or Eugene Melnyk, by the way; they knew I was right. When I was informed of their complaints about saying these players were thugs, I said, "I didn't say they were thugs. I said they *looked like* thugs."

I digress, as Ron MacLean would say. Back to the subject. Rochester was the toughest team, number one in the league overall, and the best-dressed and, most of all, the happiest. But again, we were isolated. When I went to the Bruins as coach, same thing. As an NHL coach, you only worry about the team. On the road, most teams had a road secretary take care of everything; at the airport, hands you your ticket; at the hotel, hands you your key. And this is the way it had been in my life, starting when I was 16. At 46 years old, after my last job in the NHL with the Colorado Rockies, I was, as they say, on my own. When I got the job on *Hockey Night in Canada*, I had to fly from Denver to Toronto, with a stop in Chicago. I said to Rose, "Well, what do I do? You mean I have to stand in line to buy a ticket and I have to check my own bags, and then in Chicago, find the gate to Toronto?" I was completely lost. It took me a while, but I still haven't got the hang of it yet. Luba makes sure of everything, and I have to admit, when Ron MacLean and I are on the road, I leave everything to him. And now some airlines in the States have it so you have to get your own ticket out of a machine. I just look sort of helpless and stupid. All the ladies always come and get my ticket for me. I guess they like helping a good looking, sharp-dressed guy.

I have no knowledge of emails. Luba does it (I can send a fax). Twitters, Facebooks, cell phones, BlackBerrys, I have no knowledge or interest. My mentality is a jackhammer, minor-league hockey player who thought he would play forever. No education, no trade. I'm sorry to say a lot of my teammates found themselves, much to their regret, in the same situation as me. When we were finished, we were completely lost.

* * *

I remember my mom calling, "Donald, Donald," at 5 A.M. on winter mornings, very quietly to not wake up the rest of the family. My equipment bag would be by the door and my breakfast ready, Corn Flakes and toast and a glass of milk. I would head out into the dark with my equipment bag over my shoulder, and as I left she always said, "Be careful. Rideau Public School was my school, about 4 blocks from home, and it had a beautiful outdoor rink.

We would start playing shinny hockey at 8 A.M., go home for lunch at noon, then back at 2 P.M. to play till dark. We'd come home for dinner, feet numb and feeling frozen. Mom would rub them to get them warm again, and I'd be out to play road hockey until 8 P.M. and then in for a hot bath, into my pajamas, and with a cup of cocoa, gather around the radio, waiting for Foster Hewitt to come on with the Leafs at 9:10 P.M.. The Leafs didn't broadcast the first period. We were so excited to hear Foster. He was like a God. They used to let the players bang their sticks on the boards after a goal, and it was a thrill to think you could actually hear the players and when that guy would holler, "Come on Teeder," and the crowd cheered, we were in heaven. I still have that radio. To bed we went with visions of the NHL dancing in our heads. I remember Mom crying as the train pulled out when I left to play for Barrie in the "O." I was a real home-boy—I never left home for camps or anything.

Mom, Dad, Aunt Hilda and Aunt Pansy drove up with Uncle Bill to Toronto to see Barrie and St. Mike's play. After the game, Ma took one look at me, and I'll never forget the look of shock on her face when she saw me. I had lost all my baby fat and was in shape. She thought I was sick and she said, "Oh, look at the bump on your nose." I laughed and said, "All hockey players get those, Ma." When I left home my nose was straight. If you check every hockey player you will see a little bump on the bridge of their nose from getting clipped with a stick; but again her eyes were misty.

I phoned Ma later that year and upset her again when I said I was quitting school. She said I would live to regret it, and boy was she right. When I turned pro with the Boston Bruins, I played in Hershey and was called up by Boston for a game in the semifinals against Montreal. Mom took the train up from Kingston with Aunt Tillie to see the game. After the game, Mom gave me two big shopping bags full of cookies and cakes. The players laughed at me with the bags, but on the train back to Boston, they ate all the cookies and cakes. I was always grateful that Mom saw my one and only NHL game, and as the saying goes, "Build one bridge, and you're a bridge builder."

Mom's only complaint about my coaching was for me not to

chew gum while coaching because it was "bad manners to chew gum in public." I never did figure that one out.

Mom phoned me one Sunday and said, "Must you say you were out with the boys and had some beer? It sounds so bummy," so I started to say I was out with the boys and had a few pops, and that's how beer became pops for hockey players. Somebody added wobbly pops, so you see, some good things do come out of "Coach's Corner."

It's funny how as you get older you remember little things about your parents. I had a rabbit called Brownie and as most rabbits do, she had a lot of babies, but Brownie would not take care of her babies. I remember Mom wrapping them up in a flannel shirt, putting the oven on low and keeping them warm and feeding them warm milk with an eyedropper.

I remember Mom buying me some hockey pants and I said I didn't like them. I remember the hurt look on her face—sharper then a serpent's tooth, an ungrateful child—I know I mentioned it before how when she saw my old gloves I wore in Barrie, she bought me a new pair. Now I know some people may say, "Big deal; so what?" Well, let's put it this way, we all had old rotten gloves and I was the only guy with new gloves. Yeah, the guys made fun of me, "Mommy's little boy, doesn't want her little baby to get hurt." It didn't bother me at all. My Dad was a working man and I know those gloves were expensive; but as you can see, it meant so much to me, not so much the new gloves, I could have survived with the old ones, but it was the thought, and when I look at me in the Barrie uniform with those gloves, I think of my mom.

With Santa and Cindy at the Sudbury Wolves Christmas party in 1962.

MY LIFE WITH DON CHERRY
Cindy Cherry

MY MOM AND DAD'S HOUSE WAS always the party house. They didn't have much money, so they had lots of team get-togethers.

I remember once, when Mom was preparing for a big party—it might have been the team's Christmas party—so she wasn't going to the game. Since I did not have school the next day, I went to the game with Dad. I was only 6 or 7 and had never gone to a game without my mom, so this was a pretty big deal for me. After the game, I went down with the wives/moms to wait for the husbands/dads to come out. Slowly, they were all leaving to go to my house. I was getting quite nervous; I knew my dad was always the last to come out of the dressing room, but I still remember asking one of the players if he was still in the shower. The player said he thought so, and that he would see me later.

Now, the War Memorial Arena was pretty scary when it was all empty. Just think: an hour ago, it was filled with eight thousand people; now it was eerily silent. Finally, all the lights went out. I was quite scared and didn't know what to do. I looked down the long hallway to the dressing room to see if anyone was around. There was a light coming from under the door, so I lightly knocked. Luckily, the trainer was still cleaning up. He asked me what I was still doing here, because my dad had left quite a while ago. I guess he could see I was nearly in tears, so he assured me my dad would come back for me; in the meantime, he asked, would I help him clean up the dressing room?

Can you imagine the earful Dad got when he got home and Mom asked him, "Where's Cindy?" Dad raced back to the rink; to this day, I wonder if it was because he was worried about what happened to me or because I was cutting into his party time. When he got there, I was neatly folding the towels for the next day's practice. I was sure glad to see him.

* * *

I look back on how we lived like gypsies. Mom and Dad could fit everything they needed to live for a whole hockey season in a car. At the end of the season, we would always move back to either Kingston or Hershey for Dad to work on construction in the summer. Then, wherever he was playing that year, Mom would have the necessities of life fit in the car. The basics were clothes, pots and pans, linens, my toys and, last but not least, a stereo and a fish aquarium.

Yes, a fish tank. No matter were we were, we always had an aquarium. I remember that during one party, Danny Belisle (his claim to fame was that, in the movie *Slap Shot*, Paul Newman beats him up on the ice) went fishing in my aquarium. He had me get him a safety pin and thread—a weird request at a party, but a little kid could never imagine what an elder might do . . . or need a safety pin at your house for. He then proceeded to bait the pin with Mom's roast beef. Needless to say, I was pretty upset when I saw this. I yelled for my dad again. What we didn't notice at the time was that a piece of the roast beef had fallen off the hook, and it rotted in the water, killing all the fish the next day. Hockey players' humour is like no other.

* * *

When the players came over, they loved to play Ping Pong. You have never seen Ping Pong played with such violent undertones.

My dad, knowing this, had warned the players, "Don't break the table." Needless to say, as Dad predicted, it all came to an end when there was a really tight game. That concept of needing to win by two points doesn't go over well with hockey players. Rob Walton (brother of the Toronto Maple Leafs' Mike) was going for the winning point. If there is such a thing as spiking a Ping Pong ball, he was set to do it. The ball came up high, he put his hand down in the middle of the table with all his weight on it, and that table folded like a sandwich. He went headfirst down into the middle of it—his feet sticking up in the air. I, of course, wasn't worried that our team's top goal scorer might have hurt himself; my concern was that the players broke my table. Crying, I ran and got Dad, and I don't know if he was more worried about the player or my broken table, but from the way he was yelling, I believe he was more upset that I was crying—and that Rob probably wouldn't be playing the power play anymore.

*　*　*

My mom's chili, served at our parties, was renowned. In those days, it was hard to find a place that sold that real thick-crusted Italian bread. In every city we lived in, she would seek out an authentic Italian grocery store. It always had her Romano cheese, her favourite salami, pickled eggplant, all the good stuff. I, of course, hated to go there—I referred to it as the "stinky" store. Smother that bread with slabs of butter to scoop up her chili—one of the favourite things the players liked to do. What really got her upset was when they started eating it from the pot, just to "taste" it. Mom asked one player three times to stop it, but he had had way too many beers and was past the point of heeding Mom's warnings. When Mom said to me, "Get your father," I knew he was in big trouble.

Dad told him one more time that if he was caught again, he'd be out of there. My job was to guard the chili and squeal on anyone who ate it out of the pot. Sure enough, the same guy came back, so I ran to get Dad. I knew that Dad really didn't care about the guys eating out of the pot—he did it himself on occasion (though not at one of Mom's parties!)—it was just that it upset Mom so, and he didn't want to listen to her complain about it. I guess that's where I learned that complaining is a great motivator to get something done. I also figure that this guy not heeding Dad's warning also ticked Dad off, so he grabbed him by his shirt. I can remember that his feet were hardly touching the floor. Dad told me to open the door, and he threw the guy out. He tripped down the porch stairs and fell into the snow. Dad then told me to find the man's coat, and he threw it at him. Thank goodness he did, for this was the dead of winter, and I can remember it was freezing out.

His wife then started yelling at Dad about how this was no way to treat a guest in his house. My next job was to figure out which coat was hers and retrieve it, as Dad told her to get out too. It was times like this, seeing my dad in action, that really made the impression on me that I should not cross him. It also has to be said here, in my dad's defence, that he later found out the player had a real problem and was an alcoholic, and that he had a lovely family and great kids. Unbeknownst to the owners of the team, Dad told him to stay home for the practices and games and paid him for the whole season.

* * *

When I say Mom and Dad's house was the place where the team would always meet, it served another function. You have to realize the lives these players lead. They're far away from home and their families, which is especially hard on the single guys. Holidays were tough for them. Mom, being who she was, would always invite them over for dinner. Even for game-day meals. We would have a houseful. They would never know what to bring her as a thank-you gift, so they would always bring us kids something. One player even bought me a canary. (To be accurate, when Dad was proofing my literary efforts in writing these stories, he confessed he was the one that bought the canary, and he gave it to Bill Sweeney to give to me when he was coming over for dinner. That's what dads do.)

People talk about a team feeling like a family, but we really did feel like that. Birthday parties for the kids turned into team parties. I can even take it a step further: in those days, a single guy could not have his girlfriend stay with him if she was visiting from out of town. My, how times have changed. So Mom even let the girl-friends stay at the house for weeks on end. I thought of them as sort of the sisters I never had. One girl helped Mom redecorate the bathroom. They tore it apart, then her boyfriend made it to the NHL and we never saw her again. That's the way it worked.

We counted one day how many times my parents had packed and moved around. The total got up to fifty-five times. Some people may question this type of lifestyle, not putting down roots or having some sort of stability in life. Granted, those things may have some value, but I feel the ability and ease with which we can make new friends is a far more valuable asset in life. Think of how many times one has to start a new job. The strength to assimilate into one's environment is an underestimated knack in Canada. I also found it very easy to say goodbye and move on to newer pastures. Whenever they would have a going-away party for an employee where I worked, and everyone was so emotional, I'd really think something was wrong with me. I would feel like Elaine in the *Seinfeld* episode—she ends up phoning in sick because she can't stand eating all the cake at these parties. I just don't get it, and most times I would be faking my sadness to see them go.

I was always amazed how my mom could arrive in a new city and find her way around so quickly and easily. She'd find the basics of life: grocery store, Italian specialty store, dry cleaners, hair salon, babysitters. The one time she did get tripped up was when we were in Quebec. With hand signals, she showed the stylist how much hair to take off, and they interpreted it as how much to leave on! I can still remember how upset she was. But this ability she had, in adapting to whatever life throws at you, helped me when I had to leave Rochester for Boston in my senior year of high school for Boston. I hear about people nowadays turning down a new job 'cause their kids will have to change school. How can I not relate? Not only did I have to leave, but we couldn't move into the furnished house Mom and Dad rented till October, and school started in September. So it was decided for me that I would stay that month with a family whose dad worked for the Bruins and start school while living with them—they had a daughter that went to the same school. Mom and Dad never asked if this would work for me; it was just understood it was the way it was going to be. No options.

* * *

I was a hard-nosed kid, with a personality more like my dad's than my easy-going mom's (except for when someone crossed her when it came to food). I would have been a hard kid to raise if it weren't for my dad. The fear of him made me toe the line. Fear, not of being spanked or yelled at, but of what I'd seen he would do to make a point. Hockey was our life, so when he made an example out of someone, you would heed his wrath. I always figured if he could do that to a player, with something that might hurt the team in order to get his point across, he could easily do it to me.

* * *

There was one player, John Wensink, who was like part of our family. He played for Dad in both Rochester and Boston. For some reason, once he started scoring a lot of goals, he stopped listening to Dad. Big mistake. Dad sent him further down into the minors for a few weeks to smarten him up. Mom and I didn't speak to Dad for days. Then, when John was playing in Boston, it happened again, and Dad benched him during the finals. It nearly broke John's heart, and once again, Mom and I were angry at Dad.

You could say that I thought of him like a brother, but in truth, and thirty-five years later or so, I must admit I had quite a crush on him. I told Rhonda, his wife, about that years later, while we were playing racquetball, and she said John always liked me, but I think she said it only to make me feel good. When he left Rochester to play for St. Louis, I gave him a scrapbook of all his newspaper clippings that I had kept for him over the years. I hope he still has it and looks back at all those memories fondly.

When you look back at the whole situation, you are amazed at how the lives of these young professionals are played out. He was fresh out of major junior hockey, far away from home. New team, new city, a totally different life. Dad always felt responsible for the lives of these players. He even took an interest in where they lived. As most people know who have followed Dad's career (or watched the movie), he coached a high school hockey team in Pittsford, New York, just outside Rochester. Those same parents who wanted him to coach their sons in high school eventually bought the Rochester Americans and once again made him their coach, only now it was "for real." It was important to have these players in well-established homes, somewhat like the billeting system in Junior A. Dad had one player, Eddy Scott, who lived with his single mom while playing high school hockey. Dad asked if she would let two of his single rookies—John Wensink and another player, Gary Bredin—stay with her. It was the perfect set-up for everyone. He knew they would be well taken care of, and have not only accountability to the team but to Mrs. Scott, whom they adored.

However, most Sunday games and holidays, Mom would have them over the house. Because Mom, Tim and I adored John, it was easy to forget he had a job to do, which made him accountable to Dad. I guess a few times we lost sight of that fact, and were continually angry with Dad in his decisions concerning John. There was one incident, which I will never forget. I remember it as if it were yesterday. I can remember Dad telling John, when he and Gary were over for Thanksgiving, when you're in a fight, just keep going. If you hesitate, he said, that's when you're going to get clocked. Good advice, you'd think. Then it happened. Mom and I always sat together at the games, while my brother was either in the penalty box, getting an education on life, or worse, on the bench as towel, water or stick boy. John got into a fight, and as the case had been when we watched my dad fighting on the ice, we never worried about him; we always knew that both could handle themselves quite well. It's funny to look back at that—or worse, to say it. It makes me realize how different an upbringing I have had. To digress for a moment, I can remember bartending in our first bar in Hamilton, and there was a doozy of a fight right in front of me. I thought it was quite exciting to watch, and I looked around and all the other bartenders were crying and so upset. That's when I knew my upbringing had toughened me up to the real world. How many kids can say they have cheered their dad on in a fight, while thousands watched? Sure, I saw him cut up afterwards, got him ice, and saw my mom take out his stitches, but that was our life.

Getting back to what was hardly called a fight, John had this guy out cold on the first punch. The player fell, and with all the excitement of people cheering, John, not knowing his opponent was out, kept going. After the fifth punch, a silent hush fell over the crowd. They feared they were witnessing a murder. Mom and I just looked at each other in utter horror. First, for the poor kid on the ice, but we both knew someone was going to be held accountable for this, and it would either be Dad or John, neither of which would be good. The guy ended up in the hospital, Dad went to see him that night. I'll never forget going up into the offices after the game, and seeing John sitting, in handcuffs, with a policeman. He was eating one of the leftover sandwiches, which I made for the guys in the press box (the Rochester Americans were a hometown team on a strict budget, so it was one of my jobs to be the caterer), and he commented on how delicious they were. I thought this was ironic, because one of the newspaper reporters had mentioned to one of the owners that the sandwiches were soggy. I knew why this was: the tea towels I'd put over the plates of finger sandwiches, to prevent them from drying out before game time, had been too damp. I told my dad about the writer's complaint, and he never got another inside scoop about the Amerks again. I don't think he ever figured it out it was because he complained about my sandwiches.

I don't think John ever realized how much trouble he was really in at the time, even if he was in handcuffs. He had faith in Dad, that Dad would always look out for him. The owners, on the other hand, wanted him charged with assault or attempted murder. Dad had to lay his job on the line, and told them that if John went, he went too. Needless to say, no charges were laid. Mom, however, was another story: she really gave it to Dad that night. I heard her yelling at him, saying that it was all his fault, he'd driven John to it, and he should have known better and been ashamed of himself. Poor Dad, he'd got it from everyone; owners, fans, family and the press (needless to say), had a field day on this one. Even though it was the seventies, the press got on the bandwagon about violence in sports and how someone can get hurt in a fight. Some things never change. So, at a young age, reading the papers that just ripped apart Dad, John and the sport that paid our bills, I learned that to be in the public eye, you had better develop a thick skin. If you want the benefits of being in the public eye, you'd better be prepared to absorb the slings and arrows people will shoot at you. One of my favourite expressions is "Life is not about waiting for the storm to pass; it's about learning to dance in the rain."

* * *

Before John Wensink was the Rochester Americans' resident tough guy, there was Bob Kelly. In those days, minor league hockey players were sometimes owned by the team they played for. They were almost treated like racehorses. Dad would groom them for the NHL, then the owners would sell them for quite the profit. This was Bob's story. I noticed throughout Dad's career that he had many players whom no other coach could control. There were many reasons for this. Dad was street smart—he survived more on his ability to out-think the opponent than on skill. That's why so many great coaches aren't the superstars, but the guys who are students of the game. I have seen many a cliché in movies being relevant to Dad's life. Take, for instance, *Bull Durham*. When Dad was a player in Rochester, there was many a time that an NHL team would send down a potential superstar to room with Dad, so he could enlighten the player on the fact that it took more than just skill to get by. I learned early on that many of the players who started in the minors with us, then got to go to the NHL, ended their careers with us. That old saying, about seeing the same people going up the ladder as when you're coming down it, really held true in Rochester.

There have also been NHL wives who have written books or publicly moaned about life in the NHL. I remember seeing one wife of a very famous Leaf saying that she hated going to the games, and that she would read a book during them. I believe in karma, and did this one get it. When I think of how my mom sacrificed and never complained, when I hear these women it just makes my blood boil. There is nothing worse than a whiner.

If you want the short answer to the question of why Dad can get along with players no one else can, I sort of relate it to dogs. My dogs have always been well-behaved despite not receiving any formal "obedience" training. Why is that? Basically, because I'm nuttier than they are, and they know it. Like Dad, I also love the much-maligned bully breeds. I find it funny that, if people want to describe someone as being intense, formidable, the best, etc., they say they are a real "pit bull." When you have as many real tough guys on one team as Dad had on the Bruins, there could only be one alpha male, and that was him. The way he accomplished that can be found throughout this book. I always find it amazing that, whether it's a hockey player or a business associate, even if 99 per cent of people don't like them, they will get along with Dad. So

With Max Domi (left) and Del Cherry (right).

Me and my buddies.

My #1 Blue.

Me and Shania. I'm signing pucks for her brothers in Timmins.

A cut-out of me with the FOB Wilson Angels, south of Kandahar.

With GM John Ferguson and Lanny McDonald, coaching Team Canada at the 1981 World Championships in Sweden.

My Colorado Rockies (1979–80)
Front row (L to R): Hardy Astrom, Wilf Paiement, Gary Croteau, GM Ray Miron, Coach Don Cherry, President and Governor Armand Pohan, Mike Christie, Ron Delorme, Bill McKenzie. Middle row: Asst. Trainer Bob Webster, Dean Turner, Doug Berry, Jack Valiquette, Don Saleski, Nick Beverley, Rob Ramage, Mike McEwen, Trainer Toby Wilson. Back row: Bobby Sheehan, Trevor Johansen, Lucien DeBlois, Pat Hickey, Randy Pierce, Rene Robert, Mike Kitchen.

My favourite picture with Pat Burns and his Coach of the Year award in the Boston Gardens.

My buddies never miss "Coach's Corner."

Two of my favourite guys.

"S. One of your
favourite Bouts"

That's me in the cowboy hat, wearing cowboy boots—got a blister. That's René Robert and Bobby Schmautz; we had a great crowd and beat Pittsburgh 5–0. Didn't matter, my fate was sealed: it was my last game coaching in the NHL.

This picture of the Brunelles after their son, Jonathan (second from right), didn't get drafted, gets me all choked up. See the story on page 174.

It's 5 am at Patrol Base Sperwan Ghar, Afghanistan. The soldier nearest the cut-out of me is Tyler Crooks of Hamilton, Ontario. Tyler was killed in battle. God bless him.

much so, that he constantly gets calls from other people asking him to talk to someone they can't get through to. If he chooses to talk to them, he is usually successful in swaying their opinion, but nine times out of ten he finds he agrees with the stubborn person, *and* goes back to the people who asked him to step in and tells them so.

Bob Kelly and most tough guys, such as Bob Probert, Tie Domi, Terry O'Reilly, and many others, are very soft-spoken people. I learned this very early in my life, and to this day, when I hear someone very loud and boisterous, I tend to not put much stock in what they are talking about.

It was Bob Kelly who got me started on the path to my career in dog grooming. (I had the first mobile dog-grooming unit in Canada, called Cherry's Groomobile.) His family had a shih-tzu that they didn't know how to brush. He asked me to groom it for him, and I really enjoyed it. When he made it to the NHL, he bought me a TV, and the enclosed card said, "To Cindy, thanks for everything." Looking back, I guess he was thankful to Dad for taking him from obscurity of the minors to the big time, and not just for my detangling his dog. He was one classy guy, and I still have that TV in my bedroom—and yes, it has a knob to change the channel and adjust the volume.

When Battleship Bob Kelly went to Chicago, that's when Dad had to go out and find another tough guy. That scenario mirrored the plot in the movie *Slap Shot*. Let's face it: to sell out the War Memorial in Rochester, you not only had to have a winning team, but—and this was quite possibly more important—an entertaining one. The owners weren't affiliated with an NHL team, so their operation wasn't subsidized. As a result, they were into making money. Just as Paul Newman's character had the Hanson Brothers, Rochester had John Wensink, on loan to us from St. Louis. Then Chicago and St. Louis decided they were going to have an exhibition game. To sell out the game, the Blues chose to call John up to play against the NHL's toughest guy—who just happened to be the guy he succeeded, Bob Kelly. Dad knew that John was tough, but too young to go up against Bob, so he came up with a plan. He asked Mom and me if we'd like to go to an NHL game. We both loved the big rinks, as well as staying in the same hotels as the players, so of course we said we would love to go.

Dad arranged for John to have his pre-game meal with us in the hotel's dining room. Bob heard we were in town for the game and came by to say hello to us. That's when Dad introduced Bob to John, and I'll never forget what he said: "John's my boy now, Bob." Bob got the message, and true to his respect for Dad, whenever those two lined up for a face-off together—and the crowd was going nuts—no matter how much John tried to nudge Bob to drop the gloves, Bob wouldn't.

That exhibition game was very memorable for another reason. It brought into focus for Mom and me what Dad had had to go through in his fighting days. What he thought were great tickets, right along the glass, turned out to let us see way too much detail in the game. Mom and I were particular to a different location. When the benches were on opposite sides of the rink, we would always sit on the side were we could see our team's bench, two or three rows above the screen so we didn't have look through it, and on the corner. From that point, you can see the action in all the corners as well as both benches. One other thing: we had to be in the visitors' end, so we could see the home team shooting at the net twice. That's were we have our Leaf tickets in the ACC today, but now you have to look through the protective netting. In the days before the netting, when I'd sit in the Gardens or the Air Canada Centre, I would check out the goalie to see if he was left- or right-handed so that I could judge whether the puck would be headed in our direction when he cleared it. Now, of course, we don't have to think, so I can talk even more during the game!

At this game, a fight did start right in front of us—but not between John and Bob. Steve Durbano pummelled Bob Gassoff. Durbano was a tough, scary-looking guy with a five-o'clock shadow, while blue-eyed Bob had beautiful long, blond hair that Durbano proceeded to grab in order to splat Gassoff's nose into the glass.

There was blood all over his face and the glass—it was ghastly. Mom and I were horrified. Sure, we had seen Dad in fights, one of which was so bad that even our own players came out of the dressing room to tell Mom and me that it might be a while before Dad came out because they were sewing up his third eye. Mom just looked at Dad's face afterwards and said she wouldn't have believed that a fist could do that much damage.

After the Chicago–St. Louis game, Dad asked us if we wanted to go out for dinner. We were so upset about seeing Gassoff's blood all over the place—we had bad headaches over it—that we said no thanks. Dad said, "Oh, I get it. It's okay when I'm in a lot worse fights than that, and you two are in your ivory towers in the stands, and you don't see up close what I go through. Well, welcome to the real world that I live in." And he started to laugh at us. I don't know who was angrier: Mom, because we had these seats and had to watch this bloodbath, or Dad, who realized that we'd never appreciated all his fights because we made it a point never to get that close to the action.

* * *

Dad never had curfews for his players. They just knew not to push their luck with him. The rules were that they had to be in early the night before a game and couldn't stay out too late on the other nights. But although he didn't believe in curfews, he did name certain bars that were off-limits to the players, places that were bad news for young, single hockey players who were the toast of the town. Thinking that the team couldn't survive without its top two goal scorers, a couple of rookies decided the rules didn't apply to them, and off they went to a bar that was off-limits. Sure enough, Dad got wind of it and found out they were there. I still remember the bar's name: the Orange Monkey. Dad couldn't believe they would cross him, and he made an example of them to send the message about what happens when you go against him. Even though the team was in a dogfight for a playoff spot, down they went, further into the minors, never to be seen again. Once again, Dad had to stick to his principles and send a message out to everyone (including me). His players, like Tim and me, always knew were they stood with Dad. Sure, we would test the boundaries, but all he had to say was "Don't push your luck," and we would heed the warning.

New players joining the team couldn't grasp this concept of no curfews. The team captain would have to go over to them and explain how it all worked. He would say something like, "We all have a good thing going here. Just listen to Don, and all will be well." Dad wouldn't even fine players. What he *did* do was far worse. He believed in peer pressure. That was a mighty force. They policed themselves. And if a player was caught out drinking the night before a game, the whole team paid for it during practice. Dad was the champ at making practices either fun or miserable. Don't forget that he endured the Darth Vader of hockey, Eddie Shore. He had learned from the best how to torture players.

* * *

Most kids love the Ice Capades. But I never did, because to me they represented my dad going away for about two weeks straight. The arrival of the Ice Capades in our town spelled a long road trip. Now, I always loved it when my dad came home, because he always had gifts for me in his suitcase. He came home from one road trip and told me to go into his suitcase—and there was a puppy. Every kid's dream! Mom was not pleased. It turned out that the players had a lot of time on their hands during the day, so they went window shopping and saw all these doggies in the window, just like the song, and the whole team bought all the puppies. I named her Ginger. Another time, he went away for training camp and came home with five bunnies. He sure knew how to have a happy welcome home.

The Ice Capades usually came into town right after Christmas. So JoAnn Arbour (daughter of Al) and I went down for the

Americans' last practice before the long road trip, because we were on Christmas vacation. There was always some competition amongst figure skaters (or "fancy skaters," as Dad called them) and hockey players as to which were the best skaters. While the Ice Capades team watched, at the end of the practice Al Arbour and Dad started to figure skate. I must admit, JoAnn and I were a bit embarrassed at first to see our dads act so silly. Sure, they started out as making fun of fancy skaters, but then you could see they were really getting into it—and, I might add, quite well. Obviously, I had never before seen my dad skate on one leg, arms extended, holding hands with his defence partner. Looking back, who would ever have guessed we were watching two future NHL coaches of the year showing off their skating abilities. It goes to prove, as did the CBC television show *Battle of the Blades*, what good athletes hockey players actually are.

* * *

I loved my Chevy Monte Carlo. It had beautiful spoke hubcaps. (I mentioned hubcaps to my son the other day, and he didn't know what I meant! That was scary.)

Saturday was a busy day for the old Boston Garden. If you can believe it, we played in the afternoon, and then the Celtics played at night. After our games, the "Bull Gang" who put the floor down over the ice would run you over if you got in their way. It was always cool to see the guards bring in these huge, muzzled German shepherds to sniff out any silly fan who thought they could hide in the arena and see both games for just one ticket. Trust me, that never happened.

It always fascinated me to watch the basketball players come in. They were different from hockey players in more ways than just the obvious. Their clothes were horrible. Okay, I'm sure things have changed now, but then! I was used to sharp-dressed hockey players who prided themselves in custom-made suits. These guys, because they were so tall, looked silly with off-the-rack clothes: high-water pants, with their suit sleeves practically up to their elbows. I guess they didn't have big-and-tall stores back then.

I would usually go out on Saturday nights, so I'd bring my car down to the game, which meant I couldn't park it inside the Garden like Dad did; I had to park down below, outside. I remember once, it was the last game of the season, and I was so happy that my car's spoke hubcaps hadn't been stolen for the entire season. You guessed it: that day, all four were gone. I was so upset, and was Dad angry 'cause they were really expensive back then. Frosty Forristall overheard Dad in the dressing room telling someone about my loss, and he told an off-ice official who worked the penalty box. This was the same guy who once told Dad that his car was going to be stolen Tuesday and burnt on Wednesday. Dad asked him how he knew, and the guy just stared at him. You gotta love no-fault insurance.

Needless to say, my hubcaps were put back on my car in time for the next Bruins game. I don't know which feeling was stronger: my joy at getting them back, or my awe at Dad's power to rectify the situation. Either way, I was happy.

Try to envision the scene on those Saturdays, with fifteen thousand people trying to leave the Bruins game while sixteen thousand were trying to get in to park for the Celtics game. In Boston, there are Bruins fans and there are Celtic fans and never the twain shall meet. The only overlap is with Red Sox fans. Those were trying times, getting out of the parking lot. I consider myself a very good Boston driver. Getting my driver's licence was tricky. I kept moving back and forth between Rochester and Boston, so the timing of my driver's test was always getting mixed up. Finally, I complained to Dad, and he made a call. This man came to the Garden at 5 P.M. and told me to get in the car and drive around the Boston Garden. He then gave me my driver's licence. I ask him, "Don't you want to see me parallel park? I've really been practising." He said that anyone who can drive in Boston's rush-hour traffic can drive anywhere. And boy, was he correct: they are tough drivers. Once, while leaving the Garden, I was foolishly trying to make a left turn. I was waiting forever, then I felt my car moving while my foot was on the brake. The truck behind me was pushing me out into the intersection! The driver of the car that I was about to cut off looked at me as if to say, "What the . . . ?" I just shrugged my shoulders and pointed to the vehicle behind me. The driver of the oncoming car put his car in park, got out, ran over and pulled the other guy out and proceeded to pummel him. By then, since he was now block-ing the oncoming traffic, I made a hasty retreat. I was visibly upset, and when I got home, all Dad said was that's what I get for not coming down to the game with him — and my bumper better not be damaged. Come to think of it, can you imagine doing something like that in the cars of today, with their plastic bumpers? Does the word *accordion* mean anything to you?

Dad had a Cadillac Seville that he adored. With that in mind, I still can't believe Mom and I did this. The one thing we love to do is eat out. Every year, we could hardly wait for the Bruins' wrap-up party at our all-time favourite restaurant, Kowloon's. Their pupu platter is beyond words. Well, wouldn't you know it, Dad got very sick after the playoffs one year and couldn't go, but Mom and I still made it. Driving there on Route 1, one of the busiest highways in Boston, my foot was to the floor, trying to give it gas, and I had abso-lutely no power. With no cell phones in those days, I cruised onto the shoulder where I saw an emergency phone. We got the opera-tor, but instead of asking for assistance, we asked to be put through to Kowloon's restaurant. We asked for the Bruins party, and Terry O'Reilly came to the phone and offered to call for help, but we said just come and pick us up, we are not missing the festivities. Mike Milbury picked us up, and we left the car there. The next day, Dad asked where his car was, and we told him somewhere on Route 1. He asked why we left it there, and we told him it had quit on us and we weren't going to miss the party. Boy, was he upset with us!

Speaking of Mom and me getting in trouble with Dad for our adventures in restaurants, another favourite jaunt was to Newburyport, about forty miles north of Boston, for seafood. It was right on the ocean—fresh seafood, milkshake Brown Cows, the place was a real treat. Dad was on a long road trip out west, which usually meant Mom and I went out more often. The only problem this time was that Tim was scheduled for dialysis in Boston at five-thirty the next morning. At the best of times, he wasn't supposed to have any seafood because of the salt content, but we figured he could have a hamburger. Well, sure enough, he couldn't resist and he had a few shrimp. The next day, he had to spend an extra two hours in dialysis. He normally lost three or four pounds each treatment, but this time he lost seven. Yikes! Mom and I really felt bad. What made things worse is that he told Dad what happened. Boy, was Dad angry. He called us selfish gluttons, among other things, and looking back, I guess he was right.

* * *

When Tim's kidneys started to fail, I had no idea it was that bad. I had been living in Kingston, Ontario, at the time, but decided to move back to Boston. My parents didn't see the need to tell me how sick Tim actually was when I lived up north. After seeing him spend all those long hours in dialysis, you could see that was no way to live. A transplant was the only answer, and I had a kidney to donate.

Massachusetts General in Boston is quite the hospital. We missed being on the same floor as John Wayne when he got his pig-valve transplant—they replaced one of the valves in his heart with one from a pig. I did get to see the stately room he stayed in, and met his nurse and the coffee cup he gave her. I thought that was a really big deal at the time. Mass General is a teaching hospital. Now, some people have a real issue with all these students coming around and talking about you as if you are just their guinea pig. I didn't mind at all. In fact, they did a procedure on my leg using a local anesthetic, and I got to watch.

They kept asking if I minded if several different students tried to do the procedure for Tim's transplant; I figured everyone has to learn. The one thing that didn't go over well was my incision. They tried a new procedure to close up the very large cut that went halfway around my body. They had to be very sure that the kidney they took out didn't get damaged in the process. To ensure this, they even had to take out one of my ribs, which they told me is why I was in so much pain from the operation. This new type of closure involved one very long wire. They said the advantage of this was that it didn't leave a scar. Well, when they went to pull it out in one big yank, it didn't budge. The skin had grown around the wire and it was embedded in the skin. It was the first time I had ever sweated from nerves. I told the doctor to just go for it, and so he did; the pain felt like I had been sawed in half. I told them I highly recommended that they not use this procedure again, and that I would have gladly taken the ugly scar. (After all that, mine was, in my estimation, still pretty bad.) Live and learn—they sure did. Boy, did it hurt. I really did see stars.

My brother got a private room, while I shared a room with a woman who had just had a baby. She was quite happy about the baby, but she was very sick. They'd told her not to get pregnant, because her liver was failing. But she really wanted a baby, and went for it. She and I talked a lot, and what I liked about her most was that she didn't like TV, and since we had to share one, I got to watch what I wanted. When I came back to my room after the operation, her bed was empty. I commented to our nurse that I was glad she got to go home, and they told me she had died. I didn't think she was that sick, and I know that's what sometimes happens in hospitals, but I believe they shouldn't have put us together knowing she was that close to death.

For us, being in the hospital was like one big happy family. Brad Park was in for his knee and Wayne Cashman for his back. When the Bruins games were on TV, we'd all sit together and watch. The day of one game, the referee and linesmen came for a visit and gave me a collection of cassettes—they knew the Bruins had given me what in those days was called a huge ghetto blaster. I think it's probably politically incorrect nowadays to call them that. They asked me if Dad was going to come back to visit after the game, and I said I doubted it, because visiting hours ended at 10 P.M. They looked at each other and said they were sure they could work something out so he'd make it back in plenty of time. It was really funny to watch that game and see them wave off icing and offside calls and not call penalties. Even the announcers commented on the refereeing being quite good that night.

Something I didn't find out until later was that, not only did all the Bruins give blood in our names at the hospital, but their wives did, too. I only found out 'cause Paula Schmautz complained that they wouldn't accept her as a donor because she didn't weigh enough. If only I had that problem! When Tim was writing the script for the movie about Dad, he came over to my house while my son and I were playing Ping Pong. He said he was stuck on the dialogue for the scene where Dr. Heron was telling us about what was involved in a kidney transplant; he couldn't remember what had been said and asked me if I could. I remember it vividly. The doctor was very thorough, and then asked us if we had any questions. At the time, none of us spoke up—and to tell you the truth, I wanted to ask a semi-intelligent question, just to show him we were into it. I remembered reading somewhere that people who had their appendix or bladder removed lost a lot of weight, and I was hoping this would be true in my case. The doctor looked rather stunned at the question—I could see it wasn't exactly the type he had been expecting. He gave me the bad news that the best I could hope for was a loss of a pound and a half of kidney. So I told Tim that that was about all that was said, and that I doubted the CBC would want to put that in the script. Fortunately, when he ran it by them, there were women in the room who thought all this was hilarious, so there it was, on TV for all the world to see: my issues with my weight.

I remember being in the hospital with the IV in me, complaining to the nurse to get it out. She asked me if it was hurting my hand; again, I was too embarrassed to tell her I wanted it out, 'cause I figured if it weren't in I'd drop five pounds. I look back at the photos of my time in the hospital, and I weighed all of about 125 pounds then. Too bad I couldn't have enjoyed that weight then. Just the other day, I explained to my son what the old saying, "Youth is wasted on the young," meant. When it came to my time in the hospital, no cliché was ever truer.

* * *

I see these shows on TV talking about athletes' wives. They really are silly. I told my brother that the joke is on the producers; they completely missed out on where the real action is: the wives' room. You have to figure, the players and coaches get down to the arena at least two and a half hours before the game. That's a lot of time to kill.

I can still remember my first time in the Boston Garden. Mrs. Sinden met us and brought us to a special room where she and the assistant GM's wife sat before the games. Mom said, "Oh. I thought the wives' room was over there." Mrs. Sinden said that one was only for the players' wives. Mom, having the same mentality as Dad when it came to her relationship with the players, said, "That's fine. We'll sit in there with them." When we walked in, it was overwhelming for several reasons. First, the look on the ladies' faces to see us in there. Second, for me to see Noah's Ark in the coat check. I had never seen such an array of fur coats in my life: lynx, wolf, mink, sable, chinchilla, beaver, fox . . . there was even rabbit. (Who had that? Must have been a kid's coat.) I can still remember the goalie's wife, complaining about how her full-length lynx coat shed like a real cat's fur and trying to get the hair off her black pants.

We introduced ourselves, and everyone was quite friendly. What else could they be, when you think back. Then something occurred to Mom and me: "Where's everyone else?" Meaning the wives of the big stars. We found out that there was a second floor. Talk about a hierarchy: the room on the first floor was for the wives of all the rookies, the third- and fourth-liners, and a few steady girl-friends. The food and drinks were all upstairs, and few first-floor people went up there. So up Mom and I went, to get the lay of the land. First off, we learned that the same wives brought the food time after time. Mom changed that, and got us on a rotation of who was to bring the munchies. You can only imagine how we tried to outdo each other in tasty nibbles. We exchanged recipes, and all felt welcome to share the food—none of this business that the food was only for the people who brought it. It turned out that, once we broke that barrier between the first and second floors, Mom and I preferred the first floor.

We are good talkers, but you can only talk so much; plus, the wives talked a lot about their kids, which I wasn't into, so I started to get games of euchre going. Boy, were they fun. Most of the wives were Canadian, so they played by Canadian rules—ordering up your partner meant you had to go alone to win the hand, and you score with the twos and threes, not with the fives—just the way my dad likes it.

* * *

When I look back at Dad and Mom's relationship with the players, it was something that I'm sure doesn't exist in sports today. For instance, when the Bruins went on long western road trips, we all went on a vacation together—not only the wives with kids, but even the wives that had no kids, 'cause we had such a good time.

* * *

Our house was situated where there used to be a conservation area, but with house construction going on, the streams were getting cut off and the mosquitoes were deadly. As long as there was a bit of a breeze, you were safe. We even had to spray bug repellent on Blue's back when she went out at night, 'cause if we didn't, her whole back would be covered with bugs, and when you'd wipe her down, her back would be covered in her own blood. There was one night when a bunch of the team was over, and they were having a good time outdoors, all the while being aware we were pushing our luck with the bug situation. Bobby Schmautz must have had surgery done on his knee, because he was in a full leg cast and had crutches to get around. Well, all of a sudden the wind died down and the swarms of mosquitoes and horseflies came swooping in. We all called the dogs in and ran for cover. Poor Bobby tripped on the long walk back to the house and got swarmed. He was dragging himself along the walk, swiping at the hordes of bugs on him while yelling for help. Dad and the players were killing themselves laughing; it looked like something out of a war movie. Was he ever angry. I remember Mom getting the alcohol swabs to dab his bites because they were that intense.

* * *

I was amazed at how many of the players came over to the house when it was announced that Dad was fired from the Bruins. So many that, once again, it turned into a bit of a party, and then the press showed up, and with the drinks flowing, some of the players let their true feelings on the subject be known. They had to have known that there were a lot of guys on that team who were termed one of Dad's boys, and they must have known the writing was on the wall for them too, that their time was also coming. It took Harry a year or two, but he did clean house.

That summer, Dad was hired by the Colorado Rockies. With my parents moving out west, I really didn't have deep enough roots in Boston to make it worth my while to stay there when they moved. I was sort of in limbo. I debated whether to move out with them. They say Denver is a great city, and I had never lived out west before. It might've been the start of something out there for me. So I decided to go out with them while they looked for a house—I figured, what better way to get a feel for a place than to go house-hunting?

While we were out there, we went to dinner at general manager Ray Miron's house. First thing he did was show us a book that some hockey person gave him, and its title was *What I Know About Hockey*, by Ray Miron. You'd open up the book, and it was blank. He thought this was hilarious; I thought it was demeaning. Little did I know it was the truth. Then, thinking we were dog people, they talked endlessly about their miniature poodle. From that dinner, I knew Dad had a challenge on his hands, and even though he had signed a three-year contract, it would be a miracle if he lasted. I decided I didn't want to put roots down here, get a career going, then have Mom and Dad move back east. I wasn't crazy for the west anyway. The time zone was a problem; the times when the TV shows came on were always screwed up, and I just didn't want to have to get used to it. Plus, I think I would've been the only person in Colorado who didn't ski, and I had no desire to learn.

So I decided to move back to Kingston. That proved harder than I thought. At the time, I was an American citizen, since I was born in Chocolate Town, USA: Hershey, Pennsylvania. I started the long process of trying to get my paperwork in order to get into the country. I had to prove I had relatives in Canada—got that. Then I had to prove that there was no one who could do the job I was getting. So I had my boss write a letter stating that fact. I had to prove I had a certain amount of money in the bank. Did that. I had to have a place to live. Had that too. All this was still not enough. Then I found out I could become a Canadian citizen without renouncing my U.S. citizenship, so I went down that road. It's hard not to look back and get resentful about what they made me go through. I wonder if they are still that picky today.

Living in Kingston, I got to see Dad when the Rockies came to either Toronto or Montreal. I'd drive up for the games, and sometimes, if they had a chartered flight, I'd go home with him to see

Mom and Tim. I used to do the same thing when I was going to college in Kingston and Dad was coaching the Bruins. If I, or any of the wives, were on the chartered flights, either coming or going, the protocol was that we had to sit together and not intermingle with the players. I'm sure things have changed nowadays. The players can even take their girlfriends with them, or rendezvous wherever they go. I remember one time I was carrying my very heavy suitcase (before they had wheels), and Terry O'Reilly came up and said, very loud and clear, "Here, Cindy, let me carry your bags. Then maybe your dad will put me on the power play."

＊ ＊ ＊

It was a fun thought at the time to think of us as owners of a Major Junior hockey team. Finally, to be really back into hockey, I thought, would be a real treat. Little did I know the challenges we would face. It started before we even got the team. We had what I guess you'd call the "chicken and the egg syndrome." Dad's favorite politician of all time, Mayor Hazel McCallion, said she wouldn't build a $32 million rink if she wasn't guaranteed a team to play in it, and David Branch, the president of the Canadian Hockey League, wouldn't give Dad a team if he didn't have a rink to play in. What we had was a Mexican standoff. Dad finally had to put his neck on the line to appease both of them; each of their demands would be met. Talk about pressure, but it does say a lot about their trust in Dad to come through, which he did.

The rink that was eventually built was called the Hershey Centre. When you think of the connection of the city of Hershey and its corporation to our family, it's really amazing. My dad, while playing for the Hershey Bears of the AHL, met my mom when she was a secretary in the factory. As a little girl, I remember having a sightseeing tour through the factory and seeing my grandma on the assembly line. My grandfather and most of my relatives worked for them too, with Dad working on the construction site of their Reese's Peanut Butter Cup factory in the off-season. No matter where my parents' travels had them at the time, my mom always went back to Hershey to be with her family to give birth to Tim and me.

For the naming rights to Mississauga's flagship arena, the city considered which big corporation should be approached first, and trust me, the city of Mississauga has lots of head offices in it. Top of the list was Hershey Canada, and they agreed. If you go to 5500 Rose Cherry Place—yes, that's the address—you'll see the two large Hershey's Kiss street lamps at the front doors. The City of Hershey donated them, and it's the first time any of these lamps has ever left Pennsylvania.

The other Hershey connection was when I needed my first large founding donor when I was on my ten-year quest to build a hospice for chronically and terminally-ill children, the Rose Cherry Home for Kids. I approached Hershey Canada, and they helped me when no one else would. I will forever be indebted to Rick Meyers. They are a great company.

* * *

The media was making such a big deal out of those horns that were being blasted at the 2010 Soccer World Cup in Africa. I know all about how irritating those things can be. I was the retail manager for the IceDogs and was very proud of that fact that, while we owned the team, we were number one in sales in the OHL and number two in all the CHL—second only to the Calgary Hitmen of the Western Hockey League. I saw an opportunity to make a big profit on the selling of those horns, which are really cheap. I sold at least two to three hundred per night, and were they *loud*. So much so that Dad finally said he had had enough and was sick of listening to them and that we should stop selling them.

Great. I had about a thousand of them to get rid of, so I told our public relations person to give them away as a promotion. So what does she do? She gives them away to a hockey team that rented the box beside mine in the arena. Dad never came into my box, but wouldn't you know it, that night he does. Sure enough, the kids are going nuts with the horns. He gets angry at me and says, "Didn't I tell you to stop selling those things?" I explained the situation. He can't stand the noise anymore, and goes over to their box and tells them to stop blowing them. Now the kids look sad, and every time we score, they put the horns up to their mouths, then look over at Dad and put them down. Now Dad really feels bad. Again, he blames me for putting him in this situation of looking like such a jerk. He then goes back over signs all their hockey sweaters, hats and horns and poses for individual pictures with each kid.

* * *

How many times has Dad told parents to stay away from drafts unless their son is guaranteed to go in the first round? People never listen. Our first draft was in Barrie, Ontario. Each kid drafted got to come up to our box and have their picture taken with Dad, plus much more. It was really fun. However, there was this family, consisting of the mom, dad, grandma, sister, and this clean-cut kid in a brand new suit, sitting right in front of us. He hadn't been picked, and here we were in the sixteenth or seventeenth round. He had his head down with his hands covering his face, his mom soothing him by rubbing his back, while he held back his tears. Heartbreaking! I can't stand it. I go to Dad and tell him that kid has been here since 8:30 A.M. and hasn't moved. He says, "We have closed our bidding."

And I said, "You have to do something."

Dad finds out the kid's name, phones down to our table on the floor and tells them to reopen our draft selection and call this kid's name. We watched them jumped up, hug one another—it was just great to see. Needless to say, he came to camp and I took a special interest in seeing him scrimmage with the team. He didn't make the cut, but I'm sure it was fun for him anyway.

I made up a questionnaire to be filled out by the team, and the answers were going to be put on the back of the hockey cards I was designing. One question asked what their pet peeve was. Little did I know these boys didn't even know what that meant. After it was explained to them, Jason Spezza, whose card was probably going to be the most valuable, said he didn't have one. I asked him, "How can one go through life with nothing that bothers them? My list is a mile long." I made a few suggestions and believe we settled on linesmen calling close offsides. Ah, to be young, when nothing gets to you. As I have said before, youth is wasted on the young.

* * *

I was at Bobby Orr's golf tournament, standing with the photographer who was taking a group shot of all the celebrities that were there. As he was preparing to take the shot, I was saying under my breath, "Take off those sunglasses, Jason," because I knew what was coming. The photographer looked at me as if I was nuts. Then, *bam*! Jason got it in the ribs from Dad, who was standing beside him, urging him to take the shades off and not put them on the top of his head. It takes a pro like Dad to show these rookies the name of the game. Another thing you will notice is that he will always take off his glove to shake your hand, another tradition that is falling by the wayside.

* * *

At this same tournament, Dad and Bobby were at this one hole where all the players got to take a shot, trying to beat Bobby's drive, and then have their picture taken with both of them. The last foursome came up. It was a long, hot day and everyone just wanted to get out of there. This poor woman, knowing this, is so nervous, and, with everyone watching her, flubs. She barely hits the ball, and it sort of rolls down this little hill. Dad and Bobby both yell, "Wait! Let her take the shot again—that was just practice," breaking the ice of her embarrassment. They run up to her, take a picture with just her, then with her foursome. I watched in amazement. They are two pros when it comes to making people feel comfortable, something that the new generation of athletes should learn from.

* * *

Speaking of golf tournaments, I got to see firsthand how hockey people's lingo is so much different than other people's, with the connotations that go with certain expressions. An event co-coordinator of a tournament I was recently volunteering at was explaining to Bruce Boudreau, whose tournament it was, that she had two "floaters" going around to the volunteers at each hole to give them a break during the day. You could see that Bruce didn't take it well that she called them floaters. He said, "I don't think they're floaters. They have an important role to play." I later explained to her that in the hockey world, that is one of the worst things you could label someone. I suggested that in the future she call them "rovers."

* * *

Dad sure took a lot of slings and arrows for people who were con-nected to the IceDogs who were obviously in way over their head. Then there was an article in the paper that not only crucified him, but took on our family members working for the team. My uncle, my cousin, my brother, you name it, they got it in this exposé-type article. Did it ever do a number on everyone. The only person who wasn't ripped apart was me. So we called on our friend Tie Domi to help us find out who'd dished. And he did. My dad, just the other day, was using this guy as an example when we were talking about head coaches versus assistant coaches, and how some people are just born to be second in command and destined to just pick practice pucks out of the net, which this guy does.

* * *

I hired a friend of mine to be the retail sales manager at the arena, and she ended up running the whole front office. Every day, we would eat our brown-bag lunches in the large boardroom in the back along with this guy who would read the paper as we chatted away. Every now and then, he'd chirp in to give his comment on whatever we were talking about. I, like my dad, think it is very rude to read in front of someone while we are all eating together. I know this 'cause he told me the story of the time when he was going to meet Ron at 9 A.M. in the hotel coffee shop for breakfast. He bought a newspaper to read while waiting. Sure enough, another *Hockey Night in Canada* guy comes to join them. Dad puts down his paper, and what does this guy do? Picks it up—Dad is staring at the back pages while this guy enjoys his paper.

It's like we are his entertainment for lunch. I made the mistake of mentioning this to Dad. One day, Dad was lecturing the front-office staff. Now, you have to understand, Dad is used to giving speeches to hockey players who know to give him 100 per cent of their attention and eye contact. So what happens? A fax starts coming through in the middle of his lecture, and this poor guy glances at it. Well, Dad reverts to his hockey ways and proceeds to tear a strip off of him. I am sure my telling Dad about him having that rude habit didn't help the guy's cause any. He was so shook up that after the meeting he asked to go home to go to bed and recuperate.

* * *

I was a jack-of-all-trades when it came to running that team, and a master of none. I even helped arrange for training-camp meals from the restaurant we owned. Another duty was arranging for an anthem singer. I especially wanted to be in on picking the singer when we had an American team come in. I don't know about you, but listening to some of these slow, methodical singers stretch out these two songs to take up half a period of hockey time is annoying. (Another pet peeve on my endless list?) So I decided to get one I could

MY LIFE WITH DON CHERRY

convince to speed it up: my babysitter. She could sing, and once I explained to her that her priority was to be my sitter, then an anthem singer, she had the job. As I expected, she started dating one of our top scorers on the team. One weeknight game, I was late getting home, and lo and behold, there is our top scorer on my couch, sitting in front of my fireplace, watching TV with my babysitter/anthem singer. I was upset for so many reasons. It was late for both of them to be out on a school night, the player should have been thinking about the game he'd just lost that night, and he was in the house of one of the owners—all of which are not good. I called up the mother of my sitter and told her how disappointed I was in her daughter and blah, blah, blah. Her only reply/concern/question was whether I was going to tell my dad and get the kid in trouble. Then I called the player's mom. Her response wasn't all that much better, which was to state that if I thought there was any hanky-panky going on, I was mistaken. There you had it. My question to myself was, How could I be upset with these kids when their mothers didn't see any issue? Even stranger was to witness the mothers' giddiness at the thought of their daughters involved with these young hockey players.

* * *

Our first couple of dogs were lap dogs. One was a miniature poodle; then we got a Maltese terrier. Both nice dogs, but not Dad's cup of tea. Then it was decided that enough was enough, and Dad got the dog he always wanted, which was a white bull terrier. I remember when we first brought her home as an eight-week-old puppy. The side door did not lead to the fenced-in backyard, but the dining room window did. So Dad built a three-level ramp for her to get outside. It was sort of weird for visitors to see a dog go to a window when she had to pee. It was high and narrow and, I hate to say it, 'cause Dad will get angry, but rickety. Our pup, however, didn't hesitate to gallop down it. When my dad got a little money, he eventually made that window into a patio door that led onto a deck. It was this deck that brings me to my next story.

We had an above-ground figure-eight pool. For some reason, Blue hated to see anyone jump into it. She'd go so crazy, so house rules were that she was not allowed up on the small deck that surrounded the pool. One day, Dad decided to see what she would do if she was up there while he dove in. Was her bark worse then her bite? Was she full of sound and fury, signifying nothing, as most of these yappy dogs are? Well, he learned fast! He dives in, and she nails his inner thigh and lets it rip. All I can remember is Mom saying Dad looked like a harpooned whale with the blood flowing into the pool. We were horrified and laughing at the same time. When the chlorine hit the cut, Dad flew out of the pool, blood running down his leg, and Blue ran, too. He was crazed with pain and anger that she bit him.

Our neighbour grew tomatoes, and used broken hockey sticks as the stakes to hold them up in her garden. Dad grabbed one of them and crawled after Blue under the deck were she had run to. Dad was very upset, as you can imagine, and went to hit his Blue. She got the stick in her jaws and Dad said Blue growled at him, like, "Don't do it." He then came to his senses and slowly started to back out, while Mom and I yelled, "Don't hurt Blue." To this day, I don't know who I was more worried about under the deck, Dad or Blue.

* * *

Dad enjoys nothing more in life than telling stories about Blue. That really is her, in Boston, chasing the hose in the opening of "Coach's Corner" on *HNiC*. When he is sitting beside someone on a plane and he's reading, but can see they want to talk to him, he will not be rude, but they are now fair game in being his captive audience to his beloved Blue stories. So when he does take a break and gets back to his book, he's then assured they won't talk to him again.

* * *

Blue was a very aloof dog. She wasn't what I called a "pet me, pet me" type of dog. She never ran to you when you came into the house, barked at the doorbell or did tricks. The only people outside of the family that she really paid any attention to were Rene Robert and Dad's friend Whitey Smith from Rochester. One day, Rene came over to the house with a friend who wanted to see Blue. He sits in the family room and starts calling her name, but does the unthinkable and starts snapping his fingers for her to come. Blue started to walk towards him, but once she heard the clicking of his fingers, she just turned around and walked away. Rene couldn't believe it, and she never bothered with him again.

* * *

That snapping of the fingers put me in an awkward situation on the set of the movie. In the scene were Blue is chewing on the puck underneath the dining-room table, Jared (playing Dad) is supposed to yell at Blue and take the puck away from her. Jared's a great dog person—in fact, his dog, Gus, was on the set for the whole movie, but the snapping of the fingers wouldn't have gone over well with Dad. I then had the very uncomfortable task of asking the patient and forever-understanding director, Jeff, to have Jared not snap his fingers. As with many scenes where the audience wouldn't have known the difference, the details of the film had to be handled so Dad would be happy with the end product. I can't say enough about the crew in their determination to see this through. They were a great bunch of people.

* * *

Dad always prepares himself for a quick, witty comeback. That is not to say he is a negative type of guy. I am always amazed how I can be carrying on or moaning about something, and he will put a twist on it that I'd never of thought of. There was guy going around knocking on doors, asking for donations to put a net up under a bridge that people wanting to commit suicide used to jump off of all the time in Toronto. I, of course, politely declined. Next day, Dad tells me he ended up giving the guy some bucks. I told him I couldn't believe he did that, but once again he gave me an entirely different perspective on it. He figured it would be just his luck to be driving under the bridge at the exact time someone jumped and landed on one of his beautiful cars. I learned that getting the answer you want is dependent on how you ask the question.

* * *

Another thing I try to warn people is not to use Dad as a sounding board. Dad and people like him—for instance, Tie Domi—are what I call fixers. You never whine or complain around them or they will fix a situation, and there might be a chance the situation ends up worse. These people are not easy to live with. There is always an undertone that, at any minute, there could be trouble. Mom always hated going to the movies with Dad. A lot can go wrong in a movie theatre, because there are so many variables, like someone kicking your chair or talking or explaining the movie to someone else, so it's best to avoid trouble. My son, Del, and Max Domi played tyke hockey together. I was always first to get the dressing-room key to open it up. Once the rooms got switched up, so I got assigned a new room. Of course, a guy comes in who thinks it's his room and proceeds to yell at me about how stupid some women are, how I don't know what's going on, blah blah blah, and leaves. So then Tie comes in with Max and I'm talking to myself about how I've forgotten more about hockey than this guy ever knew. Tie perks up. "What's the problem? He said *what* to you? What does he look like? Do you want me to speak to him?" You get the picture. I had to simmer him down, and I just thought, "He is just like my dad, not looking for trouble, but can and would be more than happy to address it."

* * *

There is a difference between using Dad as a sounding board and asking him his opinion. Do not ask him his opinion, unless you are going to go with it 100 per cent. Many people have casually run things by him. He gives them what he calls an answer, not his opinion. They don't use his opinion. He takes no offence, but heaven help them if they ever ask him anything again. I have heard him say more than once to people (even after I have warned them of his attitude), "Why ask my opinion if it means nothing to you?"

* * *

Tim, Dad and I, when telling a story or talking about a situation, refer to our "syndromes." It really saves a lot of time to get the gist of the story if you describe it as such. For this book, I don't feel comfortable using their real names, but one is named after an ex-GM of the Canadiens. Once, after an *HNiC* broadcast, Dad said to the GM, "Good game." Pretty standard comment, which prompted a standard, condescending reply of "They worked hard." Dad hears this as "You dumb-heads think they played well, but I, the hockey expert, know they could have played a lot better." You don't have to be talking hockey to suffer from this syndrome. For instance, a friend of mine purchased her first brand new mid-size car. I went on and on about how great it was, and what did she say to me? "Well, it's an okay starter car!" Another time, in the early '90s, when a car phone was a big deal, I was congratulating a friend whose boss had given her one. Her only reply was that I shouldn't be so easily impressed, that a phone is nothing but a business tool. All three scenarios involve people dismissing comments that are meant in a positive way.

* * *

Another "syndrome" is named after an ex-Bruin who didn't worry about money, till he had some. Then he went cheap. Dad knew he would go on the road trips with absolutely no money in his wallet. What did Dad do? He told the trainer to hold back the per diems for two whole days while the team was on the road.

* * *

One other small tidbit of information that I give to people about Dad is that he believes in shooting the messenger. I try to warn people, don't give him bad news. It might not be their fault, but somehow you are associated with it. One time, his beautiful 1990 Ford F-150 truck was making an awful noise while I was driving it. My son asked, "Aren't you going to tell Grandpa?" I told him about this syndrome, and best he figure it out for himself. Just ask Brian Williams about enlightening and pointing out a tiny rust spot on one of Dad's beloved Lincolns. The examples are endless.

* * *

Dad has always taught me, "You are what you are perceived to be." No matter if it's correct or not; you only have one shot to make a first impression.

One philosophy he had to explain to me is "Money flows with success." Dad was never one to haggle over money. When he was made coach of the Rochester Americans, he got paid $15,000 and they threw in being the GM. The going rate at that time for such a position in the AHL would have been $80,000. He didn't care, because he knew in the long run it would all work out. When he proved himself in Rochester, the NHL came calling. Again, he was glad to get the job and signed for $40,000. To give you some perspective on this, Harry Neale was getting $85,000 for coaching in the WHA. This all led to Dad being the highest-paid coach in the NHL when he signed his two-year contract with the Colorado Rockies. On the flip side of this, when he left Rochester, he wanted to leave them in capable hands, so he highly recommended a certain player to be coach. Just as this guy was about to sign his first coaching contract, he wanted it stipulated that they fly in his wife from Winnipeg each month. It was a dealbreaker, and this guy never got another opportunity to coach again, which was a shame, as Dad thought he had enough talent to make it to the NHL.

* * *

Another one he taught me, that helped me "avoid" trouble in high school, is the philosophy of "guilt by association." This one I have really emphasized to my teenage son.

One of our all-time parent-versus-child lessons involved Dad making me clean a bike I was going to give away. I did not believe that I should have to spruce it up, since I was giving it away. It didn't help that Mom agreed with me. Needless to say, my beautiful pink-and-white Schwinn gleamed when I handed it over to a kid I didn't even like.

* * *

Looking back, Dad made me address situations as a young kid that really prepared me for the confrontations of life. In Rochester— 217 Mohawk Street to be exact—a really mean old man lived behind us. He told me that if my guinea pig escaped one more time and went into his garden, he would kill it with a shovel. I tried to explain to him that guinea pigs eat weeds, unlike rabbits, which eat flowers. It fell on deaf ears. Sure enough, Beaver, my guinea pig, got loose and ran through the fence into his beloved garden. I ran into the house in tears and told Dad that Beaver was soon going to be killed. Dad calmly said I had to walk around the block, knock on the old man's door and tell him I had to go into his back-yard to get my pet. I asked Dad if he'd go and talk to him, and he said no. I then asked if he'd go with me, and he said it was my fault the guinea pig got out, and now I had to face the neighbour. It was like a death march for me. I was terrified of this old man, but I did save my guinea pig.

* * *

Living in the house on Mohawk Street, I missed by three houses being able to take the bus to school and stay for lunch. Not only did I have to walk a very great distance, but they wouldn't even let me stay for lunch. I had to go home for that, too. One day, Dad drove me to school during a snowstorm, knowing that I had to walk all the way home for lunch. He asked me about the kids on the buses. I told him they not only got bused, but they get free hot lunches. Boy, did he get angry. After that day, I got to stay for lunch, but still had to bring it, cause Dad didn't want me to eat for free.

* * *

The stories about Dad and Ron are endless. People always ask me about their relationship. It is a very unique one and hard to describe, and even I envy it. A lot of times when they are travelling together, people mistake them for two undercover policemen.

Their antics together on a plane are amusing. You know how some people put their seat back the whole way, and you get cramped? When it's done to Ron, Dad has actually taken his news-paper and hit the person in front of Ron, so they think it's Ron that did it.

If Dad wants more coffee, he will whisper to the stewardess that the guy beside him is complaining that his coffee is cold. They will come back and, in a stern voice, ask Ron if he wants more, and then Dad will pipe up that since she is here, is it any trouble to give him some?

Ron is one of those lucky people who can sleep on the plane. One time, he fell asleep before the plane took off. It was on the tarmac for over an hour as he slept. It still hadn't taken off, and Dad nudged him to wake him up because they'd arrived. He starts getting up to go, with everyone, including Dad, having a good laugh.

One time, they were leaving a parking lot very late at night. The cost was $4.50, and Ron gives the guy a five-dollar bill and tells him to buy himself a coffee. The guy fires the change back at him, and Dad yells, to make Ron feel even worse, "Yes, my good man, buy yourself a hat or something frilly."

One time, Ron accidentally called a stewardess "Dear." Dad piped up, "Did you call this young lady, Dear?" And she replied, "Yes, and I heard that!" Dad then said, "He says it all the time." Ron is probably one of the most non-condescending guys you'll ever meet, yet Dad sets him up to be the opposite.

* * *

Dad has very strict rules for drinking. First, he never lets anyone pour his beer. Sure, he knows that some beer experts say a large head releases the gases of the beer. His thought: he doesn't want a milkshake.

Dad will not go out for a few pops with you if you've eaten dinner. Lunch is okay. One day, Ron said he had just gotten back from dinner with friends and that he was ready to go out with Dad. Dad wouldn't go. He ordered beer to his room and watched TV. I asked him, "Why does this bother you so?" He just said, "I dunno, those are just the rules."

Not only can you not go out with him if you've had dinner, but you can't sit with him if you order "food." Appetizers are considered food. One time, a producer from *HNiC* came over to their table and brought his chicken wings over with him, and Dad asked him to leave. Peanuts, chips and popcorn are okay, but if you have any cheese, that is a sign that the night is now over.

* * *

Dad is very bar-savvy. He and Ron were in a bar in New York that was owned by two brothers. During the day, you'd always get fresh, frosted glasses with each round. Then they went in on a Friday night. Dad could see things had changed. Ron would finish his draft, with Dad having two sips left in his, and order another round. They would take Ron's glass and fill it back up, and pour Dad's in a new frosty mug, then give it to Dad, who would proceed to gulp down the rest and hand the guy his empty glass. Three rounds later, with Ron having the same warm glass, Dad finally had to speak up and ask Ron if he didn't see what was going on. Nothing is accidental with Dad. Everything he does has some reason or logic behind it.

* * *

When my brother first told me about the idea of making a movie about Dad, I couldn't believe it. How different is that? Then he started on the script. Rewrite after rewrite. What to put in, what to take out. All these stories. There was only one scene that I asked to have changed. Originally, he had my Uncle Johnny introducing my mom to my dad. I said no way, it was Uncle Johnny's wife, my Aunt Honey. To men, this wouldn't make a difference, but women know that a woman introducing her niece to someone holds a different light to the man that she is introducing her to. Women know good quality men more than a man does.

Sarah Manninen, who played Mom, was a shoo-in. Hard to believe she had long blond hair when she went for the first audition. The hairstylist, Heather Smith, got her hair just right, with subtle changes throughout the movie. A lot of the jewellery Sarah wears in the movie is my mom's. I figured what the heck, I might as well give it to them to use. What good was it doing in my jewellery box? I never thought they'd find an actress with a small enough wrist to wear Mom's platinum watch, which she wears throughout the movie, but they did.

* * *

Think of the pressure Jared Keeso and Sarah had on them, with us Cherrys on the set. I tried to be as humble as I could, giving them guidance on the emotion that was going on at the time. For instance, in that one scene where Dad and Mom really have it out, the night he knows he is going to be the next Rochester coach, I told Sarah, "Remember, it's not that she's angry that he has been out all night, but she is embarrassed that when they are calling, she doesn't know where he is. That's a different kind of mad." Mom wasn't an Italian who throws her hands in the air a lot, but what she did do when she was angry was shift her weight from hip to hip. I think that was the best scene in the movie. I still remember it like it was yesterday.

* * *

I can now understand why these Hollywood actresses have to be so thin. The dog they used in the movie was only a seven-month-old pup, Sully, and was it tiny. I thought to myself, "Yikes, wait till Dad sees how small this dog is." I was so surprised when I saw it on film, it looked like it weighed about forty-three pounds. In real life, it was lucky to weigh twenty-five.

For the scene of Blue gnawing on the puck under the dining-room table, I asked the trainer if she had put bacon grease on it, to entice the chewing. No, it just liked chewing pucks. Must be in the breed.

Thank goodness Jared is a dog person. In the kitchen scene, where he throws the beer cap in the sink, which Dad had a habit of doing, it bounced out and landed on the floor, and Sully grabbed it in his mouth. Jared immediately stopped the scene and went in Sully's mouth to get the cap so he didn't choke on it.

People kept asking me about this guy who was going to play Don Cherry. I told them he was a cross between a young Marlon Brando and Paul Newman. I also added that, as good-looking as he was, he was equally as mannerly and a genuinely nice person. Jared would make any parent proud.

* * *

I think the hockey scenes in this movie are the best that have ever been made. They really capture the feeling of what goes on during the game behind the bench. Those scenes of the players changing on the fly were brutal to film. We knew hockey connoisseurs would be looking for mistakes, so it was important to get the players changing in the right direction for each period. So much so, they had the footage of the actual game on the ice as reference.

As everyone knows, it was a high-stress game. Jared kept trying to look as stressed as he could be. There was only so much grimacing, pounding, hands on hips and shrugging that he could do. Finally, I suggested that when Dad got really frustrated behind the bench, he would whip his Juicy Fruit gum at the glass. It's funny when I see other coaches do the same thing when they're ticked off, and it's always at the end of the period or game. The next scene, Jared did it, and I was really thrilled.

The scene of Mom and me back in Boston, watching the game in Montreal, was fascinating for me to watch. They used actual NHL footage of that game, plus the stuff we had shot the week before, and blended it all together. Sometimes, you don't know if you're seeing Jared or Dad. What could have complicated it even more was if I had told them that the local TV station had cameras in our living room, taping us watching the game. That TV on set was exactly like the TV we had then, and I still use it in my living room today. I've lost the clicker to it, and was very tempted to take the one from the set, but they told me to not even think about it.

In that scene, Sarah and Paige Bannister, who played me (and who they cast perfectly—I'll tell you why later), could only look worried so much. The director asked me what dialogue went on during the game. I told them exactly what was said: Mom told me to stop picking at my nails and I told her I'd stop when she stopped twirling her hair—and that was about it.

* * *

We had one great party in Winnipeg to show the movie to locals and the crew. They decided to have it at the Pembina Hotel, where the movie was filmed. Boy, did it look different as a real bar than when we were there filming. I sat with Paige, eating pizza and drinking beer. Now *that* was fun. Behind us were these guys talking during the movie. I guess they figured it was more a bar than a movie theatre, so Paige turns around and tells them to be quiet. The casting person really got my portrayal correct.

Everyone really liked the movie for all different reasons, and I was quite proud of it. The most enlightening comment came from a friend of mine who is my alter ego. She is such a nice person. When I'm on a rant about who knows what, I always ask for her perspective on it, and nine times out of ten it will be different from mine, which makes me look at the situation differently. Her comment about the film, as expected, was something I had never thought of before, and, as usual, we debated it. She said, "I can't believe how mean people were to your dad." Now, *mean* would not be the word I would use to describe why things happened to Dad. I think Dad would admit that he brought most hardships on himself. The point is, though, he never complained about it. Dad had a habit of rubbing the wrong people the wrong way, and he stuck by his principles, but as he admitted in the movie, his family sometimes paid the price. As with most things, it all turned out, and karma has a way of coming through in the end, be it good or bad.

* * *

I thought being on a movie set while they were filming my life before my very eyes was surreal, but sitting in front of a computer, writing these stories, is even more surrealer. Is that a word? If not, I'm making it one, 'cause it best describes my life this past two years.

As you can imagine, Dad had to read all my stories to give his approval on what I said. I should have had a camera when he was doing so. All he kept saying was "I didn't know that . . . you better not say that . . . don't use his name," and when I was describing them taking the stitches out from my kidney transplant, he broke out in a cold sweat and had to stop reading. He didn't know that the woman beside me in the hospital died, or that not only did the Bruins players give blood at the hospital in our name, but so did the wives. He didn't know how late I was staying out during high school, 'cause it was Mom who told him to say something to me. The biggest thing that upset him was he had no idea of the challenges I had faced getting into Canada. He said, "Cindy, you should have got a little boat to sail over to Canada and filed for refugee status, gotten your free room and board, health care and spending money to pay for your clothes. You would have had it made." Then it was my turn to ask *him* questions. Why did he put John Wensink on with Bob Kelly when we played Chicago? He said he thought it was a square fight. He then confessed that he gave Bill Sweeney the canary to give to me when he came over for dinner. He knew Mom wouldn't want a bird, but if Bill gave it to me there was nothing she could do. He also told me that, as scared as I was walking alone around the block to get my guinea pig from that mean old man who was going to kill it, he snuck around the block to watch me, and said the old geezer looked up and saw him and there was no chance of him making me cry more. So, there you have it folks, I hope you have gotten a kick or two out of the hockey world we live in.

Timothy and me at the Boston Gardens.

MY LIFE WITH DON CHERRY
Tim Cherry

A LOT OF PEOPLE ASK WHEN my father started to get his over the top fashion sense. You might think in Boston. I feel Dad dressed very nicely when he coached the Bruins, but his suits weren't over the top. The first suit that was outlandish was in Colorado; specifically, his first game back in Boston.

In Colorado, our family knew it was going to be a rough ride. The team didn't get on track right away. One of the main reasons was the lack of consistent goaltending. Our number one goalie was Hardy Astrom. Dad makes fun now by saying "the only problem Hardy had was pucks." To me, Hardy was one of the goalies who would make some great, spectacular saves and then, right at a critical part of the game, would let in a soft one that would just kill the team. He played forty-nine games for the Rockies and had nine wins and a goals-against of 3.75. Hardy was nothing but consistent. The next year, after Dad had left, he played thirty games, had six wins and a 3.76 goals-against average. After that, he didn't play in the NHL. One of the main reasons for the tough time was that the team didn't have confidence in Hardy, and if a team has no confidence in their goalie, they're dead.

The team played hard and they never quit. There was a stretch when it looked like things were turning around. A goalie from St. Thomas, Bill McKenzie, started to play well, and things started to look up. He was no Patrick Roy, but he made the saves when he had to and the team had confidence in him. He started taking over the goaltending duties around the end of November, and we started to get a streak going.

Going into a three-game road trip that had stops in Pittsburgh, the big homecoming in Boston, and then Quebec, we had only lost one of our last three games with wins against Detroit, the powerful Islanders and a tie with Washington.

For my Christmas present, I was going on the road trip back to Boston. I would fly with the team into Pittsburgh, and the next night we played in Boston. I would fly home and the team would go on to Quebec to play the Nordiques.

We flew into Pittsburgh on Thursday, November 29, 1979. The next morning, we all got on the bus to head over to the rink for a practice. That night, Marvelous Marvin Hagler was to fight Vito Antuofermo for the WBC and WBA middleweight titles. Hagler was from Brockton, Massachusetts, and Dad and I watched his career take off from an unknown to the best pound-for-pound fighter at that time. Dad met Hagler a few times when he fought in the Boston Garden. He was the best middleweight in boxing, and he got passed over for title shots because nobody wanted to fight him. Dad and I were excited, because tonight was the night he was going to win the title. On the bus from the hotel to the rink for a morning skate, the guys were razzing Dad about the fight. Dad stood up and said, "I'll bet every one of you twenty dollars that Hagler wins tonight." The players all hooted and hollered, and as Dad sat down, he threw out, "And if it's a draw, I'll still pay ya."

That night, Dad and I watched the fight in his hotel room. Dad got a large room for the players to watch the fight, and bought some food and beer. It was the night before a game, so the players didn't go out; they all showed up in the room to watch the fight.

Hagler hammered Antuofermo for ten rounds. Antuofermo was bleeding—that was nothing new—and he hardly laid a glove on Hagler. I mean, it wasn't even close. For some reason, Hagler backed off after the tenth round and Antuofermo made a small comeback in the later rounds. Title fights lasted fifteen rounds back then, Antuofermo maybe won three of the last five rounds, but still Hagler won in a cakewalk.

It went to the judges' scorecards, and when the decision was announced, we were in shock. It was a draw. Dad was livid. I'm not sure if he was mad at losing money to the players or at Hagler getting jobbed. The phone rang, and Dad picked it up before the first ring was completed. Dad heard Randy Pierce, a good, tough winger from Arnprior, Ontario, on the other end. Dad had picked up the phone so fast that Randy didn't know he was on the other end. Dad heard him say, "I bet he's pissed, I'd better not bug him," and then Randy hung up.

The next morning Dad gave me a pile of twenty-dollar bills. As the players were getting ready for the morning skate, I started handing the money to the players, and the guys gave me a hard time. I gave Randy his twenty and said, "Someone called Dad last night right after the fight. Do you know who it was?" Randy looked around to see who had ratted on him. He shook his head no as the players all laughed.

We played in Pittsburgh that Saturday night, then flew out right after the game to Boston, where we would play the next night. Dad put Hardy in net against Pittsburgh, and we lost a close one 5–4. I think they scored very late in the game on another soft goal. Dad was saving Bill McKenzie for Boston. Dad was livid after the game; we should have at least had a tie. I said to Dad, "Better we lose tonight and win tomorrow."

We had a skate at the Boston Garden that Sunday morning, and Dad was mobbed by the newspaper reporters and TV stations. After all the serious questions about what it was like coming back to Boston, and whether Dad and Harry were talking yet, they asked Dad about what he was going to wear. He told everyone to be ready, because it was something special.

If Dad was nervous that day, he didn't show it, but the players were ready. In the dressing room, it felt like a playoff game. Dad had struck a pretty strong bond with most of the players on the team by then, and they wanted to win for him. Just before the guys went out for the warmup, Dad decided to show off his attire for the night. It was a crushed velvet—Dad called it burgundy, I'd call it purple—jacket. It was pretty over the top.

While Dad had his jacket on, someone called for him to do a quick interview. Dad went out into the hall, and Bobby Schmautz was waiting for him with a sock (in those days, players used to put baby powder on the blades of their sticks) full of baby powder and threw it at him. Dad turned at the last moment and it hit him square in the back. So, for the next twenty minutes I was brushing baby powder off his crushed velvet jacket. To me, that was Dad's first over-the-top jacket. It was pretty tame compared to some of the jackets he wears today.

* * *

In the old Boston Garden, the visiting team's coach had to walk across the ice to get to the bench. I was with Dad as he came out before the game. As we crossed the ice, the fans started to applaud and then give him a standing ovation. I was so proud of Dad at that moment; it was very emotional. It really did feel like a homecoming. To me, it showed how Dad really did connect with the Boston fans.

The game was pretty rough, and right off the bat, Terry O'Reilly and Ron Delorme (from North Battleford, Saskatchewan), got into a dandy fight. They would fight once more in the third. There were a few more fights in the game.

The game was tied in the third period, and Barry Smith from Surrey, British Columbia, put the puck past Gilles Gilbert for the winner. We scored one more to win the game, 5–3, right in Boston.

With a few minutes left in the game, there was a timeout for TV commercials. Now, if you ask Dad, there is a discrepancy between his memory of what happened next and mine. I was sitting at the end of the bench, and Dad came down to me to say something. As he got to the end of the bench, someone reached around and handed him a piece of paper and a pen. It's almost second nature for hockey players, and coaches, that when they see paper and pen they grab it and sign an autograph. And that is exactly what Dad did; he quickly signed the piece of paper. He didn't do it as a planned stunt if we won the game. It just kind of happened. The next thing you knew, there was a lineup of people handing Dad pieces of paper. I think the realization set in that this would really bug Harry Sinden, so Dad signed one or two more before the game got started.

We won the game, and to celebrate, the team took a bus out to our old stomping ground: Kowloon Restaurant in Saugus, Massachusetts. It was quite a celebration. The team still played well, even without Bill McKenzie. We went on to beat the Nords and then walked into Montreal and the Canadiens. We never had a streak like that again, and poor Dad was in for one tough season. Looking back, that was the highlight of our time in Colorado, and it was a good one.

Oh, and in our first game back in Denver, playing Boston, John Wensink crashed into Bill McKenzie and wrecked his knee. Bill was done for the year and so were the Rockies.

* * *

A lot of people have asked me what kind of hockey dad Don Cherry was. Dad was always positive and always had my best interests at heart.

I see hockey parents today, when Dad and I go out scouting for the OHL, and I feel sorry for some of the kids. I'm not going to paint all hockey parents with the same brush, like most of the media likes to, but I will say there is a minority of hockey parents that should take a lesson from Don Cherry.

I can honestly say that Dad never pushed me into hockey. That being said, I cannot remember going to the rink or playing hockey ever not being an integral part of the Cherry family's life. One of my earliest memories is of Dad making a rink for me in the backyard in Rochester. Dad always made a very small rink, the reason being that he wanted me to learn how to turn properly. I had to skate in small circles and was always turning.

My first real time in an organized game was at a hockey school that Dad taught at in Rochester. I must have been around six years old. The puck went into the corner, and I chased it with the defenceman. Both of us fell, the defenceman falling on top of me. Now, we didn't have full facemasks back then, or even visors. I got up and skated after the puck. I felt something trickling down the side of my face and touched my glove to my face and saw that I was bleeding. I dropped to my knees and covered my face with my hands. Not that it hurt, but that's what I thought you were supposed to do when you were cut. It was small and didn't even need stitches. Dad got some tape and made a butterfly patch. It stopped bleeding almost immediately. We drove home a few hours later. As we pulled into the driveway, Dad took off the butterfly and gave my cut a good squeeze. That hurt more than the original cut. With the blood flowing—and around the eye, it does flow pretty good—Dad smeared the blood all over my face and told me to go see Mom. I didn't know that my face looked like a bloody mess when I went into the kitchen. When Mom saw the blood, she went nuts. Dad laughed, but it almost backfired. Mom wanted my hockey career to end right then and there. Dad asked how come she saw him cut all the time and it didn't bother her, but Timothy had one little cut and she went nuts. Mom said something about Dad not being her flesh and blood and that Dad was a big galoot. Luckily, Mom let me go back to the hockey school the next day.

When I was ten, I was not that stellar a hockey player. I was a good skater and could handle the puck, but I just didn't do much on the ice—in fact, I had not even scored a goal in house league. Dad always told me that I just needed more confidence on the ice. Even with me not that, shall we say, effective a hockey player, I made the Rochester Junior Amerks travelling hockey team. We got the greatest leather jackets and the coolest uniforms. I loved that jacket, and it looked so cool at school. The only reason I was on the team was because Dad was an ex-Amerk. He knew, but I didn't. After I made the team, I sat on the bench and didn't play much. One game, I travelled all the way to Buffalo and got one shift. For some reason, it really didn't bother me, not playing. After that game, Dad sat me down and told me that I was going back to house league and that I had to give the Amerk jacket back. I was devastated. I remember crying at the thought of having to give back the jacket. But my cries fell on deaf ears. I was going back to house league, where I was going to play.

My first game back at house league, I scored my first goal. Dad was right—all I needed was confidence. I started scoring in bunches and quickly became one of the top scorers in the league. A few years later, I learned that, after I started scoring, the coach of the Junior Amerks asked if I could come back. Dad said no—he wanted me to finish in house league. I think had I known that it would have been another crying session.

Like I said, both Mom and Dad were always positive, even when I played a bad game. If Dad saw something I should do differently, he would never tell me right after the game. He'd tell me the next day on the outdoor rink. He would never say I was doing something wrong; he always said I should maybe try something like this or that and he'd show me. I can't remember Dad saying a negative thing about my hockey, and he always made it fun for me. Something all hockey parents should do.

* * *

One of the things I enjoyed most when Dad coached the Bruins, was skating on the Boston Garden ice before practice. Scott Cashman and Craig and Robbie Cheevers were around my age, and we would always skate before the practices on the weekend.

When it was an optional practice, most of the players would still show up at the rink. When this would happen, it would mostly be an east–west game: a scrimmage with players from the east versus players from the west. Many times, the players would let Scott, Craig, Robbie and me play. Most of the time, we would stay out of the way, but the players would pass us the puck and let us go in for a breakaway once in while. Cheevers or Gilbert would never let us score.

One game, I was caught around the net that Gilbert was in and I wanted to get away as fast as possible. Not that I was worried about a player hitting me with a puck, but there could have been a deflection. You don't realize how hard the pros can shoot a puck until it whizzes by you. Bobby Schmautz was coming down the wing and let a hard wrist shot go, and for some reason I stuck my stick in front of the puck (or so I think — Schamutzie could have shot the puck at my stick). It went into the top corner on Gilbert. I raised my stick like I knew what I was doing, and the players started to give it to Gilbert pretty good. He rushed out of the net and tackled me at centre ice. Moments that will live forever.

One morning, Craig Cheevers, Scott Cashman and I were tying our skates in the dressing room to go skate before a practice. Peter McNab was hanging round us, and looking back, we should have been suspicious based on the way he was acting. He and Terry O'Reilly, I think, followed us out to the ice. Now, in the old Garden, you had to cross a hallway and go through a doorway, covered by black-out curtains, and through the Zamboni entrance to get to the ice. They were chatting away to us as we entered the rink. Craig, Scott and I froze. There were fifteen thousand people in the Garden. We turned to head back to the dressing room. Peter opened the door to the rink, and he and Terry almost pushed us onto the ice. Peter said, "If you want to be a hockey player, you have to learn to play in front of a crowd." Being one of three people on the ice, with fifteen thousand pairs of eyes staring at you, is terrifying.

What happened was that, the night before, the crowd camped out for tickets to see Led Zeppelin play the Boston Garden. It was very cold that night, so the Garden management thought they'd better let them in or someone would freeze.

Terry and Peter threw some pucks on the ice and told us to skate around. We all looked at each other, trapped on the ice in front of this tired and not too friendly crowd. We skated slowly around, to the catcalls of the crowd. One of us took a shot at the net and missed, and the crowd gave us a hard time. One of us shot the puck in the net, and they all cheered. We slowly got comfortable and started to whiz up and down the ice, with the crowd yelling and hollering.

Someone threw a cookie at us and just missed. The next thing you knew, food and paper cups were flying onto the ice. Someone threw a dime, and I tripped over it, the crowd roared and it started raining coins. It was getting dangerous, as some of the Bruins were coming out on the ice and you can really hurt yourself if skate over a coin on the ice.

We were sweeping the ice clean of the junk as the rest of the team came onto the ice. Craig, Robbie, Scott and I headed off as quickly as we could.

We were in the dressing room for a short while when the team came back. They were told to get off the ice and stay in the dressing room until the cops came and said it was okay to leave.

After a few hours, they gave us the all-clear. We went to look at the empty Boston Garden, which was trashed. From what I understand, they started calling the people in line to buy the tickets, and after only a few minutes the concert was sold out. So they had to tell fifteen thousand fans that they'd spent the night in the Garden for nothing. When it was announced to the crowd that the show was sold out and there were no more tickets, they went nuts. They tore up the seats. Broke all the toilets and flooded the hallways. It was a mess. That was the first and last time that I was ever in front of a crowd that large. Looking back, if I could do things over again, I would have brought a little camera to the rink. I think of all the pictures I could have taken back then, and how much I would have treasured them now. How true that youth is wasted on the young.

* * *

In the miniseries of Dad's life, *Keep Your Head Up, Kid*, we had to cast an actor to play me. We cast a fine young guy named Ty Woods. In the script, Ty was to say how he hated the Montreal Canadiens. My advice to Ty was to say it with all the dripping venom possible, because in the era of my Dad coaching Boston, I *did* hate the Montreal Canadiens. I think the whole city of Boston hated the Habs, and hate is not too strong a word.

The rivalry between the Bruins and Canadiens when Dad coached was a classic matchup of David and Goliath. Montreal were the Flying Frenchmen and the Bruins were the Lunch Pail Gang. Now, the Habs were talented, but their toughness was well underrated, as was the Bruins' overall talent overshadowed by the team's hard work and grit. In the minds of the media and the fans, it was talent versus grit; Ali versus Smokin' Joe.

I don't think fans or even the media realize how much the lives of players, coaches or GMs and their families revolve around the game. A family's whole routine revolves around the team's schedule. That routine gets even more intense in the playoffs. Teams play every other night; the pressure and focus on winning becomes all-consuming. When the playoffs were on, it was hard for me to think about anything other than the next game. School and homework became second in my world (not to my Mom, of course) to the Bruins. I was bombarded with questions first thing every morning at school. Kids wanted to know what happened in the last game, was anybody hurt, what did I think was going to happen in the next game. The talk in school was not just from my friends, but the teachers as well. The farther we got into the playoffs, the more intense it was for me. My friends were always very good to me and never gave me grief if we lost. I really think it was because the Bruins had captured the hearts of the people in Boston. But when we lost, it was hard to take. It was more than your favourite team losing; it was watching your dad suffer in the media, and there was nothing you could do or say. Diehard fans would still go work the next day, and sports reporters would move on to the next sport. But for the team, it just ended. There were no more games, no more pressure. I didn't even watch the rest of the playoffs when the Bruins were out. Hockey ended when the Bruins' season ended.

In '77, Boston met the Canadiens in the finals and were swept in four games. I was at game four and didn't have a ticket. I was standing at the Zamboni gate, trying to get a glimpse of the game. Jacques Lemaire scored the Stanley Cup–winner in overtime. I quickly went into the dressing room. Dad was already in his office. No, the coaches didn't shake hands back then. I'm not sure when that started. Dad was sitting alone with his head in his hands. I remember his look was more of frustration and anger than one of sadness. He looked up at me and asked me to leave; he said he needed to be alone.

Dad always said the high you get from winning never equals the low you get from losing. All athletes who play at a high level are proud and competitive people, and losing, though something every athlete has to deal with, is a very tough emotion for them to handle. In pro sports, losing has such finality to it. You win, you keep going. You lose, everything stops. It's over.

Pro sports are not like the Olympics, which celebrate mediocrity by awarding medals for second- and third-place finishes. In 1977, the Bruins played their guts out, and when we got beat there was no celebrating coming in second. We just lost. Even in the off-season, I never heard Dad, Harry Sinden or any Bruins player say, "Well, we had a good season. We made it to the finals." In fact, it's tougher sometimes to lose in the finals than to get knocked out in the first round. The higher up the mountain you climb towards winning it all, the harder the fall when you lose.

The next year, we faced the Hawks in the first round and swept them in four games. Next was Philly, again. It was a war, but we beat them four games to one. We were 8–1 in the playoffs going into the finals against Montreal. This time, as Dad told me, it was going to be different. If the Bruins were going to lose, they would go out on their shields. We lost game one 4–1, but in game two we took Montreal to overtime before losing 3–2. Game three, back home, we hammered Montreal and Cheevers got the shutout, 4–0.

The games were getting rough, and you could feel the tension increase with each game. I don't think there were any fights in the first three games, but you could see we had rattled Montreal. If we had had a lucky bounce in game two, we would have been up two games to one instead of down 2–1 in games. For some reason, I was not at game four, but watching it from home. I know my mom and sister were at the game, but (I'm sure it was Mom's doing) I was not able to go. Maybe my school was slipping more than I realized. I was watching the game on TV38 in Boston. Fred Cusick and Johnny Pearson were doing the call of the game. Even though it was on a Boston station, TV38 was picking up the *Hockey Night in Canada* video feed.

There was a faceoff in the Habs' end, and Scotty Bowman put on his tough guys. Dad already had Peter McNab, Terry O'Reilly and John Wensink. Dad took off McNab and put Stan Jonathan at centre. Now, Stan was a winger, so I knew there was going to be fireworks. Our Stan Jonathan and their Pierre Bouchard got into one of the most famous and bloodiest fights in hockey history. To put it mildly, Stan gave it to Bouchard pretty good. Now, all season, when watching the Bruins on TV38, they showed replays of the fights. With great anticipation, I and the rest of the Bruins viewing faithful were waiting for the bloody replay. But now TV38 were at the mercy of *Hockey Night in Canada*. Our anticipation of seeing the blood on the ice again turned to dismay. There was a commercial, and then back to the game. No replay. Fred Cusick and Johnny Pearson were questioning on the air why we were not seeing a replay of the fight. No one in Boston knew that *Hockey Night in Canada* didn't show replays of fights. The first thing that popped into my mind was that it was because a Bruin beat up a Montreal player. When I went to school the next day, I was not alone in thinking that. All my friends, and even the teachers, were talking about how the Canadian station didn't show one of our players beating up one of their players. The great *Hockey Night in Canada* conspiracy was born. It was almost an afterthought that Bobby Schmautz scored the overtime winner and tied up the series at two games. Not only were the Canadiens public enemy number one, but now so was *Hockey Night in Canada*.

We lost the next two games, and once again Montreal won the Cup in the Boston Gardens.

The next season, we met Montreal again, but this time in the semifinals. I remember watching the news, and someone asked defenceman Mike Milbury what the team thought of playing Montreal for a third straight year in the playoffs. Some thirty years later I still remember Mike's answer. He said the first year we played Montreal, the team was in awe and bowed at the church of the Canadiens. The next year, the teams were getting a little too familiar. The Bruins started to realize that this Canadiens player was a backstabber and that Canadiens player was a little yellow. The reporter asked him about this year. Mike paused and said, "This year, we can't stand the bastards." Mike also got in trouble with the Montreal press. After a morning skate in Montreal, Mike was looking up at the Forum's ceiling. One of the Montreal reporters asked Mike what he was looking at, and Mike replied, "All the Montreal Stanley Cup banners." The reporter asked Mike if he was in awe of all the banners hanging from the ceiling. Mike replied not really; he was just thinking how chintzy they looked.

For us, this year was more than just trying again to beat the Canadiens. Dad was at the end of his three-year contract with Boston. He and Harry were having a war in the media. When playoff time came, Dad and Harry were not even talking to each other. I'm not 100-per-cent sure what started the feud. I remember there was a lot of going back and forth in the media about Dad's salary at the time. But that was more the symptom than the disease. I think it was that the pressure of trying to beat Montreal and two alpha wolves having to work together for five years took its toll. As the saying goes, only one wolf in a pack can have his tail in the air. If we won, there would have been no way Boston could not have re-signed Dad. If we lost, there was no way Boston would sign. For me, it came down to this: Bruins win, I stay in Boston with my friends, and I don't have to change high schools. We lose, I'm moving, but not sure where. That thought never really was in the forefront of my mind, it was more just wanting to finally beat Montreal.

We lost the first two games in Montreal. I remember Dad telling Mom and me that he was going to start Gilles Gilbert instead of Gerry Cheevers in net for game three. One might think that this was an easy decision, but it had more consequences for us as a family. Gerry and Betty Cheevers were good friends of Mom and Dad for many years, dating back to when Gerry and Dad won Calder Cup championships in the American Hockey League in Rochester. I went to school with Gerry's son, Craig. We vacationed together during spring break. The Cheevers and Cherrys were more than a coach and player, we were close and longtime friends. My first thought was to wonder whether Craig was going to be mad.

In game three, we won 2–1 and Gilbert was the first star. It's funny how things work in the media. Many of the media didn't say it was a good move by coach Cherry to start Gilbert in game three; they wondered why he didn't do it earlier. I think that's when I realized that most sports reporters are not much more than Monday-morning quarterbacks.

We won game four in overtime when Jean Ratelle scored the winner. So now it was down to a best-two-out-of-three series. We were beaten 5–1 in game five and returned the favour in game six with a 5–2 win. So it came down to game seven. My birthday is May 7, and my gift from Mom and Dad was to go to Montreal for game seven, which was on May 10. I would stand behind the bench and was the "stick boy" for the night.

I don't remember much of the flight up or anything up until the game. The visitors' dressing room in the old Forum was not much different than any other dressing room in any local rink, just a bit bigger. The room was quiet as the players got ready for the warmup by drinking coffee. No music, no chatter. But the room was full of tension. I remember going into the stick room to get some tape. The stick room was nothing more than a very small, hot, cinder-block room with a small table with a vise. Terry O'Reilly was working on his stick. He had the stick in the vise and was using a hacksaw to cut it down. Bobby Schmautz wanted to use the vise. He had a blowtorch in hand and wanted to fix the curve on the blade of his stick. Schmautz said something about how Terry should hurry up, and Terry said something to Schmautz he didn't like. The level of tension and willingness to do battle (armed with a blowtorch and hacksaw, no less) quickly escalated to a level where I was pretty scared. Thank goodness they both calmed down.

When the game started, I was on the bench. I was not the only one Boston had let come on the trip. The Bruins had hired a little person (who they nicknamed Tattoo after the character on the TV show *Fantasy Island*) as a gofer. He never made road trips, but the team brought him along as well. It was all hands on deck. We stood together at the end of the bench. It was tough for both of us to see over the players.

The one thing that sticks out in my mind was how loud it was during the game. There was no glass between the bench and the fans. After every play, there was this deafening roar of approval, dismay or outrage. Every time a Montreal player fell, the crowd went nuts, looking for a penalty. You couldn't hear yourself think. We were up 3–1 going into the third period. Looking back at the game now, I can't believe how well Wayne Cashman played. He was one of the older players on the team, but he was not only a leader in the dressing room but on the ice. He had scored two goals and Ricky Middelton had scored the other.

Between periods, again, not much was said, and we were full of confidence. It wasn't luck that we were up 3–1; we had dominated. In fact, it was because of some bad luck that we weren't up by one or two more goals. In the first, Stan Jonathan had a wide-open net with Dryden down and out. The puck hopped over his stick, and that gave enough time for Savard to come back and make the save. If the puck hadn't hopped over his stick, we would have been up 4–1.

Montreal got a goal quickly in the third, and then came the penalty on Dick Redmond. The ref had let a lot go, but you could just get the sense that he was looking to call *something*. The fans' screaming every time a Montreal player fell down was taking its toll. The refs are only human, and it would be impossible not to be influenced by the Forum faithful. When the ref called that penalty, it was then five power plays to one in favour of Montreal. The fans were doing their job. Dad jumped on the bench and gave the ref hell; he was yelling that the crowd had called the penalty. That's the shot you now see on the opening of "Coach's Corner."

Montreal scored and tied the game at three. There was no panic on our bench. We were still playing very well, and if it weren't for the penalties and power-play goals for Montreal, we would have been cruising along.

The game went back and forth, and the roar of the crowd was getting even louder. As the puck went into Montreal's end, the players stood up and I couldn't see the play. But in my mind today, I recall this goal in slow motion. All I heard was a gasp from the crowd, and then, saw the red light go on. Rick Middleton scored to put us up 4–3. I remember hugging Tattoo and jumping up and down. The crowd was in shock. It was almost if they were saying this shouldn't happen. I swear you could hear a pin drop.

Until the drop of the puck, the crowd went nuts. Again, it was so loud I could hardly talk to the person standing next to me. The action was mostly a blur. I didn't see what happened with the penalty for too many men on the ice. I know that Donny Marcotte was shadowing Guy Lafleur and the wingers got mixed up. I was watching the play, not the players changing. It was John D'Amico that made the call. Afterwards, he skated over and told Dad he was sorry, but he had to call it. The players were huddling around the bench, and Bobby Miller reminded the guys that Montreal would pull Dryden and we could try for the open net and not get called for icing.

Guy scored the tying goal before Scotty Bowman pulled Dryden. I was furious. I thought the play was offside. Looking back now, I guess it was wishful thinking, but it sure looked offside to me at the time.

It didn't occur to me at that time that Dad would become the scapegoat if we lost. I didn't even think about how our family would be uprooted if we lost. In the heat of the battle, you just focused on winning. I still thought we were going to win. If we did, the penalty would just have been a footnote, if remembered at all.

So now we headed to overtime. I remember filling the water bottles and Dad sitting in the chair in the shower. He had a broken stick and was tapping it against the wall. He got up and went to the middle of the dressing room. I don't recall verbatim what his speech was before the players went on the ice, but it was something along the lines that, after they'd lost the first two games, if someone had told them they would be going into overtime in game seven, he wondered if they would be happy.

The overtime was back and forth, and Gilbert was playing great. Then came the moment. No, not the goal, but the save by Dryden. I think it was Peter McNab who passed the puck out to Donny Marcotte in the slot. Dryden was looking the other way and had no idea where the puck was. Marcotte rifled it to the top left corner and started to raise his stick in celebration. The bench started to rise up. But Dryden was so big and took up so much of the net that the puck hit him on the shoulder. I was in shock. I thought we'd won the game for sure.

It was a couple of minutes later that Savard put the puck over to Mario Tremblay. I saw the look in the Bruins defenceman's eyes as Tremblay bore down on him. I swear the bench sank. It was over. Tremblay over to Lambert. Park was a half a step behind, and Gilbert just missed making a great save. It was like everything went into slow motion. I think we were all in a state of shock.

Gilbert skated over to the bench and handed over his gloves, mask and stick. I said "Great game, Gilly." He shook his head and said, "Not good enough." Then he skated into line to shake hands.

As I headed for the dressing room, an usherette tried to grab the stick off me. We got into a short tug or war until I ripped it out of her hands.

In the dressing room, it was like a funeral. All you could hear was the hiss of the showers. There were players with tears in their eyes. One of the most emotional players was Gerry Cheevers. In the press, he kept saying how bad he felt that he couldn't have won one of the first two games for the players.

Dad kept the media out of the room to let the players—I guess grieve is the right word. It was like a horrible nightmare. We just couldn't believe it happened. Before Dad left, he told the players that he was as proud of them as Scotty was of his players. It wasn't until I heard a report asking Dad about the too many men that I realized not only had we lost in such an epic way, but Dad was going to get the blame. The realization of us having to move to a new city next year also dawned on me. I didn't care. The thought of Dad getting roasted in the Boston media was more upsetting to me.

The flight back to Boston was quiet as well. Bobby Schmautz, who was sitting in front of me, turned to me and said, "That's it for you coming on road trips." He was kidding, of course. I said to him, "Well, Schmautzie, I don't think you have to worry about that." He nodded in agreement.

When we landed at Logan International Airport, about five hundred fans came to greet us. They cheered as the players came off the plane and they held signs saying how proud they were of the team. Some of the players were going to head off to one of the team's watering holes. They wanted Dad to come along, but he had to take me home. I have always felt guilty about that; that would have been the last time Dad could have gone out with the players for a few pints.

When we got home, Mom was waiting at the door with Blue. She gave Dad a beer and told him it wasn't his fault. I went to bed and I still remember Mom and Dad sitting in a dark kitchen in the wee hours of the morning, not saying a word.

My fear of Dad getting roasted in the Boston media never came true. They never blamed Dad or even tried to see who the player was that jumped on the ice. They all sang the praises of the team and how hard they'd worked all year. I can't remember a bad word being said in the press.

Of course, Dad didn't sign with the Bruins, and we moved to Denver. I have often thought about what would have happened if we had won game seven. I don't really know if we would have beaten the New York Rangers in the finals and won the Stanley Cup. Not that they were a better team—in fact, I don't think we lost to them in a couple of years. But the Bruins players gave every ounce they had in the series against Montreal, and I wonder if there would have been anything left in the tank. I know Dad would have gone back with Cheevers in net, and he might have beaten the Rangers singlehandedly.

Dad was let go after the playoffs. I still remember the "almost goal" by Marcotte and often wonder how different our lives would have been if he'd scored.

* * *

Here is a trivia question for you: Who is the only player that Dad coached in Rochester, Boston and Colorado? It was Bobby Schmautz.

As long as I can remember, Bobby was part of our hockey world. I don't really remember him in Rochester. Recently, I was looking through an old scrapbook of newspaper clippings from Rochester. One headline read, WITHOUT SCHMAUTZ, NOTHING. It seemed that Vancouver sent down him down as punishment. He went down and lit up the American league in the short time he was in Rochester. When Dad coached, he was paranoid about players covering the points. If you watch "Coach's Corner," you will see Dad hammer this point home more than a few times. He told me the first player he saw cover the points was Schmautzie in Rochester. He would stand right next to the defenceman, and the defence-man was helpless. All he could do was back out when the puck came around the boards. Dad quickly noticed that and made all his wingers stand right next to defencemen. In Boston, it was a great strategy because you need tough wingers to either make the defenceman back out or take the punishment if he decides to pinch in. In Boston, we had O'Reilly, Wensink, Cashman, Schmautz, Secord and Jonathan, along with Marcotte and Middleton. Not too many defencemen would take the punishment and pinch in.

When we went to Boston, Schmautz was already there, and that's where I remember him. He was only about five foot ten but was solid as a rock. He was one of those players that gave off energy that you just didn't fool around with. When I was behind the bench during a game, there were times I was scared of him—it was just the vibe he gave off. He was vicious with his stick and had no conscience if you crossed him. He wasn't just a stick man. Schmautzie would drop the gloves as well, but if you were smart, you just left him alone. In the Bruins' training camp, Dad would talk to all the rookies. He'd tell them if they wanted to drop gloves with O'Reilly, go ahead. Want to challenge Stan Jonathan? Good luck. Al Secord or John Wensink? Go for it. But, he told all the rookies, "See that short guy over there? Just stay away and leave him alone. If you don't, you're taking your life in your hands." The other players used to joke that he would carve his Christmas turkey with his stick.

Dad told me about one game in Detroit. A Red Wings rookie accidentally clipped Schmautz with his stick and gave him a little cut. Dad went down to him and said, "Schmautzie, he's just a rookie, he didn't mean it." Bobby nodded his head okay. Dad said that all he remembered was that, late in the game, the Wings rookie was skating up the ice and Dad didn't even see what Schmautz did, but all he saw was the kid grab his face and crumple to the ice in a pool of blood. Bobby Schmautz asked no quarter and he gave no quarter.

Dad had a close relationship with his players in Boston. I would say most all of them were his friends, but they all knew who was in charge and that there was a line that couldn't be crossed. But if I had to choose one player that was a best friend on the team, it would be Bobby.

Now, the Bruins had two great captains when Dad coached. First was Johnny Bucyk, and then Dad made Wayne Cashman captain. But Schmautzie was the straw boss. If something was up with the team, Dad could always go to Schmautzie to find out what was wrong. If a player wanted talk to Dad but for some reason was afraid, Bobby would go and talk to Dad and let him know what was going on.

Dad and Bobby were friends off the ice as well. Bobby, his wife, Paula, and their two daughters would come over to our house in the summer to go swimming and have a barbecue. When our house in North Andover needed a new roof, Schmautzie put the roof on. When it was announced that Dad was not coming back to coach the Bruins, Schmautzie was the first one over.

Going into one playoff year, I think it was the '77 playoffs, Bobby was in a terrible slump. He had not scored a goal in about fifteen games. It wasn't that he wasn't trying; it was that he was snake-bit. Every one of his shots would hit a stick or a skate. If he had an open net, the puck would jump over his stick. If he beat the goalie, he'd hit the post. I laugh when I hear media experts give the old "you create your own luck" speech when a player runs into a slump. There are times that a player just runs into a streak of bad luck, and there is little you can do but play through it. Bobby was going through one of those streaks. Dad tells me that the day before the playoffs started, Harry was in Dad's office, and Bobby came in and sat down. "Grapes, I'm playing horrible. You gotta not dress me." He did it with the right intention. Schmautzie wasn't looking for sympathy, but he felt he was hurting the team. Dad told him to beat it, in hockey terms, and that there was no way he wasn't dressing. Later, Dad gave him hell for saying that in front of Harry, for Bobby was not one of Harry's favourite Bruins. We played the Los Angeles Kings in the first round, and Bobby scored eight goals in his first eight shots on net in the series. Just like that, he had his scoring touch back.

Schmautzie lived off the ice the way he played on the ice, all-out. One day, Mom and I were driving home to our place in North Andover. The roads twisted and turned through the Massachusetts countryside. In front of us was a red Corvette. The driver sped up and slowed down and was waving to Mom and me as we were driving. Mom and I were trying to figure out who we knew that owned a cherry-red Corvette. While we were going about 45 miles an hour on not too straight a road, the driver of the red Corvette climbed halfway out of the car window and sat on the door. Schmautzie was waving at us, and as soon as we waved back, he got back into the car and sped off.

* * *

One of the many perks I had as the coach's son was that I got free hockey sticks. I played in three leagues in Boston and had a pretty busy hockey schedule. I also went through a few sticks. I quickly found out that I preferred Ricky Middleton's stick. When he would get a new batch of sticks, I would go through and pick out the one or two that I liked while he was on the ice in practice. Now, I knew my sticks, and I would usually pick the best ones. It got to the point where Rick asked Dad if he could get first dibs on his own sticks! Dad told me no more free hand at picking sticks. He would pick them for me.

Dad had the philosophy that it was no good for a child to play with a stick that was made for an adult. Back then, you didn't find sticks that were specifically made for the small hands of a child. Everybody bought an adult stick and cut it down to size. Dad always felt that he need to shave down the thickness of the stick to fit my hand properly, therefore letting me get a proper grip.

One day after practice, Dad was shaving down my sticks. Like all things Dad does, it was the work of a perfectionist. He cut it down to the proper length and then, with the stick in a vise, he would get a rasp and start to shave it down. Then he would sand it down, check the balance of the stick. He would then get a plane and balance it off. Then Dad would heat up the blade with a blow-torch and fix the curve on the stick. Ricky had a pretty wicked curve, and Dad liked me to use a straighter blade. It would take Dad about an hour to get the stick to the point where he was happy with it. Dad worked extra long on this one stick. It was a masterpiece. He gave it to me, and I shot some tape in the dressing room while Dad watched to see if he needed to make any adjustments. It was perfect. Dad had worked up such a sweat working on this stick and was about to go take a shower. Schmautzie came by and asked to take a look at it. He leaned on it, like all hockey players do to check the flex. Bobby almost fell over when the stick snapped in two. All three of us were stunned. Nobody laughed, either. Dad was really pissed, and Schmautzie felt really bad. He tried to make the point that the stick would have broken the first time I took a slap shot. Dad quickly snapped that I didn't take slap shots. I used a wrist shot almost exclusively. Schmautzie was dressed to head home, but he took off his jacket and got his best stick and said he would make a better one. He worked for about forty minutes on a stick and gave it to me. I remember I liked it. Dad grabbed it and said it was no good. If you know Dad, it could have been the best stick in the world, but he was so pissed that you just knew it was going to be no good. We all left, Dad mad and Schmautzie telling me he didn't do it on purpose.

* * *

When Dad went to Colorado, Schmautzie didn't last long in Boston. I believe he was traded to Edmonton for their first season in the NHL. When Colorado played in Edmonton, Bobby came out for warmup in a Rockies sweater. Needless to say, he was traded soon after that and he did end up in Colorado. Dad left at the end of the year, and Bobby went to Vancouver to finish out his career.

That is the sad part of the world of hockey. You make a good friend like Bobby Schmautz, and after the hockey is over, you all seem to go your own ways and things are never the same.

THE LAST WORD

I HAVE READ MANY AUTOBIOGRAPHICAL BOOKS, and at the end of these books, the writer always seems to say that he sees a lot of mistakes he made along the way, but he wouldn't change a thing.

Not me. When I look back on my life, on the long list of mistakes I made, I would change a lot of things.

It seems, as I look back on life, I was my own worst enemy. Why did I play baseball when the biggies in Boston told me not to play? That's how I hurt my shoulder and ruined my chances for the show and spent twenty-two years in the minors, riding the buses.

Why did I fight Eddie Shore when I knew I had no chance of winning? He held all the cards.

Why was I the guy to tell Toe Blake, the legendary coach of the Montreal Canadiens, that we players were being short-changed by the Montreal organization on our taxi allowances? That ticked off Toe and the whole Montreal organization. Imagine! A punk from the minors questioning the great Montreal Canadiens organization and telling them they were wrong.

As Rose used to say, "Why is it that you with your big mouth had to be the one to say something?"

Why fight the GM of the Colorado Rockies, Ray Miron, when I knew he had the ear of Armand Pohan, the stepson of the owner?

And why would I not take the Maple Leafs job that Harold Ballard offered me? He offered me a three-year contract, more money than Colorado, and a dynamite team just a player or two away from the Stanley Cup. I could have often visited my mother, who was living alone in Kingston, and I know Harold and I would have gotten along well together. I liked him, and I know he liked me.

No, I had to go to Colorado like a dummy because I shook Ray Miron's hand—the hand that eventually stabbed me in the back. Not a smart move.

It continued on *Hockey Night in Canada*—always on the edge, always pushing the envelope and being told five times, "This is your last year."

One boss was quoted in the paper sayin' I was "reprehensible and despicable," not a good reference for my next job.

Rose was never a fan of "Coach's Corner." "You're going to get fired again," she'd say.

I was fortunate. I had some smart men to bail me out, starting with Bob Clark, the lawyer who got me started coaching high-school hockey in Pittsford when I was unemployed, then hired me as coach and general manager of the Rochester Americans.

Hockey Night in Canada executive producer Ralph Mellanby stood up for me when the CBC bigwig said, "Cherry has to go."

Luckily, I had these men in my corner, and yes, of course, the Lord. Nobody could get himself out of the situations I put myself in unless he had a guardian angel watching over him.

Now I can see my problem: I had tunnel vision. Everything was straight ahead. Black and white. No grey. Just do it, and never mind the consequences, no matter who I hurt.

It seems I lived on the edge all my life, and as I said in the movie, it was an awful selfish way that I lived, thinking of nobody but myself and making it very hard on my family.

And as I head into the twilight of my life with a lot more years behind me than ahead of me, I wish I could change many things. But you can't go back.

I guess I have to go along with the saying of Popeye: "I yam what I yam and that's all what I yam."

I hope you enjoyed the book.

THE END.

PHOTO CREDITS AND PERMISSIONS

ENDPAPERS

Molson Canadian Bubba Beer Can hockey cards reprinted with permission from the Molson Coors Canada

"Damn French Canadian Shirtmakers" cartoon reprinted with permission from Sun Media Corporation

"Here are your passports" cartoon reprinted with permission from Canadian Artists Syndicate, Inc.

PHOTO INSERTS

Insert One

Page viii (top) © Steve Babineau/NHLI via Getty Images

Insert Two

Page viii (bottom) © Lianne Harrower

Insert Three

Page i (bottom left) © Rob MacDougall

Page vii (bottom) © Bruce Bennett/NHLI via Getty Images

INTERIOR

Page 258 © Rob MacDougall

All other photos courtesy of the author.

TEXT PERMISSIONS

Excerpt from "The unacknowledged wounds of war that never heal" by Catherine Ford (June 2010) reprinted with the permission of Troy Media.

Excerpt from BGen. D. C. Kettle, Chaplain General for the Canadian Armed Forces' response to the above column (July 2010) reprinted with the permission of Troy Media.

"Vet of the Month" profile on Captain Jack Cherry reprinted with the permission of Buffalo Joe Healy/RCMPgraves.com